AF600301

SHAKESPEARE'S BIG MEN

Tragedy and the Problem of Resentment

RICHARD VAN OORT

Shakespeare's Big Men

Tragedy and the Problem of Resentment

UNIVERSITY OF TORONTO PRESS
Toronto Buffalo London

Toronto Buffalo London
www.utppublishing.com

ISBN 978-1-4426-5007-7

Library and Archives Canada Cataloguing in Publication

van Oort, Richard, author
Shakespeare's big men : tragedy and the problem of
resentment / Richard van Oort.

Includes bibliographical references and index.
ISBN 978-1-4426-5007-7 (cloth)

1. Shakespeare, William, 1564–1616. Julius Caesar. 2. Shakespeare, William, 1564–1616. Hamlet. 3. Shakespeare, William, 1564–1616. Othello. 4. Shakespeare, William, 1564–1616. Macbeth. 5. Shakespeare, William, 1564–1616. Coriolanus. 6. Men in literature. 7. Resentment in literature. 8. Desire in literature. 9. Guilt in literature. 10. Evil in literature. 11. Protagonists (Persons) in literature. 12. Anthropology in literature. 13. Literature and anthropology. I. Title. II. Title: Big men.

PR2992.M28V35 2016 822.3'3 C2016-900610-7

University of Toronto Press acknowledges the financial assistance to its publishing program of the Canada Council for the Arts and the Ontario Arts Council, an agency of the Government of Ontario.

Funded by the Government of Canada
Financé par le gouvernement du Canada

For Sheila, Max, Katie, and Dominic

Contents

Preface

The title of this book requires a brief word of explanation. In the most literal sense, it refers to the protagonists of Shakespeare's tragedies. There is something colossal about these men. "They are," A.C. Bradley observed, "not merely exceptional men, they are huge men; as it were, survivors of the heroic age living in a later and smaller world."[1] Bradley's landmark study of Shakespearean tragedy has been subject to strong critical objections both earlier in the last century and, more recently, on formalist and historicist grounds. I think these objections are less decisive than might appear for reasons I will develop in chapter 1 – and of course the endless reprints of the book throughout the last century and into this one suggest that it continues to speak to the concerns of a substantial audience, if not necessarily the audience assumed by the academic commentary on Shakespeare's plays.[2] From this point of view the more serious problem with Bradley resides not so much with his aesthetics as with the anthropology underpinning his aesthetics. After making the above comment about Shakespeare's tragic heroes, Bradley does not explain why tragedy concerns itself with the representation of these colossal figures, nor why our attention to them takes place within the context of their suffering. He simply takes these things for granted. I want to dig a little beneath these assumptions; in trying to do so, my title takes on a second, more specific meaning. Anthropologists have observed that among tribal cultures there exists the political type of the big man. The big man is not, however, a chief or king. His capacity to attract followers depends not on his divine right, but upon his ambition and charisma. "His every public action," the anthropologist Marshall Sahlins writes, "is designed to make a competitive and invidious comparison with others."[3] This book is about Shakespeare's big men in both senses of the word. Shakespeare's big men are to be admired, as Bradley suggests, but they are also to be suspected of promoting competitive and invidious comparison. Identification with the tragic protagonist is inseparable from resentment of him.

The experience of this paradox, I argue, lies at the heart of tragedy. Chapters 3, 4, 5, 6, and 7 explore the ways in which this paradox manifests itself in *Julius Caesar, Hamlet, Othello, Macbeth,* and *Coriolanus*. I take it as given that each of these plays addresses the ambivalent experience of resentful identification differently. For instance, it is much easier to identify with Hamlet than Brutus. Despite his abominable behaviour towards Gertrude, Claudius, Polonius, Ophelia, Rosencrantz, and Guildenstern, Hamlet wins us to his viewpoint, and we tend to excuse his behaviour on the grounds that he is, on balance, more of a victim rather than a persecutor. We are much less tempted to make similar excuses for Brutus, whose centralizing inner conflict peaks in the play's second act only to be rapidly overshadowed by the collective action of the conspirators in the third. Antony, somewhat comically, attempts to restore Brutus's nobility at the end. In a jarring and hasty eulogy, he declares that, unlike the other conspirators, Brutus was free of envy, "the noblest Roman of them all." But Brutus's significance cannot be so easily divorced from the envy driving the conspiracy against Caesar. Identification with Brutus cannot be separated from resentment. This paradox reaches a new lucidity in *Othello*, where admiring identification with the protagonist is systematically obstructed by the presence of the play's antagonist. Iago's resentment dominates the stage until Othello becomes an echo of his more resentful counterpart. In *Macbeth*, this paradox receives yet another formulation. Here resentment is overshadowed by guilt. But guilt is also a species of alienation, and consequently works to produce the tragic effect in a different way. Finally, Coriolanus, whom Bradley described as Shakespeare's biggest big man, is variously applauded and derided by the patricians and plebeians who share in his glory even as they participate in his downfall. Yet when Coriolanus abandons his desire to burn Rome in the fifth act, he refuses the violence of the centre. This extraordinary act from Shakespeare's most violent hero creates difficulties for tragic form, which demands the protagonist's commitment to the violent agon of the centre. As many commentators have noted, in this context Coriolanus's destruction is apt to appear ironic rather than truly tragic. In laying bare the generative paradox of tragedy, Shakespeare emptied the scene of its affective power. The most perverse of tragic heroes, Coriolanus is also Shakespeare's last.

My selection of these five tragedies is not meant to be exhaustive or definitive. I could have included *King Lear*, *Antony and Cleopatra*, or *Timon of Athens*. Nor are the histories or comedies irrelevant to my theme. The point, however, is not to reduce Shakespeare's plays to a single unchanging pattern or idea. Precisely in the case of the aesthetic, the idea is not a substitute for literary or dramatic experience. This is why a theory or hypothesis about the plays must be cashed out in an analysis of aesthetic content. There is no shortcut around, or substitute for, the aesthetic text. Aesthetic form is inseparable from aesthetic content, and the content changes from play to play. In this regard Shakespeare is an embarrassment of riches. Inevitably, I have had to draw the line somewhere, and I have chosen to draw it around these five tragedies.

The chapters dealing explicitly with Shakespeare (chapters 3 to 7) represent the core of this book. These analyses will, I hope, persuade readers that Shakespeare can profitably be read from the perspective of what has come to be known as "generative anthropology." Chapter 2 explains why we need such an anthropology. Here I introduce the work of Eric Gans, whose theory of aesthetic history I find extremely useful for thinking about Shakespearean tragedy. I realize that many Shakespeareans will be more interested in hearing what I have to say about Shakespeare than in what I have to say about the anthropological specificity of language or the ethical structure of "big man" societies, so I have tried to keep my discussion of the theory as brief as possible. Readers who want to get to the pudding before hearing the proof may wish to skip chapter 2 and proceed directly to the analyses of the plays. But I recommend that at some point they return to chapter 2 because it provides the foundation upon which the analyses are built. In particular, it explains my reasons for adopting Gans's notion of the "neoclassical esthetic" to describe Shakespearean tragedy. To put it another way, chapter 2 answers the question of why anyone should bother reading Shakespeare at all. It can therefore be usefully read in conjunction with chapter 8, which explains in more detail the basic difference between generative anthropology and René Girard's related theory of mimetic violence.

I realize that the approach adopted here may strike many Shakespeareans as intolerably eccentric. I come at Shakespeare from a perspective that seems to eschew the more familiar historicist focus on the political, religious, or economic contexts of early modern drama. In chapter 1, I address this concern by showing that there are others in Shakespeare studies treading if not exactly the same path, then convergent paths heading in the same direction. Historicism no longer has such a tight grip on the kind of work we do. Other approaches, including more philosophical or anthropological approaches, are making their way from the margins to the centre. My particular approach to Shakespeare may seem somewhat unusual in the explicitness of my commitment to the idea of an "originary hypothesis," but the usefulness of the theory in the context of Shakespeare studies is not, I think, hard to demonstrate. Chapter 1 makes the case for why Shakespeareans should care about generative anthropology by showing how much common intellectual ground exists between the two. As much as possible, I attempt to explain the situation from the viewpoint of a Shakespearean rather than the perspective of a "vernacular"[4] amateur of generative anthropology. I then switch perspectives, in chapter 2, when I adopt the minimal position of the originary hypothesis. The minimality of the hypothesis is intended to be maximally inclusive, in the sense that it assumes not merely the preoccupations of professional Shakespeareans but the anthropological or vernacular preoccupations of anyone interested in what makes us human. The next five chapters are devoted to a back-and-forth dialogue between the minimal anthropological hypothesis and Shakespearean tragedy. The final chapter functions as a kind of summary of my position vis-à-vis Girard's well-known but controversial reading of Shakespeare.

Nothing I have said so far explains why we need another book on Shakespeare. Yet it is precisely this question that obliges us to formulate Shakespeare's relevance to our humanity as sharply as possible. The purpose of tracing cultural forms such as ritual or tragedy back to an originary scene from which they are hypothesized to have emerged is to grasp these institutions in terms of their minimal anthropological structure or essence. The most powerful explanation is also the most parsimonious. If we explain the origin of tragedy in ancient Greece as the emergence of a more powerful means to explain our engagement with and resentment of the big man, we have made a historical argument about the origin of a new cultural form. But to understand why tragedy should emerge at this point rather than another, we need to understand why resentment is a problem and why the preexisting ritual means for controlling it proved inadequate. But this requires us to understand the structure of hierarchical society and, more precisely, its difference from the egalitarian forms of social organization that preceded it. What motivated the first big man to appropriate the ritual centre that was denied to his egalitarian ancestors? The origin of agriculture in the later Neolithic period would seem to provide an obvious explanation, but the presence of a material cause does not explain the *ritual* aspect of the big man's appropriation of the centre. The big man does not seek mere appetitive satisfaction; he desires the symbolic prestige associated with the centre itself. But whence comes this prestige? The originary hypothesis explains the big man's desire for prestige as a fundamental element of the scene of representation. Desire for the centre is a corollary of the word that refers to its object by simultaneously interdicting it. But desire also breeds resentment. This resentment is unleashed when the appetitive object is destroyed in the collective *sparagmos*, a moment commemorated in all sacrificial ritual. But the *sparagmos* is preceded by the word in which transgression of the interdiction is first imagined within the individual's internal scene of representation. This is the aesthetic moment of the scene, the moment reproduced in tragedy.

As this brief synopsis suggests, there is no purely logical justification for the originary hypothesis. Once formulated, the hypothesis must be evaluated on the basis of its ability to provide a plausible analysis of the particular moment of history we wish to examine. It is a heuristic device that cannot be assessed independently of the results it produces. In terms of the argument of this book, the hypothesis functions as a minimal starting point from which to understand the general question of why tragedy should originate as an alternative to ritual in ancient Greece and then reemerge in Shakespeare's day as the central cultural form. The abstract manner in which I have posed the question may make it appear that my argument is purely historical and deductive – in other words, that I am not concerned with providing an analysis of the plays themselves. But precisely in the case of the aesthetic, form is revealed in content. It is only by appreciating the *irony* of tragedy, in which the suffering of the central protagonist is a condition of our identification with him, that we can gain an insight into the problem of resentment.

Acknowledgments

This book is the result of the highly agreeable task of teaching Shakespeare to many hundreds of students over the past decade. I am grateful to all of them. Nothing would give me more satisfaction than to learn that this book succeeded in speaking to them and to readers like them. It is good to see that Shakespeare continues to inspire non-experts to serious personal and ethical reflection despite the historical distance between our time and his.

I am grateful to the Social Sciences and Humanities Research Council of Canada for providing me with a grant in 2010 to get started on writing this project. Some of the arguments in this book were presented at the annual meetings of the Shakespeare Association of America, and I am grateful to my colleagues for the feedback provided on these occasions, most recently at the 2015 meeting in Vancouver. Thanks are also due to four anonymous reviewers of the University of Toronto Press for suggesting ways to make this book more palatable to Shakespeare experts. I am particularly grateful to the Generative Anthropology Society for providing me with a publication subsidy just when I needed it. It is a pleasure to acknowledge the support and generosity of this most invigorating and convivial group.

Last but not least, I wish to thank my wife, Sheila, and our children, Max, Katie, and Dominic. This book is for them.

SHAKESPEARE'S BIG MEN

1 Why Shakespeare and Generative Anthropology?

The best way to answer the question I ask in the title of this chapter is to get on with the business of reading Shakespeare via the heuristic of generative anthropology's "originary hypothesis." Before proceeding with the practical business at hand, however, let me try to locate the approach I am taking here with some of the work currently being produced in Shakespeare studies. I appreciate that the originary hypothesis, along with other examples of anthropological lingua franca I employed in the preface (and will be developing further in the next chapter), are not exactly household phrases among Shakespeareans. To some extent, the strangeness of my approach is not misleading. Generative anthropology differs in its basic assumptions and values from a good deal of current Shakespeare criticism. However, there are many contemporary Shakespeareans with whom I feel a common ground. One could even say that they are doing something very close to generative anthropology, at least as I understand it. What I would like to do in this chapter is to highlight some of these differences and, more importantly, the similarities.

In terms of the differences, historicism is a good place to begin. Historicism has been, arguably, the major emphasis in current work, but historicism's fine-grained focus on the religious context of Shakespearean drama may be separating us from our chief source of interest in Shakespeare, which is not in the end religious but literary. Understanding a play by Shakespeare does not require that you drastically revise or modify your basic moral concepts.[1] The average reader may not know much about the theological controversies of the Reformation (beyond the fact that they existed), but this same reader will nonetheless be able to grasp that morally speaking the ghost in *Hamlet* is ambivalent. No amount of additional specialized historical knowledge changes this basic fact about the reader's experience. This is not to say that acquiring detailed historical knowledge will not help to enrich or expand a reader's appreciation of *Hamlet*. But the enriching of aesthetic experience is not what is at issue. What is at issue is rather the belief that a legitimate experience of *Hamlet* depends upon the prior acquisition of specialized historical knowledge of the period in which Shakespeare wrote. I believe that claim to be false.[2]

Why then do we insist on the primacy of historical knowledge when writing about Shakespeare? I think the reason is that we have lost confidence in the aesthetic object. Having lost our confidence in Shakespeare, we instinctively imitate the sciences in a desperate effort to shore up our lost prestige.[3] Historicist specialization is thus partly an exercise in risk management and damage control. It has nothing to do with the intrinsically technical or specialized nature of our subject matter. Understanding a play by Shakespeare is not something that requires a PhD. Of course, we would like to think that a PhD equips us with specialized knowledge that in some way qualifies us to be experts on Shakespeare. How else do we justify the long years of study? But the concepts that critics deal with are everyday concepts that are accessible to anyone with moderate linguistic competence – which is to say, everyone. This fact stands in marked contrast to the concepts underpinning scientific knowledge. The concepts of science are technical and difficult to understand, but they are cognitively powerful. The concepts of the humanities are nontechnical and relatively easy to understand, but they are, as Ernest Gellner points out, "cognitively feeble."[4] This separation between the moral world of lived experience and the world described by science is a product of the Enlightenment, which drove a wedge between religion and serious cognition. No longer are these two worlds seamlessly connected. "The world in which men think seriously, and to which serious thought refers, is," Gellner says, "no longer identical with the world in which one lives one's daily life."[5]

From this angle, a book that proposes to read Shakespeare anthropologically – that is, in terms of a generative anthropology, the basic concepts of which are untechnical and open to anyone who wishes to engage in dialogue about what it means to be human – is bound to look a bit eccentric. But by no means altogether so. Despite the long ascendancy of historicism in Shakespeare studies, there are signs that the momentum is shifting. A number of recent works have argued for (or proceeded from the claim that) something like a nontechnical anthropological hypothesis of origin has something valuable to offer Shakespeare studies. Harold Bloom's "invention of the human" is probably the most striking example of this reversal of direction.[6] Bloom's challenge has largely come from outside the academic context, in the form of the books he writes for a more general readership. Shakespeare's popularity among non-academic readers is certainly relevant to the present argument, but I will postpone my discussion of Bloom until the final chapter, at which time I will address his views in the context of a more general discussion of Shakespeare and modernity. I believe that Bloom's Shakespeare can be most usefully assessed by comparing it to René Girard's Shakespeare. Here, however, I wish to consider a handful of critics who have challenged the historicist paradigm from within Shakespeare studies itself.

In his recent state-of-the-art polemic, Edward Pechter claims that Shakespeare studies is in a malaise.[7] The reason is simple. We no longer believe in what we do. Shakespeareans don't believe in Shakespeare. This is why we have been led to objects outside Shakespeare, including a Foucault-inspired understanding of history that has dominated the discipline for the last thirty years or so. Pechter himself is rather reticent about how to solve this problem, but it is clear that his sympathies lie with the romantics, who first put Shakespeare on the map as an object of aesthetic study. In this sense the subtitle of Pechter's book (*Romanticism Lost*) rather than his title (*Shakespeare Studies Today*) is more revealing of the author's general point of view. Pechter has an obvious preference for how things were done in the past, but he keeps his sights firmly focused on the (dismal) present. This contradiction pervades the entire book. One of the difficulties of Pechter's analysis, at least for me, is that though it is an excellent (and often witty) diagnosis of a real problem in Shakespeare studies, it is less helpful when it comes to providing a solution. Nowhere in the book does Pechter actually discuss Shakespeare as an aesthetic object in the manner of the romantics he so admires. Pechter himself is keenly aware that his assessment, however accurate, might be considered an exercise in bad faith.[8] Why publish a book on contemporary Shakespeare scholars rather than Shakespeare if your basic argument is that Shakespeare scholars have become harmfully distracted from their proper object? Are you not simply contributing to the distraction? It is only when one turns to Pechter's earlier study of *Othello* that one gets a sense of the kind of criticism Pechter would like to see – namely, a deeply humane and sensitive study of character that acknowledges the many textual paradoxes and ironies that combine to produce the play's powerful tragic effect.[9]

I share Pechter's desire to return to Shakespeare via his texts rather than contexts. Pechter himself enlists the support of an impressive trio of critics, including Stephen Greenblatt, Edward Said, and Stanley Fish, all of whom have gone on record arguing for a return to a "passionate engagement" with the aesthetic text.[10] More recently, Pechter's call has been answered by Richard McCoy, whose study of "faith in Shakespeare" explicitly eschews the "scholarly fixation on Reformation controversies and futile conjecture about Shakespeare's religious beliefs."[11] Understanding Shakespeare's historical context cannot, McCoy argues, explain our aesthetic fascination with Shakespeare: "Faith in Shakespeare can be sustained and explained only by the complex, subtle power of poetic eloquence and dramatic performance."[12] This focus on Shakespeare's poetry rather than Shakespeare's contexts puts McCoy closer to the romantics than to his contemporaries, as McCoy himself admits: "In seeking to define faith in Shakespeare, I have found Samuel Taylor Coleridge and other great Romantic critics and poets better guides than many recent critics."[13] What is good enough for Pechter and McCoy is good enough for me. As will become evident in the chapters that follow, I have found the romantics, from Coleridge and Hazlitt to Bradley and Harold Goddard, to be among the most reliable guides when reading Shakespeare.

In another recent commentary on the state of the discipline, Michael Bristol acknowledges the "significant record of achievement" of historical criticism, but like Pechter and McCoy, he worries about historicism's "notable lack of conviction about Shakespeare's value as dramatic art." Historicism, Bristol notes, "is dense with citation and historical references, focused intensively on the 'social, political, and economic sub-stratum' of the plays," but it gives "little attention to the desires, motivations, and social interactions of Shakespeare's characters."[14] Bristol does not argue that in order to makes sense of Shakespeare, you do not need *any* sense of history. Obviously you do. What Bristol argues (quite sensibly, I think) is that "much of this [historical] knowledge is included in the exposition of the dramatic narrative."[15] The portability of Shakespeare's sense of history – that is, its transportability from Elizabethan times to our own – means that an exclusive emphasis on the historical context outside the play tends to undermine the text's poetic aims. "In its militant aspect," Bristol writes, "historicism insists that a correct understanding can only be achieved by reference to specialized historical knowledge."[16] Bristol's solution to the problem of finding an adequate context for discussing Shakespeare is to turn to moral philosophy. This is not because he believes Shakespeare requires the authority of professional moral philosophers. On the contrary, what Bristol means by moral philosophy is captured by his idea of "vernacular criticism" – the attempt to identify and analyse, by whatever means possible, the everyday moral concepts we live by.[17] For example, seen from the viewpoint of vernacular criticism, one of the most interesting questions to ask about Macbeth is, why does he kill Duncan? It is not enough to say that Macbeth is ambitious, because Macbeth himself has argued clearly and insightfully against his own ambition. As Bristol puts it: "His assent to doing exactly what he has decided not to do is an instance of incontinence or *akrasia*, acting in contradiction to his own lucid sense of what it would be best for him to do."[18]

Bristol's idea of vernacular criticism strikes me as an attractive notion. I share his conviction that understanding Shakespeare is basically a non-technical exercise that involves dipping into our shared moral vocabulary. I prefer the term "anthropology" to describe this approach because it captures more explicitly the anthropological horizon of vernacular criticism (only humans engage in moral reflection). But this difference seems like a small one compared to the similarities. I share Bristol's concern that historicism undervalues precisely what is most valuable in Shakespeare – namely, the richness of the plays as ethical discovery procedures. Bristol's way of considering the plays is far more attuned, for example, to the problem of self-deception. His focus on desire, motive, and character allows him to grasp the ethical complexity of the situations in which Shakespeare places his protagonists. Often this ethical complexity is ignored or even derided by historicist critics. For example, in her polemic against the romantic critical tradition, Margreta de Grazia ridicules the idea that Hamlet is capable of deceiving himself when he passes up on the opportunity to kill Claudius at prayer.[19] How can Hamlet lie to himself about his motives? And how would such a lie be indicated on the stage? De Grazia finds the idea preposterous: "When the character himself has no knowledge of his intent to deceive – when he is both deceiver and deceived – how can his deception be staged?"[20] She goes so far as to argue that the idea of self-deception was invented by late eighteenth-century critics who wished to make Hamlet appear less diabolical. If Hamlet is self-deceived, then he cannot be all that bad. This idea was then seized upon by Coleridge and other romantics, until eventually we got to Freud and Ernest Jones, for whom self-deception is merely a routine case of repression. De Grazia has little use for the romantic, self-doubting Hamlet, and in particular for the theme of self-deception that is so central to the romantic interpretation of character. She believes that once we shed ourselves of this Hamlet, with its vexed division between conscious and unconscious selves, we can see that Hamlet's refusal to kill the kneeling Claudius is really just good theatre, one that we must take at face value. Hamlet decides not to kill Claudius because he wants to send him to hell. Where is the self-deception in all this?

There are two problems with this argument. First, de Grazia assumes that self-deception can be explained by comparing it, rather literally, to the epistemology of interpersonal deception. This strikes me as highly problematic. Self-deception is not straightforwardly analogous to interpersonal deception. To assume that it is leads to the kinds of absurd logical paradoxes de Grazia finds in the idea of self-deception. How can I both know the truth and not know the truth? How can I be both guilty of deception and the victim of deception at the same time? But these kinds of logical paradoxes merely show that we have missed the salient feature of self-deception, which is after all an intuitively intelligible idea to most of us. As Mike Martin points out, "It is misleading to claim that the literal, genuine, central, or full-blooded cases of self-deception are only those that parallel the epistemology of interpersonal deception," and he rightly criticizes those who seek to undermine the intelligibility of the idea by "applying a potentially illuminating analogy in a too-rigid manner." "Self-deception," Martin concludes, "can best be viewed as a set of related phenomena which are analogous to interpersonal deception in some but not all ways."[21]

The second problem with de Grazia's argument is that it ignores the prominence of self-deception as a theme in Shakespeare. Far from being a recent romantic invention, self-deception is fundamental to the Christian tradition upon which Shakespeare's drama is based. Hamlet deceives himself in the same way Macbeth deceives himself: that is, by ignoring his better conscience and listening to the voice of temptation, a voice that is personified by Shakespeare in the ghost and the witches. The fact that these ambivalent seducers are also agents of self-destruction would have been obvious to an audience attuned to moral allegory. I will have more to say about the allegorical tradition and its relevance to Shakespeare in the chapters that follow. The point I wish to emphasize here is that historicism, in its focus on context rather than text, has neglected not merely the formal complexity of Shakespeare's texts but, more specifically, the combination of formal and ethical complexity that makes up Shakespeare's understanding of human desire, motivation, and character. In short, historicism has lost its sense of the anthropological relevance of these texts for understanding ourselves.

Bristol reminds us that the assumption that Shakespeare provided ethical models for understanding human action was a commonplace among earlier critics such as Richard Moulton and A.C. Bradley. Their approach to literature was based on the idea of "the experimental adequacy of fictional worlds to model human action."[22] Bradley is often ridiculed for the "bad habit of confusing literary characters with real people."[23] But when we remember that much of what we assume about real people is fictional or hypothetical, in the sense that we don't have unmediated access to other minds, then this kind of simplistic division between fiction and reality appears less helpful. It is much better to think of Bradley as combining, as Bristol puts it, "his robust sense of literary character and his belief in the fictional reality of unobserved states of mind."[24]

Another contemporary Shakespeare critic relevant to this context is Harry Berger, especially in the keen eye he brings to discerning Shakespearean irony.[25] I have found his readings of Shakespeare to be quite brilliant. Just when you think you have sorted out the ironies of the text, Berger shows that you didn't look closely enough. Berger is not simply pursuing irony for the sake of irony. His idea of irony is bound up with a consistent and systematic *ethical* reading of the plays. The key idea for Berger is complicity. In tragedy complicity is thematized in the way Shakespeare unsettles the distinction between margins and centre. For example, we typically think of Macbeth as evil and the Scottish thanes as good, but Berger shows that Macbeth sees more clearly than his fellows the structure of evil that pushes him towards the centre. All the thanes are bound up in this more general sacrificial pattern. The brilliance of the play is that it shows us not only the rise and fall of the hero, but also the complicity of the Scottish thanes in an ongoing sacrificial ethic that includes the centralization and sacrifice of both Duncan and Macbeth.

In his approach to Shakespeare, Berger owes much to the work of the anthropological literary critic René Girard. In the pages that follow, my own debt to Girard will, I hope, become clear. In the final chapter I spell out this debt more explicitly, but it will perhaps be useful to state the basic difference between our approaches here. To put it as succinctly as possible, Girard emphasizes the collective violence of the *sparagmos*, whereas I emphasize the antecedent problem of resentment or imagined violence. Human violence is distinguished from animal violence not merely by our greater propensity for self-annihilation, but also by our capacity for representing violence before inflicting it. The two problems – the problem of absolute violence and the problem of representation – are in fact inseparable. Shakespeare's tragedies explore this relationship between violence and representation with breathtaking detail and subtlety. It is characteristic of Shakespeare's protagonists, as Bradley noted, that they imagine violence before carrying it out.

As I hope this brief introduction makes clear, reading Shakespeare as an "anthropological discovery procedure" is not a wholly eccentric idea. There are other voices in Shakespeare studies who share my reservations about historicist approaches and who lean towards the kind of vernacular or anthropological approach offered here – and by no means just those I have cited in the preceding pages.[26] My intention has not been to undertake an exhaustive survey of the current scene, but to provide readers with a more familiar context into which they can insert what might otherwise strike them as a radically unconventional point of view. This last point is something I wish to emphasize. Generative anthropology is not a technical subject for the specialist. It is for anyone interested in understanding the uniqueness of human origin. That an understanding of this origin can be accessed most conveniently through a reading of Shakespeare is only superficially controversial. Shakespeare's preeminence in the Western cultural tradition is testimony to the enduring nature of his anthropology. The romantics were the first generation of critics to take Shakespeare seriously as a thinker whose fictional worlds could also be looked at as discovery procedures for human self-understanding. They were generative anthropologists *avant la lettre*. When Pechter challenges us to regain our lost conviction in Shakespeare by returning to the example set by the romantics, I understand him to be alluding to this fact. And when he claims that until we recognize the continuing pertinence of the romantics for understanding Shakespeare we will be unable "to develop an adequate foundation on which to build [our] work," I take the challenge seriously.[27]

This book may be understood as a response to Pechter's challenge to reaffirm our conviction in Shakespeare by developing an adequate *anthropological* foundation upon which to build critical work. This does not mean that I expect all Shakespeare scholars to accept my particular version of the originary hypothesis. What it does mean, however, is that a conviction in Shakespeare requires at least some kind of *humanistic* hypothesis, however provisional or tentative it might be. To reiterate what was said at the beginning of this chapter, the plausibility of the hypothesis must be measured by the reading of Shakespeare it enables. In the next chapter, I explain generative anthropology's originary hypothesis. I then give an account of the relevance of the hypothesis for understanding the anthropological concepts of hierarchy, resentment, and tragedy. Once we are clear about these basic concepts, we will be ready to put the hypothesis to work in a reading of Shakespeare.

2 The Originary Hypothesis: Hierarchy, Resentment, and Tragedy

Tragedy, as Aristotle observed, presents us with a hero who is "better than you." The idea of the tragic hero's social superiority may not strike much resonance in us today, but in Shakespeare's day, as in Aristotle's, an individual's position in the social hierarchy inevitably had much greater significance, especially when that individual was at the top.

We must therefore ask ourselves two questions:

(1) When did longstanding (i.e., *ontological*) hierarchy originate?
(2) What function did it serve?

Before we can answer these two questions, however, we must begin by laying out the basic categories of our hypothesis of human origin.

According to Eric Gans, those categories deemed fundamental to anthropological understanding must be traceable to their appearance in the "originary scene" of human culture.[1] Because human culture is transmitted non-genetically, purely biological explanations of culture can only ever be partial. Rather than seek to imitate the methods of the natural sciences, the most powerful research strategy for the humanities is to minimize the number of our non-biological explanatory categories by tracing them to their genesis in the first cultural scene, a minimal account of which Gans proposes in his "originary hypothesis."

The most important element of human culture, and therefore of the hypothesis, is language, which is basically a means for transmitting behaviour non-genetically. As Durkheim realized, culture is above all a system of prohibitions imposed by the community on the individual. Far from being a window onto the world as empiricist philosophers from Hume to (the early) Wittgenstein have believed, language provides humanity with the means for refusing reference to the outside world. If our concepts really were the result of abstracting from our perceptions, then thought would quickly spiral into the anarchy of free association. As Ernest Gellner says in his criticism of empiricist theories of language and concept formation, "anything can be associated with anything."[2] In fact the opposite is the case. Our concepts are constrained by language. Language is the specifically human means for constraining cognition and behaviour. As the evolutionary anthropologist and neuroscientist Terrence Deacon has shown, language is a system of *symbolic* connections that override the more fundamental, perceptually based *indexical* associations built by the individual's sensorimotor system.[3]

The question this argument begs, however, is why cultural or linguistic constraint should be necessary at all. Gellner believes that it is the genetic plasticity of humans that leads to the origin of cultural constraint.[4] If humans are to live socially in homogeneous communities, they at least need to think like each other. Culture is the means for producing this like-mindedness. "Man is born genetically free," Gellner says, "but is everywhere in cultural chains."[5]

What is lacking in this insightful and witty formulation is a sense of the constraining effect of language not merely on cognition but also on human action. Borrowing from Jacques Derrida's idea of language as *différance* and reinterpreting René Girard's originary scene of scapegoating, Gans proposes that language originates as the *deferral* of mimetic conflict.[6] Language, like religion itself, is a solution to violence. When two hands reach for the same object, both cannot possess it. This "pragmatic paradox" is only surmounted when mimesis is allowed to continue, but this time not as the imitation of the other (Girard) but as the imitation of the object. When both subject and other-model abort their appropriative gestures and interpret their actions as a shared representation of the object, mimetic conflict is deferred.

But this deferral is not the end of human conflict. The word defers the immediate threat of mimetic crisis by sublimating animal appetite into human desire, but in doing so it produces the corollary of desire, which is resentment. In the first moment of desire, the word points the subject towards the object. But in attending to the word, the subject experiences resentment at not having the object. This experience leads the subject to return to the object in a characteristic oscillation between word and object that is the hallmark of the aesthetic.

The aesthetic is the principal cultural means for deferring the resentment generated by the subject's experience of dispossession from the central object. But appetite is not indefinitely deferred. The conclusion of the originary event occurs when the appetitive object is divided among the members of the human periphery. This division can never match the individual's aesthetic experience of the undivided whole. The asymmetry between the individual's aesthetic experience of the centre and the economic conclusion to the originary event provides the characteristic tension between universal morality and particular ethics.

The moral idea that we are all created equal is a consequence of the symmetrical exchange of linguistic meaning on the periphery. Comprehension of the word is independent of one's position in the social hierarchy. But the moral equality implicit in the exchange of words gives way to the economic reality of the exchange of things. The latter is rarely a symmetrical affair, for the simple reason that whereas words are easily produced, things are scarce. It is only very recently – that is, in technologically advanced, industrial society – that the exchange of things approximates the moral model of the exchange of words.[7] Human history is characterized by different solutions to the problem of economic distribution. The institution of the big man emerges at the beginnings of agrarian society. Shakespeare's thematization of resentment occurs in the late stages of agrarian society. Divested of the sacred guarantees that assured their status at the apex of society, Shakespeare's kings return to their original condition as charismatic big men.

We are now in a position to provide preliminary answers to our two questions concerning the origin of social hierarchy. Invidious ethical and social hierarchy originates with the big man's usurpation of the sacred centre, in which locus only the god previously resided. Functionally this usurpation integrates desire more fully into the system of economic redistribution.

The principle of the big man is simple. In egalitarian hunter-gatherer society, differences in social status are temporary.[8] More precisely, they remain subordinate to the fundamental difference between god and human, or, as per the hypothesis, between the sacred centre and its profane human periphery. Egalitarian societies may tolerate a small number of socially superior individuals, such as shamans and even certain kinds of headmen or chiefs; but their status as "first among equals" means that their significance never overshadows the more fundamental difference between centre and periphery.[9] The shaman may represent or imitate the god, but he is never a substitute for it. "What makes the big-man different," Gans argues, "is the essentially economic nature of his functions."[10] The chief of an egalitarian hunter-gatherer band does not hold a monopoly over the means of production, for the simple reason that the means of production are beyond his control. The prey animals of hunter-gatherer societies are by definition a scarce and mobile resource. Even supposing a single hunter or group of hunters to be capable of killing enough animals to feed an entire tribe for many months, the production of this surplus would be pointless, for the meat would soon spoil.

All this changes with the advent of agriculture in the Neolithic revolution. The desire that was formerly restrained by ritual sacrifice now becomes a reality of human praxis. The universally experienced desire for unique possession of the ritual centre now has the potential to be more fully integrated into the economic exchange system. The big man is not merely a temporary representative of the god of the sacrificial feast; he is a permanent usurper of the centre. The foodstuffs that he distributes in the potlatch-like feasts he presides over are the products of his (and his dependents') labour.[11]

Why should the big man work harder than his fellows merely so he can become the centre of attention at the feasts over which he presides? Gans explains the praxis of the big man in ethical terms as the integration of "producer's desire" into the economic exchange system.[12] It is difficult not to feel slightly sentimental about the egalitarian ethic of hunter-gatherer societies. But this ethic is not based on the abstract moral idea that "all men are created equal." It is based on the far more constraining idea that all men are *equally inferior* to the central locus of desire in which place alone the god, not a human, resides. In the ritual scene, producer's desire remains incapable of being fully integrated into the distribution system. Ritual solves the problem of producer's desire by reducing *all* to the status of equally insignificant consumers compared to the provider of the feast, which is the god. In the division of the object in the sacrificial feast, each may appropriate his share and none thereby gains access to a surplus by which he could gain an advantage over his fellows. Producer's desire is thus wholly sublimated or purged within the context of the sacrificial feast.[13]

In contrast the big man's desire is not sublimated or purged in ritual but made the basis of an ethical praxis that functions outside the narrow constraints of the ritual scene. The big man's labour takes place away from the centre, in the cultivation of the crops and animals he will later redistribute during the ritual feasts that guarantee his centrality within the community. The big man thus achieves in reality what could only be imagined by the individuals of the more rigidly egalitarian ritual system. The transformation of the big man into a sacred king is, one might say, an inevitable consequence of this first step in social differentiation. But what the historical phenomenon of the big man enables us to see more clearly is that far from being an irrational aberration of human history, as the Enlightenment *philosophes* believed, the tyranny of sacred kings is in fact a rational function of the exchange system itself. Today the well-nigh complete integration of desire into a consumer market makes the ritual constraints imposed on producer's desire in primitive egalitarian societies appear curiously quaint – when, that is, they are not sentimentalized as evidence of a superior implementation of an abstract Christianized morality that is in reality unknown to them. The sacred king's obnoxious wealth is far closer to us in spirit than the hunter-gatherer's rigid adherence to a strictly observed communal and egalitarian ethic. We tolerate wide disparities in wealth today not because we believe in the sacrality of kings, but because we believe in the right to fulfil one's *desire for significance* – what the American Declaration of Independence succinctly describes as the "inalienable right" to "the pursuit of happiness."

But this mobilization of desire brings its own problems: in particular, a mature form of resentment that is no longer abstractly directed at an inaccessible sacred centre but at the centre's real human occupant. Girard's study of ritual sacrifice, in which the cultural order is periodically renewed by the sacrifice of an "emissary victim," belongs to this stage of social and cultural evolution.[14] The expulsion of a scapegoat or "king of disaster" is a corollary of the big man's usurpation of the centre.[15] Shakespeare's tragedies are meditations on the theme of "the death of kings," and it is unsurprising that Girard should find in Shakespeare something of a kindred spirit, one whose understanding of sacrifice anticipates his own. Yet Girard's deep affection for Shakespeare is in the end subordinate to his greater fidelity to Jesus's antisacrificial message in the Gospels. Shakespeare may satirize the sacrificial assumptions of the theatre, but he cannot ultimately escape its sacrificial mechanisms without abandoning the stage altogether. For Girard, there is an element of bad faith in Shakespeare's theatre; in order to succeed, the playwright must give the audience the violence it craves.

Girard's ambivalence towards Shakespeare is traceable to his ambivalence towards representation, whether it be in myth, literature, or philosophy. Gans's more sanguine notion of representation as the deferral, rather than the forgetting, of violence allows us to appreciate better the specific contribution of the aesthetic in the ongoing cultural project of deferring resentment and the collective violence that attends it. It also allows us to pinpoint more accurately Shakespeare's position in a sequence of historical aesthetics, from the classical aesthetic of the ancient Greeks to the neoclassical, romantic, and modernist aesthetics of the post-classical era. Each of these aesthetics marks a new approach to the central ethical problem of deferring resentment. "From preliterate societies down to the archaic empires of Egypt and Mesopotamia," Gans writes, "the deferral of resentment and, consequently, the operation of the esthetic remain firmly under the control of the ritual center."[16] But in ancient Greece, "the esthetic becomes for the first time the central principle of a cultural institution."[17]

Why did the aesthetic separate itself from ritual to found an institution of its own? Gans explains the origin of literature as a response to the increased mobility of desire in the wake of the dissolution of the archaic empires founded on ritual sacrifice and the distinction between centre and periphery of the originary scene. Already the big man's praxis had shown the centre to be occupiable by a human. In usurping the ritual centre, the big man contributes to its desacralization. But this first step in the long historical process of humanizing the centre leads to a corresponding increase in resentment. It is sacrilegious to resent a god, but not a human. Once the big man opens the path to the centre, he unleashes and exacerbates the forces of resentment. As long as only a very few big men are able to satisfy producer's desire, which among other things requires a good deal of hard work, the ritual system of constraint will remain effective in controlling the resentments of the consumers of the big man's feast. No doubt brute coercion is all that is required to transform the big man's guests into his enslaved subjects. This is indeed the fate of the agrarian states that follow the emergence of the first big men of the Neolithic. These much larger hierarchical societies are no longer ruled by charismatic big men but by sacred kings. But the big men of the small island societies of Melanesia studied by Marshall Sahlins are not yet the authoritarian rulers of the agrarian state.[18]

We can thus postulate a period of development from the first big men of the later Neolithic through to the last great agrarian states of Egypt and Mesopotamia, during which producer's desire and consumer resentment were held in balance by ritual sacrifice. The liberation of art from ritual in ancient Greece is a response to this change in the relative forces of individual desire and collective resentment. Ritual sacrifice seeks to constrain resentment by sacralizing the centre as forbidden to desire. As Girard has shown, the emissary victim is first reviled then deified.[19] In the first moment, he is regarded as the cause of the disorder afflicting the community, which is why he must be expelled. But once he has been expelled and peace thereby restored to the community, he is regarded as a god, a bringer of peace and harmony. Much of the force of Girard's study of sacrifice in *Violence and the Sacred* comes from his insistence on the collective violence, whether explicit or implicit, that precedes the transformation of the victim into a god. This insistence carries over into his analysis of Shakespeare, in whom Girard sees an almost obsessive mimetic intelligence. It is also why Girard regards *Julius Caesar,* with its multiple scenes of collective violence, as "the essential and indispensable work" when it comes to "the scapegoat or victimage mechanism."[20]

My interpretation of Shakespeare's "theater of envy," though sympathetic to Girard's attempt to read the plays in the context of a fundamental anthropology, emphasizes the individual's internal scene of resentment rather than the collective act of sacrificial violence. The distinction has significant consequences for our anthropology – and, consequently, for our interpretation of history. This is especially the case when it comes to judging Shakespeare's relevance to modernity. Where Girard reads *Hamlet* apocalyptically as an allegory for the modern situation in which revenge could mean total annihilation of our species (e.g., in a nuclear holocaust), I regard the play as a meditation on resentment and the pernicious effects it has on the prince. To extrapolate from Hamlet's predicament in Elsinore to the predicament of humanity in a nuclear age is a breathtaking gesture, but it is not one I am prepared to make, at least not in the way Girard proposes.

Let me put the point in terms closer to Girard's understanding of modernity. Resentment is indeed a central problem, not just for Hamlet or Shakespeare but (as Girard implies) for all humanity. But this problem cannot be reduced to an opposition between revenge and no revenge that we moderns must face up to. Self-annihilation will always remain a possibility, now as at the origin. The task of deferring resentment is ongoing. More precisely, the goal of culture – and of literature too insofar as it is a part of culture – is to increase the degrees of individual freedom by minimizing the constraints on desire that lead to resentment and thence to violence. The paradox of the market is that it succeeds in this task by multiplying the opportunities of desire. But multiplying the opportunities of desire also multiplies the opportunities of resentment. If my neighbour has acquired the latest high-tech computer gadget, will I not want one too? And won't the experience of not having the latest gadget merely fuel my resentment and therefore my desire to acquire a similar object, indeed perhaps a better, newer one with yet more high-tech features? This paradox in which resentment is "purged" by recycling desire back into the system is the secret source of the market's strength.[21] Gans writes that an "ethical system that generated no resentment would truly bring about the end of history – whence the unconscious irony of applying this term to modern market society, which operates by generating and plowing back into the system an ever greater volume of resentment."[22]

I find this statement extremely apt. It pithily describes the view taken in this book. At the dawn of hierarchical society, the big man's usurpation of the centre is functional rather than fixed; his claim to significance is based on his economic success. The attempt to constrain resentment by attributing to him a pre-existing ontological hierarchy of the sacred is an ex post facto justification of this functional success. Yet by the same token, his centrality cannot be maintained *indefinitely* without a certain amount of coercion. For who shall replace the big man when he is too old to work or dead? The obvious answer is one of his kinsmen – a younger brother or son perhaps. And to assist the newcomer in his role as inheritor of the big man's position, it would be helpful to have an a priori justification for it. So the big man becomes a king who rules by divine right rather than by his wits and charisma. And just in case you suspected that the king was not as sacred as he claimed to be, there was always the king's army to remind you of his sacred right to rule.[23]

This is the fate of agrarian society after the big man. But in the margins of the agrarian empires of Mesopotamia and Egypt, there arose the society of the ancient Greeks for whom "centrality had become relative rather than absolute."[24] Greek tragedy exemplifies the aesthetic demystification of the big man's sacred power. Rather than sacralizing him as a god, tragedy humanizes him as someone with whom the peripheral spectator voluntarily identifies. This is a demystification of ritual sacrifice, for which an equivalent identification with the humanity of the victim would risk destroying the functionality of the rite. Desire for the protagonist's success is an admission of the openness of the centre to the periphery. But in tragedy this identification with the protagonist's desire is then purged when the protagonist is revealed to be a criminal guilty of transgressing the social order's most sacred taboos, as in Oedipus's twin crimes of parricide and incest. It is this latter moment of tragedy that Girard objects to, the equivalent of the *sparagmos* or tearing apart of the victim in ritual sacrifice. But what Girard fails to see is that this paradox, in which the form of tragedy is revealed in its resentful or sacrificial content, is the very essence of the human. High art gives us privileged access to the originary scene of human conflict, but this conflict is itself a product of the means contrived by humans to control it. Hamlet's attempts to defer his resentment through the various aesthetic spectacles he imagines (from the ghost to the player's Pyrrhus speech, to the Mousetrap play) are successful up to a point. But what these attempts also make clear is Hamlet's obsessive attachment to the scene he despises. Hamlet's delayed violence towards the king eventually explodes in a series of brutal murders that ends only with the stage littered with corpses. Tragedy purchases our good conscience at the cost of the protagonist himself, who must be sacrificed for his crime of usurping the centre of our scenic imaginations. The lesson is not simply the negative one that revenge is bad and Hamlet was wrong to kill (for we have ourselves willed Hamlet to undertake his revenge, and the play would not be a satisfying tragedy if we had not). Girard displays a peculiar tone deafness when he chides the entire critical tradition for supporting Hamlet's quest for vengeance on the king, as though Girard himself were somehow immune to the aesthetic effect produced by Shakespeare's play. But one does not have to be a saint in order to appreciate the ironies of Shakespearean tragedy.

These ironies arise from the same paradox that generates the deferral or aesthetic "homeostasis" between sign and referent in the originary scene. The collectively produced sign points the peripheral subject to the central object. But without the sign, the object is insignificant. So the subject returns to the sign, the formal closure of which once again represents the aesthetic object as a complete and beautiful whole. But this aesthetic relationship between sign and object cannot be maintained indefinitely. The desire sustained by the deferral of the aesthetic sign is eventually discharged in the ensuing *sparagmos*, when the central appetitive object is divided among the members of the originary human community. The violence of the *sparagmos*, the rending of the sacrificial victim, is the originary moment of human evil.

It is only after the big man's usurpation of the centre, however, that a human rather than a god is made the object of the *sparagmos*. The sacrifice of a human victim paves the way for purely aesthetic representations of the scapegoat in tragedy, thus setting the stage for the artwork as an "anthropological discovery procedure."[25] In classical tragedy the protagonist remains ignorant of his status as a usurper of the centre. The centre's dependence on the human periphery is not thematized. Instead sacrifice is regarded as the just punishment of the gods inflicted on the protagonist, whose desire has unknowingly exceeded the sacred interdiction of the centre. This is the element of fate that so strongly pervades Greek tragedy. In Sophocles's masterwork this sense of fate or impending doom is made inseparable from the play's irony. Oedipus sets himself the task of uncovering the identity of Laius's killer, but each discovery he makes only draws him closer to the identification of himself as the cause of the pollution in Thebes.

In Shakespeare's "neoclassical" tragedy the centre's dependence on the periphery is thematized in the play itself. "The neoclassical esthetic," Gans writes, "is uniquely characterized by what it adds to the classical: the representation of the scene of representation itself as the locus of significance."[26] Our paradoxical identification with and vilification of the central victim is now thematized as a constitutive element of the aesthetic scene. No longer an unselfconscious embodiment of centrality, the neoclassical protagonist finds himself displaced from the centre he desires. The roles of Brutus, Hamlet, Iago, Macbeth, and Coriolanus are one in their resentment of the centre. Brutus represents the first stage in the representation of resentment in Shakespeare's mature work. Here resentment structures the scene but without yet touching the self-consciousness of the protagonist himself. Brutus never once admits to his resentment of Caesar. Instead, resentment is projected onto Cassius and the other conspirators, which allows Brutus to believe that he is free of resentment. But Shakespeare has shown us otherwise in his brilliant staging of Cassius's seduction of Brutus. Every time the crowd roars from offstage in approval of Caesar, Brutus squirms and Cassius prods a little further. The scene exemplifies the dynamics of resentment. Forced to play second string to the imperial Caesar, Brutus fantasizes about his return to the centre in his role as defender of the republic. The shrewd Cassius sees this and strokes Brutus's ego accordingly. Brutus's resentment is finally disclosed to us in Cassius's superbly exaggerated and scandalous story of Caesar's girlish decrepitude. Cassius modestly reflects back to Brutus the envy that Brutus himself will never admit to.

3 Brutus's Neoclassical Irony

In the second scene of *Julius Caesar,* Caesar and his train cross the stage on their way to celebrate the feast of Lupercalia. Caesar's progress is briefly interrupted by a soothsayer who delivers his famous warning, "Beware the ides of March" (1.2.18). Caesar pauses briefly, but then dismisses the soothsayer as a "dreamer" (1.2.24) and passes on. The crowd follows, except for one man, who remains onstage. A second man, noticing the first man's reluctance to follow, also turns back. What follows is a typically Shakespearean inversion of public and private scenes. Caesar's public theatre moves offstage, and we are forced to imagine its continuation via the periodic offstage roars of the enthusiastic and admiring crowd. What remains onstage is rather a private scene that attacks the very legitimacy of the public scene that preceded it. As far as Cassius and Brutus are concerned (for it turns out they are the two who stayed behind), Caesar is a usurper whose ambition must be cut short.

The scene between the two men begins in a quiet, subdued fashion. Cassius asks, "Will you go see the order of the course?" (1.2.25). Brutus's curt reply, "Not I," seems intended to dismiss both the query and its speaker. Cassius, however, will not be shaken off lightly, for he repeats his invitation, this time more insistently – "I pray you, do." Brutus is now obliged to explain his eccentric behaviour, his reason for shunning Caesar's pageantry:

I am not gamesome. I do lack some part
Of that quick spirit that is in Antony. (1.2.28–9)

There is a brief pause. Has Brutus, normally so restrained and guarded, revealed too much of himself? Is he slightly ashamed at his peevish reference to Antony's "quick spirit," a reference that will be echoed later by Caesar when the great man, rather uncharacteristically, compares the lean and spare Cassius to the fat and contented man who loves music and plays? We know Antony to be one of Caesar's favourites, and Antony, Caesar says, is a great lover of plays. But Brutus too is one of Caesar's favourites. Is there the slightest hint of resentment in Brutus's voice? Does Cassius pick up on it? The moment passes quickly, but not too quickly for the hawkish Cassius, who seems to be making Brutus slightly uncomfortable, for the latter attempts to excuse himself a second time: "Let me not hinder, Cassius, your desires; / I'll leave you" (1.2.30–1). This is a polite but firm hint that Brutus wishes to be left alone. I am not gamesome like Antony, but don't let my antipathy to sports and public shows hinder you. Please follow the others. The final curt statement, "I'll leave you," signals that as far as Brutus is concerned, the conversation is over.

But Cassius isn't so easily brushed off. Why not? Why does he so persist in intruding on this man's personal space? Brutus obviously wishes to be left alone. Can't Cassius take a hint? It cannot simply be that he notices a friend in distress and wishes to help him, for we know that Cassius has other motives. In fact the whole notion of Cassius's friendship to Brutus is shot through with irony. For what kind of a friend says the sort of things Cassius says? But then, of course, the whole notion of friendship is radically undermined in this play, the central line of which (and the one which everyone remembers) is "*Et tu, Brutè*? Then fall, Caesar!" (3.1.78). What finally killed Caesar, one feels, are not the knives of the conspirators, but the fact that the last one was borne by a friend. Not that this means Caesar himself is guiltless when it comes to choosing fame over friendship. To the contrary, the whole point of the play's very first scene seems to be to show us how friendship suffers when the glare of the spotlight elevates one man above another. It takes a very special kind of person to not let his desire for fame stifle his obligations to friends and family. "O you hard hearts, you cruel men of Rome, / Knew you not Pompey?" (1.1.36–7). The message of the opening scene seems to be that Rome has begun, like a universal wolf, to prey upon itself. Pompey's defeat is Julius Caesar's triumph. But what has become of Rome when a triumph is held after one of Rome's own has been defeated? With friends like these, who needs enemies?

But let us return to Cassius, who now explicitly appeals to his friendship with Brutus:

Brutus, I do observe you now of late.
I have not from your eyes that gentleness

> And show of love as I was wont to have.
> You bear too stubborn and too strange a hand
> Over your friend that loves you. (1.2.32–6)

Again, on the surface this seems sincere, the kind of thing a true friend *would* say. Why are you so detached? What's on your mind? You seem a bit out of sorts.

But to read the lines in this way assumes that Cassius will follow through with his concern in the way that a friend should. If Brutus is undergoing some sort of moral or spiritual crisis, then shouldn't Cassius at least listen to what Brutus has to say? Or if he refuses to divulge anything, then shouldn't he tactfully back off until Brutus is ready to talk?

Cassius does none of this. Indeed, what seems to be driving Cassius is rather the opposite. He is looking for confirmation of hunches he already has, hunches based on keen observation. Why has Brutus not followed the others to observe the course? What has prompted him to separate himself from Caesar and his followers? What is buried deep within his breast? Is Brutus conflicted over his own friendship with Caesar? Does he find the fame heaped upon his friend difficult to bear, even intolerable? Could the noble Brutus be *envious*?

Now how would you test such a hypothesis? Consider the difficulty. You cannot simply come straight out and say, "Look here, you seem mighty envious of Caesar. Is that true?" Such a pointblank accusation would surely be met with an equally pointblank denial. Envy is not something one confesses to readily, especially if you are noble patrician who has an honourable reputation to uphold. In such an environment, the need to repress such a thought must be very strong indeed.[1]

As Leslie Farber remarks, envy's "talent for disguise" explains the "infrequency of studies of the subject."[2] It follows that in order to catch envy, you must approach it undercover, moving from bush to bush, in a zigzag and deviating fashion. Like a con man or analyst, your true agenda must remain quite unnoticed by the unsuspecting victim or patient.

This is the tactic Cassius pursues. He notices that Brutus's eyes do not emit the gentleness and show of love they used to. This is simultaneously a clue for Cassius and a warning to us. When the protagonist's love wanes, envy rises. Cassius sees the clue and probes deeper.

And he gets what he's looking for: an admission that his patient is deeply conflicted inside. "Vexéd I am / Of late with passions of some difference" (1.2.39–40), Brutus says, before turning to apologize to Cassius: "poor Brutus, with himself at war, / Forgets the shows of love to other men" (1.2.46–7).

This sounds promising to the sly Cassius. All is not well inside poor Brutus's heart. Cassius now pursues a slightly more aggressive tactic. He is no longer probing delicately; he is actively engaged in a little mimetic transference:

> Then, Brutus, I have much mistook your passion,
> By means whereof this breast of mine hath buried
> Thoughts of great value, worthy cogitations. (1.2.48–50)

Cassius is validating Brutus's inner conflict by implying that it is somehow related to his own buried conflict. Brutus's passion, which Cassius says he "mistook" as personal displeasure towards him, has caused him (Cassius) to bury his "thoughts of great value." But he now realizes that he was mistaken; he doesn't need to hide his feelings from Brutus. The whole strategy is designed to encourage Brutus to "get in touch" with his feelings of envy towards Caesar.

So Cassius means exactly the opposite of what he says. He hasn't mistaken Brutus's passion at all. He had suspected envy all along. The trick now is to coax it out of Brutus.

"Tell me, good Brutus," Cassius asks, "can you see your face?" "No, Cassius," Brutus replies, "for the eye sees not itself / But by reflection, by some other things" (1.2.51–3). Brutus doesn't know it, but he is about to be tempted by envy. Cassius says:

> I, your glass,
> Will modestly discover to yourself
> That of yourself which you yet know not of. (1.2.68–70)

The whole conversation between Cassius and Brutus is an elaborate code in which words like "worthy cogitations," "thoughts of great value," "virtue," and – most significantly – "honor" really mean *envy*. "I love / The name of honor more than I fear death" (1.2.88–9) Brutus boasts. "I know that virtue to be in you Brutus," Cassius replies, stroking

Brutus's ego. "Well," he continues, "honor is the subject of my story" (1.2.90–2). If Cassius were being truthful, he would have said "envy is the subject of my story" for what follows is a brilliant example of envy mongering:

> I was born free as Caesar; so were you;
> We both have fed as well, and we can both
> Endure the winter's cold as well as he.
> For once, upon a raw and gusty day,
> The troubled Tiber chafing with her shores,
> Caesar said to me, "Dar'st thou, Cassius, now
> Leap in with me into this angry flood,
> And swim to yonder point?" Upon the word,
> Accoutred as I was, I plungèd in
> And bade him follow; so indeed he did.
> The torrent roared, and we did buffet it
> With lusty sinews, throwing it aside
> And stemming it with hearts of controversy.
> But ere we could arrive the point proposed,
> Caesar cried "Help me, Cassius, or I sink!"
> I, as Aeneas, our great ancestor,
> Did from the flames of Troy upon his shoulder
> The old Anchises bear, so from the waves of Tiber
> Did I the tirèd Caesar. And this man
> Is now become a god, and Cassius is
> A wretched creature and must bend his body,
> If Caesar carelessly but nod on him.
> He had a fever when he was in Spain,
> And when the fit was on him I did mark
> How he did shake. 'Tis true, this god did shake.
> His coward lips did from their color fly,
> And that same eye whose bend doth awe the world
> Did lose his luster. I did hear him groan.
> Ay, and that tongue of his that bade the Romans
> Mark him and write his speeches in their books,
> Alas, it cried "Give me some drink, Titinius,"
> As a sick girl! Ye gods, it doth amaze me
> A man of such a feeble temper should
> So get the start of the majestic world
> And bear the palm alone. (1.2.97–131)

From a strictly logical point of view, this long speech can only be seen as a diabolical joke. In its highly personal and salacious details, it resembles our own gossip media, which daily broadcasts the embarrassing misfortunes of the rich and famous. Never once does Brutus challenge Cassius's outlandish claims. Has Cassius really engaged Caesar in this rather fanciful-sounding swimming contest? Did he really haul Caesar on his back across the Tiber to save the great general from death? And what about the blatant overstatement and gratuitous self-aggrandizement? Isn't this all a bit tasteless? Does Cassius really fancy himself a modern-day Aeneas? And so what if Caesar cried out for water when he was sick? Does any of this have anything at all to do with the real Caesar? It is sensationalism and self-serving melodrama of the most vulgar kind. Is this the sort of thing one would expect an honoured member of the patrician class to indulge in? Surely Brutus cannot be swayed by such lowbrow tactics? So why does Cassius descend to this level?

The diatribe is an excellent example of what the philosopher Harry Frankfurt calls bullshit.[3] As an analytic philosopher concerned with the logical status of our propositions, Frankfurt is perplexed by the rich human capacity for bullshit. Why is there so much of it? Doesn't anybody ever bother to check the facts?

Bullshit, Frankfurt observes, is not quite the same thing as lying. The liar deliberately hides the truth. He knows what the truth is, and his lie is designed to conceal it from you. This shows a certain respect for the truth because in order to lie, you must first know what the truth is. The bullshitter, on the other hand, has no similar concern for the truth. What he says might be true or might be false, but it hardly matters, because what the bullshitter aims to conceal is not the facts but "what he is up to."[4] Nonetheless, what brings both liar and bullshitter together is the fact that they both misrepresent themselves as truth tellers. The only difference is the liar knows what the truth is. The bullshitter, on the other hand, hasn't a clue. He chooses his facts as he pleases – or, if they are inconvenient to his purpose (as they generally are), he makes them up. His sole objective is to pull the wool over our eyes by whatever means possible.

I confess I very much admire Frankfurt's analysis of bullshit, which is admittedly an exceedingly common occurrence in everyday life. Despite my great admiration for Frankfurt's analysis, however, I think this is the wrong way to approach the problem. It makes a very dubious assumption. It assumes that words and things can always be neatly and tidily separated from one another. Once the separation has been made, we can rearrange the whole picture to sort out the wheat from the chaff. We can sort out the facts from the non-facts. We can separate the words that are genetically and historically related to their objects (the facts) from the words that are orphaned from the world (non-facts). This last category can then be easily ignored as nonsense or, as Frankfurt elegantly puts it, bullshit. And bullshit is not fit for philosophers.

This is all very well, but we are still left with the question Frankfurt begins with. Why is bullshit so prevalent? Frankfurt shows us why we *shouldn't* be so prone to bullshit, but he hasn't explained why we do in fact like it so much. His exercise therefore remains purely hypothetical, strangely abstracted from the historical reality of its intended subject matter. The philosopher remains dumbfounded by the presence of so much bullshit. But surely philosophers are not themselves totally immune to bullshit?

The problem with this picture is that it applies only to a very specialized type of language use. Furthermore, there is the question of the type of society in which this picture, where propositions must be measured against the facts, must be privileged above all else. Most people, most of the time, are not so concerned about whether their statements correspond to reality *all the time*. Admittedly, *we* are concerned about this much of the time, but by and large most societies are remarkably more relaxed about the logical status of their propositions. Correspondence to the facts is usually regarded as a relatively minor consideration. Correspondence with the other, especially if this other is the priest or some other person of special importance, usually trumps correspondence to the facts.[5]

Cassius's envious and slanderous account of Caesar must be understood in this sense. If Brutus does not challenge him on anything he says, then presumably Cassius can take his silence as a kind of implied consent. The actual logical status of the slander is less important than the slander itself. This is in fact the beauty of slander. Who cares if it's true or not? What we want now is a salacious story about the inadequacies of someone whose celebrity has become, for whatever reason, intolerable.[6]

This is why Brutus does not challenge Cassius. His very posture and body language indicate that he is extremely uncomfortable with all the attention Caesar is getting. But he cannot admit to being envious because doing so would betray his personal sense of honour. An honourable gentleman such as Brutus does not participate in the unseemly scandalmongering of the hoi polloi. And this is precisely why Brutus needs Cassius. Cassius is that part of Brutus that Brutus must hide from himself.

Is Cassius an *exemplum* of envy in something like the sense of an old medieval morality tale? I think this is exactly what he is. And I think we still have something to learn from those critics who emphasize Shakespeare's indebtedness to the medieval mystery and morality plays and, more broadly, to the moral background of Christianity.[7] From this perspective, Cassius may be said to have a symbolic function that goes beyond the purely "realistic" psychological interpretation of his character. Envy is not simply being communicated from one individual to another. Rather, it is being allegorized as itself a character. Cassius *is* envy. His function in the play, at least in this critical temptation scene, is to personify a sentiment we all experience but rarely acknowledge as our own. Brutus, like most of us, is no Prospero. Rather than admit to envy, he disguises it as something noble, a desire for honour and freedom. But this is merely an elaborate self-deception. Cassius's function in this scene is to illustrate the extent of this self-deception. He is the uncanny within Brutus, the mouthpiece of the unconscious modestly discovering to Brutus that of himself which he yet knows not of.

Shakespeare gives us plenty of indications that Brutus should beware of Cassius:

> Into what dangers would you lead me, Cassius,
> That you would have me seek into myself
> For that which is not in me? (1.2.63–5)

Allegorically speaking, we can say that envy is at war with its opposite, love or fidelity. And this creates the tragic inner conflict of which Brutus himself is only dimly aware. (Arguably, he never advances beyond this condition of tragic self-deception.) The excuses he makes to Cassius for being melancholy and neglectful of his friends are evidence of the oncoming inner storm. We hear from offstage the crowd's roar of approval for Caesar. Brutus immediately looks up and says, "I do fear the people / Choose Caesar to be king" (1.2.79–80). Cassius sees his opening and pounces: "Ay, do you fear it? / Then must I think you would not have it so" (1.2.80–1). Brutus's laconic response fails to conceal the tension within himself: "I would not, Cassius, yet I love him well" (1.2.82). I hate Caesar for his ambition, but I love him as a friend. The stage has been set. The inner conflict between love and resentment is about to unfold in Brutus's heart.

The point I wish to emphasize is the inward nature of this conflict. The political battle for Rome is, for Shakespeare at any rate, represented as an inner struggle for Brutus's soul. Brutus is at war with himself. This is not to say that the other characters do not have their internal struggles too. They do, and Shakespeare often gives them their due. But he does so without allowing them to dominate his focus on the protagonist. *Julius Caesar* is not quite typical in this respect. Given Shakespeare's general tragic pattern, which is more fully developed in the later tragedies, the play should really be called *Brutus*, for it is Brutus who receives the most extensive treatment in terms of the inner conflict. On the other hand, *Julius Caesar* deals with politics, and this focus on the collectivity rather than the individual inevitably shifts attention from the inward crisis to the external political crisis, the latter being, as Girard shows, also a sacrificial crisis.[8]

For Girard, the tragic hero is a mimetic double. His desire is mirrored in the desires of those around him. In this sense, Brutus, Cassius, Antony, Octavius, and Lepidus, as well as all the members of the original conspiracy, are supplements or "imitators" of the immortal Caesar. Even Caesar is merely reproducing the desire of his predecessor, the vanquished Pompey, who is referred to nostalgically by the tribunes in the first scene of the play. All are rivals competing for the same thing, the bloody centre stage that is Rome. In terms of the particular scene we have been discussing, we can say that Cassius's resentment is a more developed or mature version of the embryonic resentment in Brutus. Whereas Cassius has already committed himself to the conspiracy, Brutus has not. By tracing the conspiracy back to its source in resentment, Shakespeare shows us that the origin of tragedy lies not without but within the individual. This idea of tragedy is radically different from that of the Greeks.

This doubling of the scene of classical tragedy within the protagonist himself is in fact the point of the second scene of the play, which unpacks the classical scene's unproblematic representation of the centre as a fixed locus of attention. The scene begins with the appearance of Caesar surrounded by his "court." The occasion is a religious festival, the Lupercalia, and Caesar appears at its head with all the pomp and ceremony of a sacred figure. Our view of the centre mirrors that of the onstage audience, which functions much like the chorus of a Greek tragedy. We easily participate in the general adulation of the central figure. But this natural tendency to imitate the periphery's collective identification of the centre is subsequently undercut when our attention is shifted to two figures who emerge from the periphery to dominate our attention for rest of the play.

What is remarkable is Brutus's initial reluctance to accept the central usurping role. Brutus is no Richard, Duke of Gloucester. Instead, he must be wooed into the centre by Cassius, who takes this early opportunity to express his envy and hatred of Caesar. This expression of resentment by a member of the periphery undercuts the preceding public scene in which Caesar's centrality seemed assured. The whole point of Cassius's diatribe against Caesar is to undermine Caesar's legitimacy, both in the mind of his immediate interlocutor (Brutus) and also in the minds of the auditors and readers, who are otherwise predisposed to admire this legendary historical figure.

This focus on the periphery's resentful representation of the centre also explains why Shakespeare chose to title the play *Julius Caesar* rather than *Brutus*. Brutus's centrality is supplemental to Caesar's. The more self-conscious and introspective Brutus is haunted by the unreflective and unselfconscious Caesar. The neoclassical aesthetic stages the protagonist's self-conscious discovery of his marginality with respect to the centre, a marginality the classical protagonist is by definition never conscious of. Oedipus never doubts the legitimacy of his possession of the centre; the latter depends on him, not he on it. Aristotle's notion of the *peripeteia*, when the protagonist discovers that all his efforts have led not to success but defeat, underscores the classical protagonist's ignorance of his dependence on the periphery. Who knew the centre could be so vulnerable to defeat?

In contrast to the classical protagonist's ignorance of his vulnerability at the centre, Shakespeare explicitly stages the passage of the protagonist from anonymous periphery to desirable centre. Cassius's diatribe against Caesar is punctuated by the offstage shouts of the crowd as they express their approval of Caesar. The real centre is elsewhere; Brutus is all too aware of that. Cassius's heavily sarcastic portrayal of Caesar merely reinforces the scandal of the periphery's exclusion from the centre. Every time Brutus hears another shout from offstage, Cassius is there to amplify the indignity of Brutus's anonymity.

The most intelligent comment Caesar makes in the entire play occurs when he reenters the stage. He takes one look at the brooding Cassius and says to Antony,

> Yond Cassius has a lean and hungry look.
> He thinks too much. Such men are dangerous.
> . . . .
> Seldom he smiles, and smiles in such a sort

As if he mocked himself and scorned his spirit
That could be moved to smile at anything.
Such men as he be never at heart's ease
Whiles they behold a greater than themselves,
And therefore are they very dangerous. (1.2.194–5, 205–10)

Considered in purely psychological terms, Caesar's observation is totally out of character. It comes, so to speak, from out of the blue. Caesar is not given to remarking on his own vulnerability. How can we explain this uncharacteristic self-consciousness of his vulnerability?

Recall that, to this point, our view of Caesar has been strictly of his public persona. We have been privy to no private misgivings or soliloquies or asides. As we learn from Casca later, Caesar's actions have been one long public spectacle, epitomized by his theatrical refusal to accept the crown presented to him by Antony. But here he is suddenly overwhelmed by a brilliant insight into Cassius's inner being. Whence comes this extraordinary percipience? The oddity is that after divining the truth about Cassius, Caesar immediately forgets it. His is truly a split personality: one moment full of insight, the next totally devoid of it.

But the oddity disappears when we consider the moment in terms of its larger symbolic or allegorical structure. Cassius, I have argued, is not just another character. He also has an allegorical function vis-à-vis the protagonist. This function is to reflect the flaw within the protagonist. In this regard, he resembles somewhat the cartoonish figures of the older morality plays. Cassius's extended resentful commentaries on Caesar's inadequacies are modified manifestations of this moral tradition. We are being warned of an approaching conflict within the protagonist, and the tragedy is that the protagonist isn't aware of it. This is the reason why Cassius insinuates himself only gradually into Brutus's mind. What we are witnessing is the inexorable overthrow of the protagonist's mind by resentment, with increasingly violent consequences for the social order.

So Caesar's curious split personality is an analogue for the split personality of the protagonist. Envy, like a soothsayer in the street, confronts us daily, but we pass it by without a second glance, confident in our immunity to it. Of course, we easily discern it in others, but never in ourselves. In this sense, we are no different from Brutus or Caesar. And this is precisely why it requires a dramatist to point its dangers out to us. "Into what dangers would you lead me," Brutus asks Cassius

(1.2.63). If "I do fawn on men and hug them hard / And after seem to scandal them ... then hold me dangerous," Cassius replies (1.2.75–8). But Brutus never sees the danger. He is too distracted by Caesar's ambition to notice the beam of resentment in his own eye. So Shakespeare gives the most percipient lines to Caesar:

> Such men as he be never at heart's ease
> Whiles they behold a greater than themselves,
> And therefore are they very dangerous. (1.2.208–10)

Caesar hits the nail on the head. Wherever there is inequality among men, there will be resentment. Since inequality is a fact of life, so is resentment. The tragedy is that everybody in the play refuses to recognize this elementary truth. Instead resentment is always turned into something else that sounds much more dignified and noble. What does Brutus see as he stares envy in the face?

> But wherefore do you hold me here so long?
> What is it that you would impart to me?
> If it be aught toward the general good,
> Set honor in one eye and death i'th'other
> And I will look on both indifferently;
> For let the gods so speed me as I love
> The name of honor more than I fear death. (1.2.83–9)

Instead of envy, Brutus sees honour and something called the General Good. Honour and the General Good are Brutus's translations of envy. Brutus turns envy into a respectable political ideal. No doubt this is what Leslie Farber meant when he referred to envy's talent for disguise. For who can deny the beauty and nobility of the General Good? But notice there is another figure with the General Good: Death. For Brutus, death is something we naturally fear. But this fear can be overcome by loving the General Good more fervently. What Brutus doesn't see is that Envy and Death are in fact deadly twins. When Brutus gives himself over to envy, he leaves a trail of death behind him.

But envy has not won yet. There is a second temptation in the form of the letters planted by Cassius. This temptation takes place in Brutus's orchard. The internal conflict manifests itself in the form of four successive soliloquies. Once again, Brutus is torn between his personal friendship towards Caesar and his fascination with the General Good:

> It must be by his death. And for my part
> I know no personal cause to spurn him,
> But for the general. (2.1.10–12)

Should he kill Caesar for the General Good? Is she worth such a sacrifice? Consider Brutus's argument:

> And to speak truth of Caesar,
> I have not known when his affections swayed
> More than his reason. But 'tis a common proof
> That lowliness is young ambition's ladder,
> Whereto the climber-upward turns his face;
> But when he once attains the upmost round
> He then unto the ladder turns his back
> Looks in the clouds, scorning the base degrees
> By which he did ascend. So Caesar may.
> Then, lest he may, prevent. And since the quarrel
> Will bear no color for the thing he is,
> Fashion it thus: that what he is, augmented,
> Would run to these and these extremities;
> And therefore think him as a serpent's egg
> Which, hatched, would, as his kind, grow mischievous;
> And kill him in the shell. (2.1.19–34)

As most readers see, Brutus's argument is purely hypothetical. One might paraphrase it as follows. Life is a one-way ladder. (Ambition knows no climber-downward.) It follows that lowliness is in fact a condition of *all* positions on the ladder. (If you're only looking ahead of you at the next rung up, it doesn't matter where you are on the ladder.) The exception, of course, is the topmost rung. When you get to this point, you become insufferably arrogant because you have no one above you to make you feel lowly. Caesar is not yet insufferably arrogant, but it is only a matter of time before he gets to the top. Brutus cannot bear the thought of that. Therefore, he must kill Caesar before he gets there.

If we pause for a moment to consider the logic of this argument, we can see how peculiar it really is. First of all, one does not kill someone for purely hypothetical crimes. Brutus may turn out to be correct in his prediction about Caesar's insufferable arrogance, but that in no way means that he is right to take action *now*. What if he turns out to be wrong? If we kill people for purely hypothetical crimes, then everybody is guilty, and we may as well smash all the eggs.

But this invites a second, more puzzling question. Is the crime Brutus imagines actually hypothetical? It is quite possible to argue that Brutus is not talking about a hypothetical situation at all. Caesar is, in plain fact, an ambitious and power-seeking maniac who will stop at nothing short of supreme power over the whole empire. When it comes to ambition's ladder, there don't seem to be many more rungs left for Caesar to climb. We're not talking about hypotheticals here, we're talking about reality. But Brutus doesn't make this argument. Why not? If Brutus is not talking about Caesar, whom is he talking about?

The answer, of course, is that Brutus is talking about himself. More precisely, Brutus thinks he is talking about Caesar, but Shakespeare shows us that he is really talking about himself. In other words, he is engaged in some fairly high-level philosophical self-deception. Brutus is the man at the foot of ambition's ladder, poised to make the first fatal step on its upward slope. We should not worry about Caesar, Shakespeare is saying. Caesar is already far gone, his head in the clouds scorning the base degrees below him. "I am constant as the northern star," Caesar says, with "no fellow in the firmament" (3.1.61–3). But when he says this, the daggers are already glinting in the morning light, and he soon falls to the base degrees that he thought he had left behind for good.

So the hypothetical situation Brutus imagines actually refers to himself. And in this case, the description is perfectly accurate. He has not yet committed himself to young ambition's ladder. Certainly he has thought about it. But he has not yet acted. His appetite for self-love, for fame and celebrity, has been whetted by the envious Cassius. We have already seen that. But we all suffer from envy. The question is, how do we deal with it? Shakespeare is inviting us to examine this question by observing Brutus.

Consider the structure of the scene. Recall that it is nighttime. Brutus cannot sleep. This is never a good sign. Characters who cannot sleep have something weighing heavily on their consciences. "Sleep no more," says the voice in Macbeth's head. "Farewell the tranquil mind!" cries Othello, neither poppy nor mandragora shall ever medicine him to sweet sleep again. Even Hamlet finds himself threatening to drink hot blood during the very witching hour of night. Brutus is no different:

> Since Cassius first did whet me against Caesar,
> I have not slept. (2.1.61–2)

Brutus's four soliloquies map the gradual deterioration of his mind, as the light within is slowly extinguished to merge seamlessly with the darkness around him. Brutus's serving boy, Lucius, allegorizes this descent. The name means light (from *lucis*). He is first associated with a taper, which Brutus asks him to fetch. Thereafter each of Brutus's four soliloquies is punctuated by Lucius's entry and then exit from the stage. First he delivers the taper and the letters (planted by Cassius for Brutus to discover); then he confirms the day of the month (the ides of March); and finally he announces the arrival of the conspirators, whom he cannot identify because their "hats are plucked about their ears, / And half their faces buried in their cloaks" (2.1.73–4). Symbolically, the boy represents innocence and light. Later, before the battle of Philippi, he is associated with music, which he plays before falling into an innocent sleep (while Brutus remains in a state of restless wakefulness, soon to be visited by Caesar's ghost). His youth and innocence contrast the envy and jaded cynicism of the conspirators.

By the time the conspirators enter, light has almost been completely extinguished by dark. Brutus and Cassius draw apart to discuss matters among themselves, and Shakespeare focuses our attention on the remaining conspirators who argue about where exactly on the horizon the sun will rise.

> DECIUS: Here lies the east. Doth not the day break here?
> CASCA: No.
> CINNA: Oh, pardon, sir, it doth; and yon gray lines
> That fret the clouds are messengers of day.
> CASCA: You shall confess that you are both deceived.
> Here, as I point my sword, the sun arises,
> Which is a great way growing on the south,
> Weighing the youthful season of the year.
> Some two months hence, up higher toward the north
> He first presents his fire; and the high east
> Stands, as the Capitol, directly here. (2.1.101–11)

This is not simply small talk inserted by Shakespeare to pass the time before we hear from Brutus and Cassius again. It continues the theme of light with which the scene opened when Brutus called for Lucius:

> What, Lucius, ho!
> I cannot by the progress of the stars
> Give guess how near to day. (2.1.1–3)

The state of Brutus's soul is mirrored by his failure to discern the light around him. He cannot tell when the dawn shall come. Nor does he realize that his salvation is reflected in the sleeping innocence of the boy. His complaint – "I would it were my fault to sleep so soundly" (2.1.4) – is really a cry for help to be rid of the "hideous dream" (2.1.65) haunting his mind. The conspirators mirror Brutus's self-deception. They too are confused about where redemption is to be found. They believe they are authors of a new dawn, but they disagree about the most basic of matters, including the position of the rising sun.

As John Vyvyan has observed, Shakespeare uses light in an almost sacramental fashion, as the "outward sign of an inward grace."[9] When the light fails, or when the protagonist is struggling to find it, we know that he stands at a precipice and is in danger of losing his way. Brutus's call for light at the beginning of this scene is typical, as is the conspirators' confusion about the position of the rising sun. Claudius, too, calls for light when his conscience has been rattled by Hamlet. "Give me some light" (*Hamlet* 3.2.267), and there is the beautiful hymn to dawn by Horatio that signals the end of the night's terrors and the fading of the warlike apparition haunting Elsinore castle: "But, look, the morn in russet mantle clad / Walks o'er the dew of yon high eastward hill" (*Hamlet* 1.1.172–3). Macbeth's downward path is accompanied by a desire to shun the day and associate himself with the "seeling night" that will "Scarf up the tender eye of pitiful day" (*Macbeth* 3.2.49–50). Othello, contemplating the sleeping Desdemona, associates her with light and subconsciously intuits the full horror of his intended crime: "Put out the light, and then put out the light" (*Othello* 5.2.7).

When Shakespeare turns our attention to Brutus and the conspirators in 2.1, we witness how eager Brutus is to grasp the rungs of ambition's ladder. Cassius makes three separate proposals: to swear an oath, to sound out Cicero, and to kill Mark Antony. But each time Brutus overrules him in the most authoritarian fashion. He rejects the oath on the grounds that virtuous Romans do not need to swear their loyalty.

He objects to the inclusion of Cicero because "he will not follow anything / That other men begin" (2.1.151–2). And he rejects the plan to murder Antony because this will make their course seem too bloody.

Each reply reveals how self-deluded Brutus has become. First, Brutus disguises the murder in a cloak of honourable-sounding political rhetoric. He rejects the oath because he believes that since all true Romans share their disaffection for tyranny, they will automatically agree to murder Caesar. To swear an oath would be tantamount to admitting that this is not the case. Second, he rejects Cicero because he is jealous of him. Cicero is the one man, besides Caesar himself, whose reputation might overshadow Brutus's. Finally, he rejects the murder of Antony, not because he is repelled by the idea of his murder, but because he believes he can deceive the people into accepting Caesar's murder as a public good:

> Our course will seem to bloody, Caius Cassius,
> To cut the head off and then hack the limbs,
> Like wrath in death and envy afterwards;
> For Antony is but a limb of Caesar.
> Let's be sacrificers, but not butchers, Caius.
> We all stand up against the spirit of Caesar,
> And in the spirit of men there is no blood
> Oh, that we then could come by Caesar's spirit
> And not dismember Caesar! But, alas,
> Caesar must bleed for it. And, gentle friends,
> Let's kill him boldly, but not wrathfully;
> Let's carve him as a dish fit for the gods,
> Not hew him as a carcass fit for hounds.
> And let our hearts, as subtle masters do,
> Stir up their servants to an act of rage
> And after seem to chide 'em. This shall make
> Our purpose necessary, and not envious;
> Which so appearing to the common eyes
> We shall be called purgers, not murderers.
> And for Mark Antony, think not of him;
> For he can do no more than Caesar's arm
> When Caesar's head is off. (2.1.163–84)

As far as Brutus is concerned, the murder of Antony is supererogatory, Antony being but a limb of Caesar. Cut off the head, and the limbs become useless. What Brutus fails to grasp is that resentment will not die with the sacrifice of Caesar. Antony's paean to revenge, as he stands over Caesar's bloodstained corpse, is the ironic counterpart to Brutus's speech on the beauty of sacrifice:

> And Caesar's spirit, ranging for revenge,
> With Ate by his side come hot from hell,
> Shall in these confines with a monarch's voice
> Cry havoc and let slip the dogs of war. (3.1.272–5)

Brutus believes he can control the resentment unleashed by the *sparagmos*. And he believes this because his vision of the murder is extremely idealized. In his mind, it is all perfectly rational and peaceful. The onlookers will not be horrified by the murder of Caesar. On the contrary, they will admire the conspirators as they gracefully carve the body of Caesar. The killing will be undertaken with the greatest tact and delicacy, and it will therefore be impossible to resist the seductive beauty of the event.

As Girard points out, the metaphor of carving has an aesthetic dimension that Brutus opposes to the image of excessive violence.[10] Brutus is like the physician who wants to heal the patient by injecting him with a little bit of the infectious disease but not enough to overwhelm him entirely. But the fatal error Brutus makes is to believe that his vision of the murder is universally shared. When he attempts to turn his imaginary sacrifice into a real one, it all goes horribly wrong. The sacrifice of Caesar leads not to the desired unification but to further violence and chaos. Girard describes this as a sign of the historical decadence of the institution of sacrifice. When the sacrificers get too self-conscious about the violence they are inflicting on the victim, they begin to lose heart in their undertaking. The sacrifice becomes a hollowed-out symbol that fails to persuade anyone of its vitality or necessity. Ritual society cannot tolerate too much of this sort of decadence. Eventually disorder breaks out. This is, Girard says, the situation that occurs in *Julius Caesar*. Brutus has opened Pandora's box of undifferentiated violence.

Actually, Girard goes one step further. He says that not only Brutus but Shakespeare has opened Pandora's box. In writing *Julius Caesar*, Shakespeare discovered the real, shocking violence underlying human social organization. People need scapegoats upon which to vent their frustrated desires. It is impossible, Girard says, *not* to have a frustrated desire. Desire is always imitated, and therefore sooner or later people will end up desiring the same thing. Sooner or later, my model (the one whose desires I imitate) will become my obstacle and therefore my antagonist. This is the "mimetic crisis" and it is vividly portrayed in *Julius Caesar*. The mimetic crisis is Girard's term for what happens when mimetic desire bursts its banks, so to speak, and is no longer contained by the orderly system of levies and dams that has been put in place by religion, through its various rituals of interdiction. In Girard's theory, the containment of mimetic desire is performed by ritual sacrifice, the coming together of the community to vent their buried hostilities on a suitable victim (i.e., someone whose death is unlikely to promote revenge and therefore unlikely to promote further violence). In the act of sacrifice, the victim is transformed into a god, the bringer of peace, a symbol of the unity of the community, whose members now return to their lives refreshed in the knowledge that violence has once more successfully been kept at bay. Brutus's metaphor of carving is designed to convey this idea of sacrifice as an orderly ritual that will expel all violence from the community by concentrating it on a single victim. But instead of unifying the community, the assassination tears it apart. Conspiracies sprout overnight. Cinna the poet is attacked by the Roman mob in a grim parody of Brutus's sacrifice of Caesar. What is going on?

Shakespeare, Girard says, has put his finger on the brutal underbelly of human culture. What distinguishes Shakespearean tragedy from all other tragedy, including the tragedy of the ancient Greeks, was the clarity with which Shakespeare understood mimetic desire and violence. *Julius Caesar* goes straight to the "foundational murder" upon which human culture is built: "It is the first and only tragedy that focuses on this murder itself and nothing else … Its real subject is the violent crowd."[11] That is why the murder of Caesar takes place in the middle of the play. Shakespeare did not want us to be distracted by either Caesar or the conspirators. He wanted, rather, to portray the overall dynamic of the social order. And this order is built on a foundational murder. Brutus's problem is that he cannot think *outside* this sacrificial system. He wants the murder to be beautiful so that it will not incite further violence. But he can think of no other way to solve the crisis except by murdering Caesar: "He goes as far as he can in the direction of a nonviolence that he cannot embrace. Brutus is seeking an impossible middle ground between a violence too impure not to exasperate the crisis and a violence so pure that it will be no violence at all."[12]

Girard's reading requires us to accept that Shakespeare was deeply ambivalent about the theatre's use of violence. Brutus's ambivalence is also Shakespeare's ambivalence. Both men fear the public stage of violence but they see no other way to control it than by permitting it to appear on this public scene. But in collapsing Brutus and Shakespeare, Girard collapses the distinction between the violence of the *sparagmos* and the aesthetic contemplation that precedes it. The key distinction that Shakespeare is inviting us to contemplate is not the difference between violence and non-violence, but the difference between the private and public scenes of representation. As long as Brutus can contemplate the murder of Caesar as a purely aesthetic object, he is guilty of no crime other than resentment. The tragedy is not that Brutus is resentful, but that he finds no means to vent his resentment other than by murdering Caesar.

What Girard misses is the role of the aesthetic in deferring resentment. It is true that the aesthetic accomplishes this deferral by explicitly representing violence. But the representation of violence is still the deferral of violence. In contemplating Shakespeare's play, we are not engaged in actual violence. But nor are Brutus and the conspirators in 2.1. They are *for the time being* not engaged in any acts of violence. The problem occurs when their resentment is no longer satisfied with a purely aesthetic deferral. But when this change occurs, they are no longer in the realm of the aesthetic.

Brutus's imagination takes him as close as possible to the desirable centre without actually inciting violence. He can imagine it in this superbly tranquil fashion precisely because, as the sole author of it, he is perfectly in control of it. That is why he behaves in such an authoritarian manner towards his fellow conspirators. He will tolerate no rival vision of the centre. This egotism is a necessity of the aesthetic representation of the centre, which has to demonstrate the legitimacy of the protagonist's usurpation of it. Where Brutus goes wrong is in attempting to translate his private aesthetic vision into a political reality. As always, the centre is the locus of competing desires. The utopia in which those desires are magically unified into a harmony of souls exists only in Brutus's mind. The authoritarian manner in which Brutus overrules the other conspirators is an ironic reminder that the private aesthetic scene is in conflict with the public one.

Their preparations for the assassination complete, the conspirators depart. Brutus cautions each one of them not to betray their purpose, but "bear it as our Roman actors do" (2.1.227). They must hide the monstrous visage of the conspiracy in smiles and affability. The external façade disguises the resentment buried within. Alone once more, Brutus calls for Lucius but gets no answer. He muses that the boy must be asleep. The larger significance of what he says eludes him:

Boy! Lucius! – Fast asleep? It is no matter.
Enjoy the honey-heavy dew of slumber.
Thou hast no figures nor no fantasies
Which busy care draws in the brains of men;
Therefore thou sleep'st so sound. (2.1.230–4)

Brutus envies the boy's innocence. But his envy of the boy is quite unlike his envy of Caesar. Caesar is in the centre; the boy is not. Brutus imagines the boy as free of all desire and therefore of all envy. But this is pure sentimentalism. The real point is that the boy's anonymity, his wholly peripheral status, disqualifies him as a rival for the tragic centre, which tolerates those of the patrician class alone. Unlike Caesar or Cicero, the boy poses no threat to Brutus. He therefore can be sentimentalized as free of resentment.

Brutus projects onto the boy an idealized view of the centre as purged of all desire. But this is the condescending admiration of a superior, who knows that the inferior will never be able to challenge his desire. Is this not Brutus's downfall in his judgment of Antony? In representing Antony as but a limb of Caesar, he underestimates the universality of desire and of the resentment that accompanies it. Brutus persists in believing that resentment does not motivate his bid to usurp the centre.

Instead of the boy, who remains fast asleep in the neighbouring room, Brutus is visited by his wife Portia, who has noticed his absence from the bedroom. She is upset by his strange conduct. He has neglected all food, talk, and sleep, and has behaved dismissively towards her. What is the meaning of his antisocial behaviour? Brutus tries to excuse himself by saying he is in poor health. But she sees straight through him:

No, my Brutus,
You have some sick offense within your mind,
Which by the right and virtue of my place
I ought to know of. (2.1.268–71)

Like Cassius earlier, and like the boy and the conspirators in this scene, Portia represents more than simply a concerned and attentive wife. She also represents an aspect of the protagonist's self. In the play's second scene, Cassius embodied envy, which tempts Brutus towards the conspiracy. When we next see Brutus, alone in his orchard, envy has taken root and grown. He is now openly contemplating Caesar's death, his imagination compelled by the hideous image of the murder. The growth of envy within Brutus is allegorized by the growth of the conspiracy. Cassius arrives with six new conspirators. As envy rises, Brutus's innocence declines. The boy falls asleep, and Brutus cannot wake him. Now Portia enters and, appealing to Brutus's "vows of love" (2.1.273), begs him on her knees to unfold himself to her. The stage directions here are crucial. Brutus is obviously moved by this show of love and fidelity, and one feels that he is about to confess his soul to her. "O ye gods," he says, "Render me worthy of this noble wife!" (2.2.304–5). But just at this moment we hear a knock from offstage. Brutus says: "Hark, hark, one knocks. Portia, go in awhile ... Leave me with haste" (2.2.306, 310).

Brutus stands at a precipice. It is not too late to turn back from the brink. But instead he orders his wife to leave. The decision is fatal. Lucius's description of the stranger says it all: "Here is a sick man that would speak with you" (2.2.311). Portia was not fooled by Brutus. She saw the sickness within him. But he chose to ignore her. Instead he embraces the sick Caius Ligarius. This new conspirator is not physically sick. He arrives with a bandage around his head, but he soon discards it when Brutus asks him to join the conspiracy:

> I am not sick, if Brutus have in hand
> Any exploit worthy of the name of honor. (2.1.317–18)

When Brutus declares that he has such an exploit, Ligarius is miraculously cured: "By all the gods that Romans bow before, / I here discard my sickness!" (2.1.321–2). Brutus gets his first taste of the centre's charismatic power in his recruitment of Ligarius to the conspiracy. The power he seems to wield over this sick man, who so dramatically recovers his appetite for life, must be truly awe-inspiring to Brutus. It is typical of Shakespeare, however, to show that what the protagonist believes to be the path to life is in fact the path to death. Brutus believes he is making "sick men whole" (2.1.328) by expelling tyranny from Rome. But what Shakespeare shows is that Brutus only succeeds in encouraging what lies at the root of all tyranny: the disease of resentment. The irony of Ligarius's lines is unmistakable to us, if not to Brutus: "I follow you / To do I know not what" (2.1.333–4). In aiming to dismantle Caesar's tyranny, Brutus has created his own. Ligarius hasn't a clue what Brutus wants him to do, but he will follow him anyway.

There is one point I should address here before proceeding further. I suggested that Portia represents a possible source of salvation for Brutus, but rather than choosing the path of love, he chooses the path of death. He rejects Portia and instead welcomes into his home the sick conspirator Ligarius. Before dismissing her, however, Brutus makes a promise to her:

> And by and by thy bosom shall partake
> The secrets of my heart.
> All my engagements I will construe to thee,
> All the charactery of my sad brows. (2.1.306–9)

Does Brutus follow through on this promise? Many readers feel that he does. They cite the obvious nervousness and anxiety Portia exhibits while Brutus is in the Capitol preparing to assassinate Caesar. Surely her anxiety indicates that she knows about the assassination? And if she knows about the assassination, does this not refute the idea that she represents Brutus's better conscience?

The text, however, is not as unambiguous as I have just made it appear. First, the immediate evidence would seem to suggest that Brutus does *not* follow through on his promise. For the scene ends with Brutus making the same promise to Ligarius. In response to the latter's query about what it is they are about to do, Brutus says,

> What it is, my Caius,
> I shall unfold to thee *as we are going*
> *To whom it must be done.* (2.1.330–2; my emphases)

"Set on your foot," (2.1.332) Ligarius replies, and the scene ends with Brutus saying, "Follow me, then" (2.1.335). The conclusion seems unmistakable. Brutus leaves his house immediately with Ligarius. There is not enough time to explain the assassination to Ligarius before they leave. They will discuss the matter on the way to fetch Caesar, the man "to whom it must be done."

Why are these small details important? Because they show us that Brutus was insincere in his promise to Portia. It was a promise he did not intend to fulfil. The very fact that the promise is sandwiched between two urgent requests for her to leave ("Portia, go in awhile," "Leave me with haste") suggests that he is using it as a means to get rid of her, to put her off. But why? Because Portia makes Brutus feel deeply ashamed of himself. In her presence, Brutus gains something of his former self. He sees the evil of his intended action. But he will not admit to it. Instead he makes excuses. That is why he affects concern for Portia's health. But this is merely a pretext to be rid of her. He is not really concerned for her health. He is much too wrapped up in himself. Portia's refusal to be put off by him shows that Brutus himself is unconvinced by his own excuses. When she turns the tables on him and suggests that he is in fact the sick one, he is almost ready to concede that she is right. His conscience sits on a razor's edge and seems about to tip in her favour. But then the fatal knock is heard, and Brutus retreats back into his shell of self-deception. The sight of her is once more unbearable to him, and he ushers her from the room. The promise is a pretext to buy himself more time. Allegorically Portia represents Brutus's better conscience, and so he cannot tolerate her presence when he contemplates the deed he is about to commit. It is impossible for envy to flourish in the presence of love.

If this is true, why then does Portia later behave as though she is aware of the conspiracy? Just before the assassination takes place, Shakespeare gives us a glimpse of her, outside her home, in a state of extreme nervousness. She orders Lucius to run to the senate house, but neglects to explain what he should do there. She imagines sounds and rumours emanating from the Capitol. She checks the clock and refers to the soothsayer's prophecy. Finally, unable to contain herself, she bursts out with these words: "O Brutus, / The heavens speed thee in thine enterprise!" (2.4.41–2). And then she is immediately worried that she has betrayed herself to the boy, who is standing by all the while. Surely this shows us that she is aware of the conspiracy?

My response is twofold. First, Portia never explicitly admits to knowing anything about the conspiracy. The closest she comes is in the lines just quoted. But what exactly does "enterprise" refer to? It could refer to the assassination, but it could refer to something else. We simply don't know. Further, if we interpret this scene as definitive evidence that Portia does know about the conspiracy, then we are left with the difficulty of explaining how she knows about it. As we have seen, Shakespeare takes care to show us that Brutus leaves without divulging his secret to her.

But let us set these practical difficulties aside. Let us suppose for argument's sake that Brutus did divulge his plan to Portia. How does this affect the interpretation we have been pursuing? Well, for one thing it suggests that Portia is not Brutus's salvation. He has told her of the assassination, and she has done nothing to prevent him. On the contrary, she seems to be in league with him, at least morally and spiritually – "The heavens speed thee in thine enterprise!"

Although I find this interpretation problematic for reasons I have already stated, it is still possible to reconcile her actions on the morning of the assassination with the general argument that Shakespeare uses his minor characters to reflect aspects of the inner conflict of his protagonists. Not only does Portia now fail to sway Brutus from his course, she is herself inexorably drawn towards the centre's violence. She cannot resist "imitating" Brutus's desire (and therefore his envy and hatred of Caesar). In this regard, she is like the auditor or reader who is also swept up in the tragic action. It is a necessity of tragic form that we identify with Brutus, that we sympathize with his desire and resent the obstacles that stand in his way. On one level, we want him to succeed in his quest for the centre. This desire is only natural and to be expected; it is a condition of all aesthetic experience.

So Shakespeare is consciously playing with us here. In the first scene with Portia, he hinted that *we* stood at a crossroads. We had an opportunity to identify with Portia rather than Brutus. But if Portia were to succeed in her quest at this moment, if she were able to persuade Brutus to draw back from the precipice, then the tragedy would be ruined. Caesar would not have been murdered, and Brutus and Portia would have lived happy but boring and uneventful lives.

What we want, on the other hand, is a good tragedy, something with a bit of tension and preferably a dead body or two. So, like the sick man Ligarius, we fling ourselves over to Brutus's side. We shamelessly and blindly follow Brutus through to the completion of his bloody enterprise. So it is *we* who have cast Portia aside in our eagerness to observe the protagonist, whose envious desires mirror our own. What is left of her is a helpless woman consumed with nervous guilt for what she cannot prevent. Neither a full-fledged conspirator nor an innocent and ignorant bystander (like the boy), she is forced to sit on the sidelines and anxiously watch the spectacle unfold, hoping that Brutus will succeed but fearing the violence she knows he will suffer. In other words, she is just like us.

Incidentally, I am in pretty good company in my interpretation of Shakespeare here. Kenneth Burke argues that Shakespeare cleverly acknowledges our own culpability in Caesar's murder.[13] That is why Antony is so successful. He is the route to our expiation for participating in Caesar's murder. And Roy Battenhouse makes a similar remark in a different context when he suggests that Horatio is partly culpable for Ophelia's death because rather than protecting the poor girl, as Claudius had asked him to do, he allows himself to be distracted by the promise of Hamlet's return.[14] This is a subtle comment, but not too subtle, I think. It is certainly in keeping with Horatio's penchant for ghost stories. Hamlet's letter promises Horatio more thrills for his eager imagination, which may well be as foul as Hamlet's: "I have words to speak in thine ear will make thee dumb" (*Hamlet* 4.6.24–5). Battenhouse does not extend his comment about Horatio to the audience member, but I think this is a natural inference to make. Indeed, Harold Bloom makes exactly this inference.[15] Horatio, Bloom argues, is a proxy for the audience. We too are attracted to the scene of Hamlet's desire, to the foul "imaginations" (*Hamlet* 3.2.82) he, like Brutus, cannot tear himself away from. When Ophelia dies, it is the signal that the cat will mew and dog will have his day. The audience will get the bloody conclusion they have been looking for. As each protagonist plunges into the abyss, their better consciences are reduced to silence.

So Portia is Shakespeare's sly reference to the audience's single-minded desire for a tragic victim. Portia must be thrust aside for Brutus to continue on his downward course. It is not just Brutus who is attracted to the hideous dream inside his mind. We are too. And we expect to see the fruits of that dream performed before us on the stage. There are, however, consequences to our identification with Brutus's hideous desires. Kenneth Burke says that we are in need of expiation for Caesar's death and that is why we end up siding with Mark Antony. But why do we need such a violent expiation?

Recall Antony's private eulogy to Caesar. He is alone, standing (or perhaps kneeling) beside Caesar's dead and remarkably bloody body. (The body must be sufficiently bloody to allow the conspirators to bath their hands in blood "up to the elbows.") He begins by begging Caesar's pardon for appearing so meek and gentle towards his murderers. Then he calls Caesar "the noblest man / That ever livèd in the tide of times" (3.1.258–9). But the bulk of the soliloquy is given over to a frank and heartfelt desire for revenge:

A curse shall light upon the limbs of men;
Domestic fury and fierce civil strife
Shall cumber all the parts of Italy;
Blood and destruction shall be so in use
And dreadful objects so familiar

That mothers shall but smile when they behold
Their infants quartered with the hands of war,
All pity choked with custom of fell deeds;
And Caesar's spirit, ranging for revenge,
With Ate by his side come hot from hell,
Shall in these confines with a monarch's voice
Cry havoc and let slip the dogs of war,
That this foul deed shall smell above the earth
With carrion men, groaning for burial. (3.1.264–77)

This is indeed a fitting way to celebrate the death of a great man. How else is Antony to get our attention after Brutus has set such a seemingly unbeatable precedent? A solemn state funeral with a procession of public mourners would no doubt be more dignified and certainly more peaceful. But let's face it: as a dramatic spectacle it hardly compares to civil war and quartered infants.

Antony's speech should be compared to the prologue in *Henry V*, the play Shakespeare wrote immediately before *Julius Caesar*:

Oh, for a Muse of fire, that would ascend
The brightest heaven of invention!
A kingdom for a stage, princes to act
And monarchs to behold the swelling scene!
Then should the warlike Harry, like himself,
Assume the port of Mars; and at his heels,
Leashed in like hounds, should famine, sword and fire
Crouch for employment. (*Henry V* 1.0.1–8)

What the chorus promises the spectator is a spectacle fit for a king, something that will satisfy the spectator's desire for blood and violence. The ambiguity between onstage and offstage monarchs is intentional. You (the offstage monarch) will behold Harry (the onstage monarch) fight his bloody war with France. And a very rousing fight it promises to be too. The first three acts tantalize our desire for this great spectacle, the amazing victory of English foot soldiers over the fully armoured French cavalry.

Antony is doing something similar in his eulogy for Caesar. We have just witnessed Brutus's bid for aesthetic supremacy, and it appears to have been an excellent success. After all, he has just dispatched the most famous general in human history. How can that be surpassed?

Both Brutus and Cassius seem to be aware of this new benchmark in the history of (the representation of) violence, because they both comment self-reflexively on the originary and foundational status of their actions:

> CASSIUS: How may ages hence
> Shall this our lofty scene be acted over
> In states unborn and accents yet unknown!
> BRUTUS: How many times shall Caesar bleed in sport,
> That now on Pompey's basis lies along
> No worthier than the dust! (3.1.112–17)

But Antony, the great lover of plays, remains singularly unimpressed by Brutus's stage violence. Brutus has given the audience one dead body and, though one can hardly deny the excellent pedigree of his chosen victim, Antony promises to deliver a bit more bang for his buck. He will give us civil war and quartered infants.

The first two acts have been devoted more or less wholly to Brutus and, in particular, to Brutus's inner envy, which has led to the death of Caesar. What is there left to show the audience?

What is left is precisely what was there at the beginning: envy. But this time it is no longer Caesar who must be envied, since he is dead, but whoever appears to be his successor. This is the point of the third act of the play, which climaxes not with the murder of Caesar, but with the verbal sparring between Brutus and Antony as they compete for the now-vacant centre. Brutus's strategy is to place himself in the centre by ascending the pulpit, only to vacate it promptly by pointing to something greater than himself: Rome. This must be why he is so eager to hand the pulpit over to Antony. He sincerely believes that envy can be transcended by acknowledging that we are all citizens of Rome. The murder of Caesar was necessary to free Rome of tyranny. Brutus loved Caesar, but he loved Rome more.

This idea of love is very abstract. It is hard to picture love of one's city or country except in the concrete terms of *personal* love. One loves one's family and friends first, one's country later. Brutus's oration before the people of Rome misses this elementary point about love. He offers a very terse, even aggressive speech about how his fellow Romans must love their country more than any man, even if that man be Caesar himself: "Who is here so base that would be a bondman? If any speak, for him have I offended. Who is here so rude that would not be a Roman? If any, speak, for him have I offended. Who is here so vile that will not love his country? If any, speak, for him have I offended. I pause for a reply" (3.2.29–34). "None, Brutus, none!" cry the crowd. And, indeed, how could they not? Who would like to admit, amidst of mob of zealously patriotic Romans, to being a vile bondman, a hater of Rome, and a traitor to his country? Brutus is like the professor who looks scornfully at his students and asks if there are any stupid enough not to have understood what he has just said. Reply comes there none.

As many readers have noticed, there is the further irony that immediately after Brutus has finished his speech, the plebeians scream for Brutus to be a new Caesar. This is irony indeed, but it also shows the naiveté of Brutus's argument. His strategy for keeping the centre free of rivalry is to represent it as the locus of an equally shared fraternal love. We all share equally in our love of Rome. Therefore we all possess the centre "equally." But his actions prove the very opposite. By ascending the pulpit, Brutus centralizes himself above the citizenry. And this is immediately grasped by the plebeians, who promptly deify him as another Caesar.

The strategy could hardly suit Antony's purposes better. Once Brutus is deified as the next Caesar, it is a relatively simple matter for Antony to put the people into some discomfort about what they have just done. For by what right do they now centralize Brutus? O you hard hearts, you cruel men of Rome, knew you not Caesar? In fact, Antony's job of generating guilt for the victim is a good deal easier than it was for the tribunes Marullus and Flavius, who were scandalized by Caesar's pompous grandstanding after he defeated Pompey. Marullus and Flavius sought to remind the people of their love for Pompey, but they were without the visual aid of a fresh corpse to stir the people's guilt for what they had done. Antony, however, has Caesar's body conveniently to hand, and it proves decisive in swaying the people against Brutus. When he lifts Caesar's mantle and shows the people where the daggers have pierced Caesar's body, he encourages them to identify once again with the man they seemed to have forgotten so quickly. They are now full of sympathy for Caesar and indignant at the brutality he has suffered. Moments earlier, they had applauded Brutus and elevated him as another Caesar. They had identified with his desire for the centre and his envy of Caesar. They had believed in him and wanted him to succeed. But now, with Brutus firmly seated in the centre as another Caesar, they fear the consequences of their imitation of the protagonist's desires, and they side with Antony in order to expatiate for the "sin of desire." Desire and envy give way to horror. Shakespeare is giving us a textbook example of catharsis. Identification with Brutus now gives way to the shock at what his audience has allowed him to get away with. Brutus must pay for his crime, and Antony will be the instrument of the audience's revenge.

Kenneth Burke is right to regard the Roman crowd as performing a kind of classic Shakespearean double entendre. The onstage audience ironically mirrors the reactions of the offstage audience. The long scene in which Antony plays with the crowd, tugging them Iago-like to his desired conclusion, is a reprise of his soliloquy on revenge. Like the chorus of *Henry V*, Antony's soliloquy justifies his claim to our attention. Brutus and Cassius have provided spectacular fare to this point. In fact, they have gone one better than the rather paltry dumbshow Caesar had performed before the crowd during the Lupercalia. We had not been privy to that particular spectacle. Instead it was reported to us in admirably precise detail by the envious Casca. Shakespeare seems to have decided that such dumbshows are not worthy of our direct attention. Instead he puts Caesar's theatre into the background and gives us, as foreground, the background of Caesar's spectacle. In other words, he turns the scene inside out, thereby showing us what drives the spectacle in the first place.

It is envy of the centre that drives the crowd to cheer each time Caesar rejects the proffered crown. The crown is the symbol of tyranny for the Roman citizenry. In symbolically rejecting the crown, Caesar affirms his loyalty to the people. The plebeians eagerly lap up this crude allegory. In his summary of the spectacle, Casca does not disguise his contempt for the people's reaction to Caesar's showboating: "If the tag-rag people did not clap him and hiss him, according as he pleased and displeased them, as they use to do the players in the theater, I am no true man" (1.2.258–61). Casca's envy shows itself in his snobbery. He affects a superiority to the tag-rag people who enjoy Caesar's antics, but he never stops to ask why he so eagerly attends the spectacle, or why he is so keen to share its details afterwards with Brutus and Cassius. When the learned Cicero addresses the crowd in Greek (the language of learning and therefore of considerable cachet for the would-be snob), Casca has no idea what the famed rhetorician is saying.

Brutus is as contemptuous of Casca as Casca is of the people. He calls him "blunt" (1.2.295) and obviously finds his lack of irony and vulgar manner extremely distasteful. But it is precisely these qualities that make Casca relatively harmless next to men like Cassius and Brutus. He is a follower, not a leader. He is a consumer of envious shows rather than a producer of them. Brutus, however, is no mere consumer. He aims no less than to upstage Caesar himself. That is why he spends so much time explaining to the conspirators how the assassination must be performed. If Caesar gives the people miserable dumbshows, Brutus will stage for them a real tragedy, one which the people will be simultaneously attracted to and repelled by – in other words, one with some real catharsis.

Brutus's lecture to Cassius about why they should not kill Antony may be fruitfully compared to Hamlet's lecture to the players about how to perform the Mousetrap play. "Oh, it offends me to the soul to hear a robustious periwig-pated fellow tear a passion to tatters, to very rags, to split the ears of the groundlings, who for the most part are capable of nothing but inexplicable dumbshows and noise. I would have such a fellow whipped for o'erdoing Termagant. It out-Herods Herod. Pray you, avoid it" (*Hamlet* 3.2.8–14). Like Hamlet, Brutus is aiming for something rather more subtle, something that cannot be captured by the inexplicable dumbshows of the mystery plays. In those plays the line between good and evil was much clearer and therefore much easier to discern. Brutus longs for this moral clarity, but his own troubled conscience reveals how distant such moral clarity has become for him. Rather than suiting word to action in the direct and untroubled manner of the Vice or hero of the religious stage, Brutus seems to be caught in the gap between word and action, between outward appearance and inner reality:

> Let not our looks put on our purposes,
> But bear it as our noble Roman actors do. (2.1.226–7)

Like Hamlet's, Brutus's language is riddled with a heightened concern for the gap between the private and public scenes of representation. Between the acting of a dreadful thing and the first motion, all the interim is like a hideous dream. Brutus is all too aware that his inner world is radically at odds with the public one. Nonetheless, the public scene is the only one he has available to him. This creates problems for Brutus when he usurps this scene. There is something almost pathetically sentimental about the way Brutus explains why he killed Caesar, as though he realizes he has no choice other than to become Caesar's assassin, just as Antony (or someone else) will become in turn his assassin: "I have done no more to Caesar than you shall do to Brutus ... I slew my best lover for the good of Rome, I have the same dagger for myself when it shall please my country to need my death" (3.2.36–7, 44–7).

Does Brutus secretly long for his own death? After the assassination, Brutus seems to be sleepwalking through a play he doesn't quite fit.[16] His cursory remarks to the crowd seem insincere and out of character, as though he were wearing a mask that obscured his inner self. The real Brutus, we feel, is the one we saw in the orchard, the one riven by inner conflict, unsure of what to do and horribly conscious of the crime he is contemplating. But now, when he speaks to the plebeians, this Brutus, the internally conflicted Brutus of the soliloquies, seems to have disappeared. His speech reminds me of the kind of public service announcements used by the government to remind us of the ill effects of smoking or teenage pregnancy. It is wooden in the extreme.[17]

Consequently, audiences find Antony so much more persuasive. It doesn't matter that Antony is being deceptive. On the contrary, this is precisely the point. In Antony's speech, we immediately see the layers of irony. For what drives Antony's deception is a heartfelt desire for revenge. This is what makes Antony's speech far more real to us than Brutus's "public service" remarks about freedom. Brutus's interiority fades from view, and instead we get this rather unconvincing cardboard figure. With Antony, however, we see the deception, which only adds to the fullness of the character. We see the irony and the sarcasm in his repeated reference to the conspirators as "honorable," and this disjunction between appearance and reality, between the outer and inner worlds, helps us to see Antony as a flesh-and-blood person rather than a mere cardboard cutout.

It is almost as if Brutus's tragedy is over too quickly. It lasted for two marvellous acts and then abruptly fades from view. When Caesar dies, Brutus no longer has a purpose to his existence. What sustained him (and what made him so interesting as a character) was his resentment of Caesar, but with Caesar dead his resentment no longer has a target. The tension between inner and outer worlds disappears. All that is left is Brutus's public role as Caesar's assassin. What is there left to do?

Of course, there is plenty of excellent theatre still to come. But where in all this do we learn more about Brutus's interior life? We catch occasional glimpses of it. For example, we see him shudder before Caesar's ghost. But what seems remarkable about this encounter is precisely how perfunctory and unremarkable it is. It does not set off the kind of self-doubt and guilt we see in Hamlet or Macbeth. Nor can we simply put this down to Shakespeare's desire for historical verisimilitude in the fashioning of Brutus's famed stoicism. For how then do we reconcile this stoic Brutus with the extremely unstoic Brutus Shakespeare gave us in the orchard on the eve of the assassination? What seems most striking about Brutus in the second half of the play is how pompous he becomes. His quarrel with Cassius shows a complete lack of self-irony. Brutus indicts Cassius for taking bribes, but then hypocritically asks Cassius for money because he considers himself too noble to raise money by "vile means" (4.3.72). Brutus sounds just like the lofty Caesar before he was overwhelmed by the conspirators.

And perhaps this is Shakespeare's point. *The Tragedy of Julius Caesar* is the tragedy of becoming like Caesar. This is exactly what happens to Brutus. He gets stuck in somebody else's tragedy. The final irony of the play – one embodied in the play's title, which names not the protagonist but the protagonist's model – is that Brutus is condemned to repeat the role of his more famous and illustrious predecessor. Once Brutus has usurped the centre, there is nothing left for him to do except await death and hope that it will bring him the same glory it brought Caesar. This notion seems to be what lies behind Brutus's slightly comical remark that his suicide and defeat will generate more glory for him than for Octavius and Antony. It is impossible to read these lines without irony. This is the same man who killed Caesar for his ambition. Yet here he is imagining how he can turn his defeat into a glorious victory. Brutus goes to his death attempting to emulate Caesar. If it means killing himself with the same dagger that killed Caesar, so be it. Hopefully, doing so will bring him a little bit closer to his distant model and rival, the immortal Caesar. Antony's final eulogy does nothing to dispel this irony:

> This was the noblest Roman of them all.
> All the conspirators save only he
> Did that they did in envy of great Caesar. (5.5.68–70)

Michael Long notes that Antony's eulogy for Brutus "grates on our ears with tragic irony" because the "things which serve in the Roman mind to redeem him from being a mere conspirator are for us the very things which made his life so bleak"; the Roman "civic code proves itself so inadequate for life, nobody has learned anything."[18] A.P. Rossiter, whose nose for Shakespearean irony is, I think, greatly to be trusted, describes Antony's eulogy as glib and sentimental, and compares it to the similarly "flat, hurried, twisted off" ending of *Coriolanus*.[19] Rossiter's larger point is that Shakespeare's penchant for irony, his habit of deliberately undermining the dignity of his characters, is precisely how we can most usefully identify the distinctiveness of Shakespearean tragedy. Shakespeare's sense of tragedy is indelibly mixed with his sense of comedy, and in particular his sense of comic irony; the latter is a "mockingly *critical* function, which criticizes by making game of what men respect, admire, feel sympathy towards."[20]

From a purely dramatic point of view, Caesar is the archetypal big man. His mere presence on stage is sufficient to generate his centrality. When he enters the scene, all eyes automatically turn towards him. As Caesar's rival, Brutus is forced to play the role of the envious outsider. But Brutus's resentful stance already demonstrates the irony of the neoclassical aesthetic, which represents the stage not merely as a centre but as a centre with a periphery. Whatever Caesar may think of his immortal self, his centrality would not exist were it not for the actions of the periphery. The play's opening scene shows the plebeians taking a holiday to enjoy the spectacle of Caesar's triumph. The obvious displeasure of the tribunes, who seem to have misjudged things by betting on the wrong horse, demonstrates that the periphery is where the real action lies. Caesar may be the big man, but his fate is firmly in the hands of his public, who are capable of elevating him to the greatest of heights but also of bringing him crashing to the ground. By foregrounding the resentful actions of the periphery, Shakespeare illustrates the central irony of the neoclassical aesthetic, which requires not that the protagonist simply appear on the scene as a transparent incarnation of the centre, but that he undergo an internal struggle in his quest to achieve it. As A.C. Bradley noted, Caesar possesses clear analogies to the big man of classical tragedy.[21] Next to him Brutus is a much smaller figure. But this decrease in stature is made up for by a greater volume of resentment. Unlike the classical figure, the neoclassical protagonist is aware of his displacement from the centre, and this displacement manifests itself in resentment – resentment in which the audience member willingly participates. Shakespeare places the central event of his play, the assassination of Caesar, into the mind of Caesar's onetime disciple and follower. Brutus's public agon for the centre first manifests itself in an inner moral struggle as he wrestles with the idea of Caesar's assassination. This inner struggle is the characteristic feature of Brutus's neoclassical irony.

In his next tragedy Shakespeare will explore the problem of a hero whose consciousness of the neoclassical predicament far exceeds Brutus's. Hamlet does not merely resent the centre; he is also aware that his resentment is what gives the scene its integrity. His fascination with the various revenge figures of the play, from Pyrrhus to Lucianus to the ghost itself, reflects his awareness that resentment is itself an "antic disposition," a role to be played on the stage. Hamlet's much-remarked calmness in the fifth act has less to do with any newfound inner peace than with sheer mental exhaustion on the audience's part. After having his protagonist self-consciously delay his usurpation of the centre for almost an entire play, Shakespeare finally relents and gives the audience the awaited denouement. Brutus made the mistake of killing Caesar in the third act, consequently leaving himself with no central figure against which to define himself. Hamlet makes no similar mistake. He nurses his resentment – and consequently the audience's – for as long as dramatically possible. Hamlet's neoclassical irony makes Brutus's look like child's play. It takes Hamlet a matter of minutes to hook us with his filthy imagination. And once we are hooked, he never lets go. Only Iago rivals Hamlet when it comes to the aesthetic mastery of resentment.

4 Hamlet's Filthy Imagination

In *Julius Caesar* Shakespeare's analysis of resentment – and of the role of the aesthetic in purging it – remains partially obscured by his historical subject matter. Brutus's envy of Caesar is given centre stage for the first two acts, but once Caesar is murdered, Brutus becomes rather less interesting, and our attention shifts to Antony. Ultimately Brutus fails to distinguish himself successfully from his more famous historical predecessor. He remains overshadowed by the very man he resents. Kenneth Burke's idea of the play as a sacrificial contest between "a Caesar-principle and a Brutus-principle," in which Antony continues "the function of Caesar in the play," strikes me as accurate.[1] Caesar is more powerful in death than in life because he continues to live through Antony. And Antony, the great lover of plays, is Shakespeare's way of allowing his audience to expatiate for the central sacrificial act of the tragedy: the murder of Caesar.

In *Hamlet* Shakespeare maintains for the first time an unbroken focus on the inner world of the resentful protagonist. What lasted for two brief acts in *Julius Caesar* now spans an entire play. Brutus in his orchard dreaming of Caesar's sacrifice anticipates Hamlet imagining various figures to purge his resentment of Claudius. The ghost, Pyrrhus, and Lucianus are all vehicles for the aesthetic sublimation of Hamlet's resentment.

Brutus had imagined Caesar's death as a beautiful cathartic release. When he recommends that the conspirators show restraint in the murder by carving Caesar as a dish fit for the gods rather than hewing him as a carcass fit for hounds, he is attempting to communicate this aesthetic vision. Hamlet's lecture to the players admonishing them not to overdo Termagant or ham it up too much is the counterpart to Brutus's speech to the conspirators. Like Brutus, Hamlet is a bit of a snob when it comes to the aesthetics of his personal "theater of envy."

Let us briefly recall Eric Gans's definition of the classical aesthetic.[2] The classical aesthetic stages its subject matter unselfconsciously. Whoever is in the centre deserves to be there because that is the way things are. Since it is natural for humans to admire their superiors, it is natural for us to pick them as objects for aesthetic representation. This tendency is what Aristotle describes when he says that the tragic hero is someone "better than you." The case of Greek comedy is a bit more complicated because it reverses, or ironizes, the tragic identification with the centre. In comedy, you tolerate the representation of the lower sort precisely because the low figure is an object of ridicule. You laugh because this would-be tragic figure is so clearly ridiculous. Like Bottom performing the tragic role of Pyramus, the comic figure turns out to be an impostor, which ironically makes him worthy of the audience's continued (condescending) attention.

The picture gets significantly more complicated in the Renaissance. Thanks to the moral teachings of Christianity, it is no longer so easy to accept the classical world view in which all men are ranked on a rigid and immobile hierarchy. Of course, hierarchy still exists. The classical picture of a Chain of Being is still referred to with reverence and respect. But the Protestantism inherent to Christianity, with its highly unorthodox notion of universal moral equality, is beginning to make a dent in the Platonic idea of a natural, God-given social hierarchy. This shift does not deny the hypocrisy of the church itself, which frequently affirmed the necessity of the old hierarchy. But the ancient belief in a Great Chain of Being is fundamentally at odds with the idea that God had incarnated himself in a lowly human being.

What is the consequence of this ongoing moral and ethical revolution for aesthetic history? If the protagonist of classical tragedy deserves to be on stage simply because he is ontologically "better than you," what happens when you deny the reality of this ontological distinction? You get a situation like the one Shakespeare depicts in the second scene of *Julius Caesar*. You get a resentful Cassius bitterly denouncing Caesar's centrality. In other words, you turn the classical aesthetic inside out. Instead of identifying with the superior central figure, you identify with the one who points out the superior's secret inferiority.

It is the secretiveness of this identification that is key. The neoclassical protagonist is always something of a *conspirateur*. He knows that the centre is not what it appears to be, and his job is to point this out to us.

Thus the protagonist is also an ironist. His slogan is "I am not what I am." The line is Iago's, but it could serve as a watchword for all Shakespeare's resentful protagonists. They know that the centre is vulnerable to attack, and they use their superior knowledge of the scene against their less-knowing rivals, over whom they maintain a constant and invincible aesthetic authority, just as the playwright does over his audience.

This exclusive focus on the protagonist's resentment betokens a greater awareness of the complicity between protagonist and audience. Richard III, Hamlet, and Iago thrill us with their ironic asides. We alone are privileged to know what they are up to, and we gleefully participate in their superior mastery of the aesthetic scene. In contrast, a character like Julius Caesar stubbornly insists on behaving like a classical figure. "For always I am Caesar" (1.2.212), he imperiously proclaims – just after he has, in an uncharacteristic moment of critical self-irony, expressed his fear of the envious Cassius. For the neoclassical protagonist, the state of being in the centre does not easily coexist with the ironic awareness of his displacement from it. This contradiction or tension between centre and periphery, which will be lucidly described by Hamlet in his most famous soliloquy, accounts for the bipolar reactions Caesar provokes among readers. Is he a hero or an idiot? On the one hand, he shows genuine tragic nobility, as for example in his stoic attitude towards his own death, despite the many ominous portents that presage its violent imminence. On the other, his refusal to acknowledge what is so obvious to those around him strikes us as slightly ridiculous, a delusional belief in his own invincibility. But this contradiction is easily explained by the difference between the classical and neoclassical aesthetics. Caesar is a classical protagonist stuck in a neoclassical play. The resulting irony is almost unbearable. Despite the litany of ominous portents that smack him almost hourly in the face – the soothsayer's warning, his nightmare, Calpurnia's dream of his statue spouting blood, the strange and bloody sights in the Capitol, the negative omen of the augurers, not to mention Cassius's lean and hungry look – Caesar maintains to the last a belief in his invulnerability. When Brutus stabs him, his whole world turns suddenly and quite unexpectedly upside down. *Et tu Brutè*? The line is a question, and for the first time in his life Caesar does not have an answer.

After Caesar's "classic" death, Brutus's seems like a farce. But this is a problem endemic to neoclassical tragedy. Aware of the complicity between centre and periphery, the neoclassical protagonist can never truly be surprised by his death. On the contrary, he seems to have prepared himself for it all too well. Is this why the ghost haunts the parapets of Elsinore castle? Is he embittered by the rather unspectacular manner of his death? Is this why Hamlet insists on replaying his father's death *as a tragedy*? Hamlet is exceptional in his self-reflexive awareness of the aesthetic scene. But even the unreflective Coriolanus anticipates his own sacrifice when he abruptly aborts his attack on Rome. And as we saw in the previous chapter, Brutus's first order of business after he murders Caesar is to present his dagger to his auditors and generously proclaim that he too is ready to die when they see fit to dispatch him. They do and he does.

In *Hamlet* Shakespeare's depiction of the problem of resentment reaches new heights. Before he utters a word, Hamlet shows his hostility to Claudius and his court. Dressed in black on an occasion intended to celebrate the new king's marriage and coronation, Hamlet menaces the court with his ironic posture and sardonic asides. Readers and critics have diligently read back into the play the irony that they have first learned from Hamlet himself. We hear, for example, how Claudius's opening speech is a masterpiece of doublethink. Claudius explains how he has married Gertrude

> as 'twere with a defeated joy –
> With an auspicious and a dropping eye,
> With mirth in funeral with dirge in marriage,
> In equal scale weighing delight and dole. (1.1.10–13)

The conclusion is incontrovertible. Claudius is a villain! The promiscuous mixing of contrary emotions can only mean one thing: a devious and sinister mind. Anybody who can treat language with such disrespect must be capable of goodness knows what crimes.[3]

The eagerness with which many readers jump to this conclusion is truly remarkable. The critical impulse to scapegoat Claudius is no doubt the reason why G. Wilson Knight's 1930 essay, "The Embassy of Death," has gotten so much mileage, based as it is on the highly original assumption that, morally speaking, Claudius is in fact the better man compared to Hamlet.[4] As long as playgoers and readers insist on demonizing Claudius and deifying Hamlet, Knight's essay will never go out of fashion. Critics will learn to rephrase their hatred of Claudius and idolization of Hamlet in new and highly inventive ways, but as long as the basic assumption underlying their analyses remains the same, Knight's essay will maintain its freshness and originality.

Knight is very good at pointing out Claudius's admirable qualities, the most important of which is his leadership. His opening speech, delivered under extremely trying circumstances, is a model of tact and imagination. For let us not forget, these are troubling times. The old warrior-king is dead, but the business of the state must not be neglected. In particular, there is the defence of the country to consider. Already Norway threatens Denmark's borders. Is this not reason enough for Gertrude to throw herself at the nearest strong man? Claudius deals admirably with the situation. Horatio had anticipated – with rather too much gusto, one feels – a full-scale military conflict, but Claudius devises a nonviolent solution and avoids any bloodshed. Knight is duly impressed by this fact and notes how naturally it seems to come to Claudius, who appears to be a nonviolent and peace-loving man by nature, a promoter of health rather than sickness, of life rather than death.

Claudius's diplomatic skills should not be underestimated. Judging by Horatio's earlier remarks – again, delivered with a certain sadistic gusto (the setting is crucial: it is the dead of night, the guards are extremely jumpy, and there is a ghost lurking in the shadows) – diplomacy would not have been the old king's preferred manner of dealing with Norway. On the contrary, old Hamlet ruled by the sword, not by the word.

Knight's reversal of the traditional view of the play amounted to a heresy, and no doubt heresy is precisely what Knight intended. But the fact of the matter is that it is quite possible to read the text in the manner Knight does. There is no obvious misreading involved. He simply chooses to emphasize aspects we tend to overlook or ignore. More crucially, he prefers whenever possible to take Claudius at face value, to give him the benefit of the doubt rather than read too deeply and too suspiciously into his words and actions. This preference is particularly notable in Knight's remarks on the opening court scene. Are Claudius's overtures to Hamlet genuine? Does he really want to look on Hamlet as a father would a son? Is he sincere about grooming Hamlet for the throne? Knight answers all these questions in the affirmative. And why not? The fact that Claudius later condemns Hamlet to death in England and, when this fails, orchestrates the shenanigans with Laertes and the poisoned sword, is a response to Hamlet's violence, which includes first the not-so-subtle death-threat in the Mousetrap play and then the murder of Polonius.[5] Can one really blame the king for taking defensive action at this point?

And yet we most certainly do blame Claudius. For all Knight's arguments to the contrary, we find it very difficult indeed not to read Claudius as the villain of the piece. Why? In strictly objective terms – for example, in terms of who has killed more people – one would have to condemn Hamlet. Of the play's eight deaths Hamlet directly contributes to six, whereas Claudius has a hand in only two, not counting the murder of the old king, which occurs before the play starts.[6]

Our obsession with Claudius's villainy does not come out of the blue. On the contrary, it comes from the play's highly engaging and extremely verbose protagonist. Hamlet is a master ironist, someone who knows a thing or two about the difference between being and seeming, between what one thinks secretly to oneself and what one permits oneself to say aloud in public. The very fact that we feel obliged to search for double entendres and ironies in the king's opening speech shows how much of Hamlet has rubbed off on us when we judge the other characters, especially Claudius. It takes a great deal of effort, perhaps even a streak of impish perversity, *not* to judge him by Hamlet's standards. This is in fact a great compliment to Claudius. This is no stagy Caesar with his head in the clouds surprised that his position is vulnerable to the menaces of the Brutuses and Cassiuses of the world. No, Claudius is all too aware of the threats that lurk in the margins of his court and his kingdom. His opening speech is in fact a brilliant pre-emptive strike, an attempt to deflect or defuse any resentments that his rather unexpected good fortune might occasion in others. For it must be said, there is a question mark concerning the unseemly haste with which he moved to replace his dead brother, both in the Queen's bed and on the throne; the latter evidently comes with the former, hence the winning reference to Gertrude as the "imperial jointress" of the state. So in this, his first public speech to the people, Claudius artfully manages to include everybody in his warm glow. Polonius must be particularly pleased, for he singles out his son Laertes for special mention.

But despite his best efforts at cheering everybody up – to share with those less fortunate than himself his remarkable good fortune – there are still those who will complain and moan about their lot. What is to be done with them? In particular, what is to be done with the sulky prince, who is so obviously making his displeasure known by his absurdly eccentric antics? Doesn't he have any sense of taste or tact?

Claudius has two choices. He can simply ignore Hamlet and let him stew in his own resentment, or he can attempt to coax him out of his resentful posture. Quietly having him removed is a possibility, but this is not Claudius's preferred method of dealing with annoyances. We know he is a man of great patience. After all, he waited until his brother had been married for at least thirty years before falling in love with his brother's wife.[7] The underhanded measures he takes later in the play are strictly defensive, when Hamlet has forced his hand. If Claudius were a habitual evildoer like Richard III, he would simply eliminate his nephew at the first opportunity.

In fact, Claudius's initial tactic is to be gently but sternly paternalistic. He ignores Hamlet's sarcasm, which could easily become the occasion for a damaging exchange of insults, and allows Gertrude to appeal to her son's better nature. When this leads only to more sarcasm from Hamlet ("Ay, madam, it is common"), including a barely disguised put-down of Gertrude herself, whom Hamlet accuses of vulgar insincerity, he steps in to deliver a lengthy and carefully wrought speech that chides Hamlet for his "obstinate condolement." Never is he insulting or hectoring. On the contrary, it all makes very good sense, especially to an audience less sensitive to the hurt feelings of the romantic outsider. The very length of the speech demonstrates Claudius's desire to bring Hamlet into the spotlight with him. His earlier address to the court was only eight lines longer. Now he devotes a second magnificent speech to Hamlet alone. And there can be no doubt about Claudius's intentions with respect to Hamlet. He intends to groom him for the throne. It is time this young man *grew up*. There will be no going back to the life of a carefree and irresponsible student in Wittenberg. Hamlet must remain with Claudius in the spotlight as "Our chiefest courtier, cousin, and our son" (1.2.117).

How does Hamlet respond? There are in fact two responses. The first one is the superficial one. It is intended not for us but for Claudius and his court. Here Hamlet grudgingly accepts the proposal, but not without a last dig at Claudius by implying that he is only agreeing to his mother's wishes, not his uncle's: "I shall in all my best obey you, madam" (1.2.120). Again, Claudius overlooks the insult, and seeks to make the best of a bad job. "Why, 'tis a loving and a fair reply. / Be as ourself in Denmark" (1.2.121–2). And with that he brings the entire scene to a grand conclusion. He will drink to Hamlet's health that very night, and the cannons will echo the king's approval. This behaviour is typical of Claudius. Guns shall be fired in feasting and ceremony, not in war.

But Hamlet has a second response up his sleeve. This one takes place outside the public scene occupied by Claudius and his court. It is private, reserved for our ears alone. We have, it's true, already received some strong hints of Hamlet's secret opinion on the matter. His very first line is addressed more to us than to Claudius. "A little more than kin and less than kind" is an attempt to upstage the king by ironizing what he has just said. *Kind* is a pun on *kin*, to which it is also etymologically related (compare *genus* and *genetic*). Claudius is not of Hamlet's kind; rather, their relationship is unnatural, ultimately incestuous. This assertion looks forward to the ghost's main accusation that, contrary to appearances, his death was in fact "foul and most unnatural" (1.5.26), and his brother Claudius an "incestuous" and "adulterate beast" (1.5.43). But we are getting ahead of ourselves. At this point, all we have to go on is Hamlet's wordless and resentful posture, which manifests itself in three sardonic one-liners delivered in rapid succession: "A little more than kin, and less than kind"; "Not so, my lord. I am too much in the sun"; and "Ay, madam, it is common." Each of these lines is said ironically. There is a literal meaning for the onstage audience, and an ironic meaning for us. It doesn't matter that the puns are in bad taste or rude, for we delight in them nonetheless. There is a certain intellectual game being played here, and just to grasp the double meaning encourages us to see this shiny, happy world of Denmark in a darker, ironic light. We start to doubt the external appearance of things. Perhaps Claudius is not what he's cracked up to be after all. Maybe he is being a bit *too* friendly. And as for Gertrude's reference to the common nature of death, well, maybe Gertrude's perfunctory mourning of her late husband was a bit *too* common. Indeed, it is quite vulgar, the way she lifted her skirt so eagerly for the younger brother.

You can see that once you start playing Hamlet's game, it is very hard to stop. Scandalmongering is a terribly enjoyable pastime. Who can resist the pleasure of seeing the high and mighty brought low? Tragic irony is entertainment in its purest form. The only difference between us moderns and the Greeks is that they reserved tragic irony for the highest members of their society. We are not so choosy. When the ladder of ambition becomes available to all, as it has in the market-driven world of today, there is no point in distinguishing between those who have nobility in their blood and those who do not. Tragic irony is now a daily occurrence open to all. Shakespeare sits somewhere in the middle between the Greek's extreme reverence of hierarchy and our own rather more casual attitude. His protagonists look upon hierarchy with a good deal of irony, but not enough to reject it altogether. If Hamlet really were like us in his world view, if he privileged mobility over hierarchy, he would have ignored his uncle and headed straight back to Wittenberg, where he could have gotten a degree in theatre and enjoyed a successful career in the German equivalent of Hollywood, like Goethe's Wilhelm Meister. Instead he is condemned to play out a tragedy in Denmark. He is resentfully aware of the centre's violence, yet unable to take his eyes off it. In this he is both like us and unlike us. He is like us in being aesthetically fascinated by the centre's violence, but he is unlike us in being condemned to the violent world he otherwise so shrewdly observes. This irony, which is the central one of the play, makes Hamlet unique in his self-consciousness of the tragic scene.

So Hamlet's second response is reserved for us. And he wastes no time in giving it as soon as the stage empties and he is alone. The play's first soliloquy is a paean to resentment. All the "uses of the world" seem "weary, stale, flat, and unprofitable" (1.2.133–4). Denmark is "an unweeded garden / That grows to seed" (1.2.135–6). Next to his father, who is a veritable "Hyperion," Claudius is a "satyr" (1.2.140). As for Gertrude, she is no better than a "beast" (1.2.150). In fact she is worse, because a beast "Would have mourned longer" (1.2.151). And then, to cap it all, Hamlet comes to his ominous and sinister conclusion:

> Oh, most wicked speed, to post
> With such dexterity to incestuous sheets!
> It is not, nor cannot come to good. (1.2.156–8)

The most obvious thing to note about this soliloquy is how prone to exaggeration Hamlet is. His father is like the Titanic sun-god Hyperion, whereas Claudius is a satyr. Gertrude goes from being the submissive and adoring wife, hanging on her husband "as if increase of appetite had grown / By what it fed on" (1.2.45–6) and like "Niobe, all tears" (1.2.149), to being a beast "that wants discourse of reason" (1.2.150). Hamlet insists on putting Claudius in as negative a light as possible by comparing him with the old king. This idolatry of his father reaches its zenith in the closet scene, when he compares the two brothers, predictably idolizing his father on the one hand and denigrating his uncle on the other:

> See what a grace was seated on this brow:
> Hyperion's curls, the front of Jove himself,
> An eye like Mars to threaten and command,
> A station like the herald Mercury
> New-lighted on a heaven-kissing hill –

A combination and a form indeed
Where every god did seem to set his seal
To give the world assurance of a man.
This was your husband. Look you now what follows:
Here is your husband, like a mildewed ear,
Blasting his wholesome brother. (3.4.56–66)

John Vyvyan calls Hamlet's idolatry of his father "romantic nonsense."[8] We have only to look at what the ghost himself says to see that Hamlet's idea of his father is very far from the truth:

I am thy father's spirit,
Doomed for a certain term to walk the night,
And for the day confined to fast in fires,
Till the foul crimes done in my days of nature
Are burnt and purged away. (1.5.10–14)

What were these "foul crimes" committed by the old king? Given the unpleasant nature of his reckoning, it seems doubtful that these are merely venial sins. Indeed, judging by the picture painted by Horatio, Hamlet's father was not above a little violence himself. The current troubles with Norway date back to a most heroic moment in Danish history, when Hamlet's father dared old Fortinbras of Norway to mortal combat. Vyvyan suggests that "morally speaking, there was little to choose between the late king and the living one."[9] René Girard agrees. More precisely, Girard sees Shakespeare as reiterating the perennial theme of fraternal violence.[10] The point about the two brothers is that they are the same. They represent the undifferentiation of mimetic violence. Hamlet's hyperbolic description of his father is a case of protesting too much, a desperate attempt to conceal what he knows to be true by flagrantly arguing the opposite. That is why he holds the two portraits up to Gertrude. He is hoping she will affirm precisely what he cannot see: namely, the vast difference between the two brothers. What is key for Girard is the origin of all this violence in undifferentiated mimetic rivalry. The troubles in Denmark can be traced back to the original combat between the two warrior-kings, old Hamlet and old Fortinbras, both of whom were pricked on to fight each other by, as Horatio says, "a most emulate pride" (1.1.87).

Girard's larger argument is that Hamlet's problem is his failure to extricate himself from the mimetic rivalry infecting the entire

Danish court. Hamlet sees the problem more clearly than the other characters, but he too is ultimately subjected to the mimetic rivalry he so clearly discerns in the two brothers. When Laertes returns from Paris to avenge his father's death, Hamlet finally has a rival whom he can emulate. "By the image of my cause," Hamlet says, "I see / The portraiture of his" (5.2.77–8). The play is now free to reach its natural conclusion in the final bloodbath. This violence, Girard says, lies behind all tragedy. For Girard, the key difference is in the relative perspicacity of the playwright in discerning the ultimate source of violence in mimetic desire. In this respect Shakespeare excels above all others. *Hamlet* is a revenge play against revenge.[11]

But this reading of the play misses the difference of Hamlet's violence, which is not really concerned with the brute fact of violence, but with its *representation*. More precisely, Hamlet's predilection for playacting is an attempt to purge himself of the violence he harbours internally as resentment, which is potential rather than actual violence. Resentment is initially "repressed," or more exactly, unspoken, but it emerges rapidly to take centre stage. As in Brutus's unconscious imitation of the envious Cassius, Hamlet's first stage appearance reflects the structure of resentment. His ironic posture towards the king and his court is a prelude to the outpouring of his resentment in the first soliloquy. The idyllic picture of a king and queen in love, ruling over a strong and united Denmark, is brutally punctured by the prince's resentful commentary, which forces us to reassess our view of the public scene. Claudius's theatre is being upstaged by Hamlet's.

Why are we so willing to yield to Hamlet's viewpoint? It is not enough to cite his greater charisma or intelligence. No doubt he is more charismatic from a certain point of view, and there can be no questioning his intelligence. But Claudius is not lacking in either charisma or intelligence, and we have seen that when it comes to politics, he is a shrewd judge of men.

The reason that we are more likely to adopt Hamlet's point of view is that he is, quite simply, more interesting. His *private* theatre of resentment is more interesting than Claudius's *public* show of mirth in funeral and dirge in marriage. Claudius shows neither guilt nor resentment until much later in the play, and by then it is too late. We have already pledged our allegiance to the more interesting character.

Reconsider our options. On the one hand, we have Claudius's cheery picture of Denmark. The one exciting thing that Claudius offers is the threat of Fortinbras, but he deals with this diplomatically rather than by leading his troops into combat, which a more warlike prince would have done. (Think of Hal or Antony unleashing the dogs of war.) He even wants to downplay the resentment of the one character who seems to be a bit interesting to us. By coaxing Hamlet into sharing in his glory, he hopes to neutralize the prince's resentment.

Now consider the alternative: the ominous and resentful black-clad figure of the prince. His resentment makes him a natural show stealer. He displays a flagrant disregard for the rules and talks contemptuously to authority figures, including the king himself, which shows he has an independent spirit. In his first soliloquy he offers us an extremely fascinating viewpoint. Denmark, he says, is ruled by an incompetent and lecherous drunk, who has married a shallow and sex-addicted queen. The mention of incest adds a certain prurient exoticism to this picture of sexual appetite run amok.

Now whose viewpoint is more interesting? Unquestionably it is Hamlet's. It doesn't matter whether his view is true or not. Indeed, as we have seen, it is unquestionably *not true*. Claudius is neither a drunk nor a lecher. Gertrude is not always looking for an excuse to open her legs and make love over the nasty sty. Nor was Hamlet's father a godlike sun king. But none of this matters when it comes to whose story is more interesting. What we want is a story that we can really sink our teeth into, something about which we can feel some moral indignation. This requires a certain amount of poetic license or exaggeration. It is hard to get resentful about things that are obscure or fuzzy in their moral outlines. Good and bad must be clearly signposted. They must have sharp and crisply marked borders separating the pure from the impure. Hamlet's first soliloquy fulfils exactly the same function as Cassius's diatribe against Caesar. It fills us with indignation towards the centre.

Of course, Hamlet's resentment isn't as obviously fabricated as Cassius's. In the earlier play, Shakespeare very pointedly depicts Cassius as a *personification* of envy. Cassius is meant to reflect the unspoken or repressed envy in Brutus – which explains Cassius's caricature of Caesar. The outlandishness of Cassius's claims is truly striking. For this reason, I find Harry Frankfurt's analysis of bullshit an appropriate text to juxtapose with Shakespeare's. Cassius is almost Iago-like in the way he takes Brutus by the nose. He says exactly what Brutus wants to hear – that Caesar is weak, that many people wish that he, Brutus, were their leader, that Brutus's name gives him the reputation as defender of the republic, and so on.

If this is Cassius's function in his first exchange with Brutus, what is Hamlet's function in his first soliloquy? It must be something similar. Just as Cassius is leading Brutus by the nose, so Hamlet is leading *us* by the nose. He is winning us over to his side against the king and the queen. After listening to Hamlet, we begin to have serious doubts about the cheery picture of Denmark painted by Claudius and supported by Gertrude, Polonius, and the rest of the court.

I can already hear the chorus of objections. How can I say that Hamlet is leading us by the nose? Cassius may be full of bullshit, but surely Hamlet is justified in his resentment? His father has died, his mother remarried in unseemly haste, and his uncle usurped the throne. Surely these are reasons enough for Hamlet to be resentful?

No doubt Hamlet has plenty to be resentful about. (Who doesn't?) But these reasons do not explain the sheer magnitude of Hamlet's resentment in the play's second scene. T.S. Eliot, in a now famous essay, commented on this fact when he noted that Hamlet's hostility towards Gertrude is totally out of proportion to the facts of the case. As Eliot put it, Hamlet's resentment lacks an "objective correlative."[12] Eliot regarded this as evidence that Shakespeare's sources had overwhelmed the playwright's intentions. For once Shakespeare's genius couldn't save him. His usual facility for adapting his sources failed when confronted by the brutal facts of the Norse revenge story, recorded by the medieval scribe Saxo Grammaticus sometime in the late twelfth or early thirteenth century. Consequently we are left with this absurd disproportion between Hamlet's inner resentment and the facts of the revenge plot. The attempt to impose the former on the latter fails because Hamlet's resentment is an inadequate motive for revenge. The conclusion, Eliot says, is "irrefragable": "Shakespeare's *Hamlet* ... is a play dealing with the effect of a mother's guilt upon her son," but "Shakespeare was unable to impose this motive successfully upon the 'intractable' material of the old play."[13]

As other critics have pointed out, Eliot understands the problem but draws the wrong conclusion.[14] The real problem is Hamlet's resentment, which does indeed seem out of proportion to the facts of the case. But the solution Eliot proposes – that *Hamlet* is a failure – is a bit drastic, to say the least. It is also extremely perverse, for it explicitly goes against the grain of the conclusions of the majority of playgoers and readers, who have decided that *Hamlet* is among the greatest works of literature ever written.

What Eliot puts his finger on is the originary or foundational status of resentment in the play. Resentment is not merely being objectively described; it pre-exists everything else. Eliot's "objective correlative" is curiously like the "state of affairs" of the philosopher. Just as the philosopher measures truth by the facts of the case, so too Eliot measures Hamlet's resentment by the facts of the case as they are represented in the play. But, alas, he finds that Hamlet's resentment is "in *excess* of the facts as they appear."[15] The play, Eliot concludes, must be a failure.

But if Hamlet's resentment is in excess of the facts, so much the worse for the facts. If Hamlet does not have a scenario adequate to his resentment, then he will have to invent one.[16] This is exactly what Frankfurt says about the bullshitter. The bullshitter does not care about the facts. What he cares about is that he has *our attention*. And Hamlet most certainly has got ours in his first soliloquy.

Recall Cassius's function. Cassius reflects back to Brutus that part of himself he yet knows not of. Does Hamlet have a similar mirror that reflects back to him an unconscious aspect of himself? The most obvious candidate for this function is the ghost. The ghost reflects back to its beholder the beholder's own resentful preoccupations. Marcellus and Bernardo are troubled by the military preparations in Denmark. They feel ill at ease and long for a strong hand to lead them. What do they see? They see a shape remarkably like the old warlike king. Note that Shakespeare stresses the inconclusiveness of the evidence. The guards think it is the old king, but they are not sure. And this is precisely why they need Horatio to confirm their as yet unproven hypothesis. Note also that not all the guards see the apparition. Francisco, though he is "sick at heart" (1.1.9) and keen to be relieved of the watch, has seen no ghost, not even a mouse stirring. Presumably he does not share the same anxieties as Marcellus and Bernardo. Is he perhaps loyal to Claudius? Shakespeare does not provide us with an answer. We never hear from Francisco again.

Horatio's character is among the most curious in the play. Not only does he confirm the guards' suspicion that the apparition is the king, he gives a detailed explanation of why it now stalks Elsinore castle. Its martial and warlike form are a dual reference to the current war preparations in Denmark and the time when old Hamlet and old Fortinbras fought one another, in single combat, to decide who was the superior warrior. As it happens, old Hamlet won that contest, and now his ghost looms over Elsinore. It is almost as if he sits in judgment over the next generation of fighters. Who will succeed him as the next warrior-king?

Consider the candidates. There is young Fortinbras, whom Horatio describes as "Of unimprovèd mettle hot and full" (1.1.100). He appears to be the keenest to show the legitimacy of his claim to the violent centre vacated by the last king. Then there is the current pretender to the throne, the old king's brother, Claudius; but he hardly fits the bill of a true warrior-king. There is young Hamlet, the son and heir of the last king; but again he seems a bit too intellectual compared to his swashbuckling father. Finally, let us not forget Laertes. He seems rather more suitable. Like Fortinbras, he is headstrong, violent, and unlikely to let polite manners stand in his way when it comes to the central business of killing. When he comes storming vengefully back to Denmark, the rabble behind him cry, "Laertes shall be king!" (4.5.109). Evidently they know a hero when they see one. They sense the natural link between violence and aesthetic centrality.

Let us set Fortinbras and Laertes to one side for the moment to consider the oddballs in this group: Claudius and Hamlet. With all due respect to Girard's argument that Claudius and Hamlet's father are indistinguishable fraternal rivals, the remarkable thing about Claudius is how *unlike* his brother he is. Instead of taking the sword to Fortinbras and showing this young man who's boss, Claudius proposes a nonviolent solution by writing to the "impotent and bed-rid" (1.2.29) uncle of young Fortinbras. The pen is mightier than the sword. In general, this is not true – or, more precisely, it has been true only in very recent human history.[17] Nonetheless, Claudius's letter miraculously has its intended effect. One cannot help wondering if Shakespeare's reference to the impotent and bed-rid Norway is also a veiled reference to his audience members, who have no choice but to accept the script that the playwright has written for them. Claudius's nonviolence is really a form of sublimated or deferred violence. Who knows what his letter to Norway actually said? But the image of the Norwegian king as impotent and bed-rid reminds us rather vividly of the impotent and bed-rid older brother as he slept in his orchard on that brisk autumn afternoon. Claudius quite literally filled that ear with poison. Is Shakespeare winking at us? Is he filling our ears with poison too?

It is hard to avoid some version of this conclusion. For the one thing that the two most obvious rivals for the centre, Claudius and Hamlet, share is a love of words. This love of words is anticipated by Horatio, who functions as a kind of prologue or chorus figure. James Calderwood remarks that the name's etymology suggests "speaker" or "orator," and certainly this fits with Horatio's function both at the beginning and end of the play.[18] Horatio, one feels, comes to share the watch with Marcellus and Bernardo not because he wants to disprove their theory, but because he can't resist a good ghost story. After all, he has been sufficiently persuaded by their story to brave the severe chill of a Danish winter night. And he does not exactly protest when Bernardo invites him to listen to the story a second time:

> Sit down awhile
> And let us once again *assail your ears,*
> That are so fortified against our story,
> What we have two nights seen. (1.1.34–7; my emphasis)

Horatio is in a position analogous to the playgoer or reader. The poet has but a few minutes to hook his audience before their attention wanders. Horatio has heard this report about a ghost haunting the castle, and he is sufficiently interested to check it out for himself. No doubt there were many in the original playhouse audience who had heard similar reports about Shakespeare's play. Even on the play's opening night one could not help but have this thought, given the existence of an earlier revenge play, the so-called *Ur-Hamlet*, with its ghost shrieking like an oyster wife, "Hamlet, revenge!" What is our author going to do with this rather tired old revenge theme?[19]

Horatio is immediately hooked by the story he hears from the two guards. Not only that, he becomes a more powerful interpreter of the ghost than the original storytellers. He quickly and easily slips into the role of chief storyteller. Not only does he confirm the identity of the ghost, he now speculates as to the exact cause of its nightly visitations. Horatio speaks far more than any of the other characters in this scene. He has our attention, and he does not give it up until he meets Hamlet, who in turn becomes an even more powerful interpreter of the ghost. Hamlet is the only character who can converse with the ghost or (it is the same thing) hear its story.

But before we get to Hamlet, we have to pass through Claudius and his brilliant court scene. The contrast could not be more apparent. The first scene takes place at night, the guards are jumpy, and a ghost haunts the ramparts. The second scene takes place during the day, in the brilliant light of Claudius's colourful court. After the sinister appearance of the ghost, Horatio breathes a huge sigh of relief when day breaks:

> But, look, the morn in russet mantle clad
> Walks o'er the dew of yon high eastward hill. (1.1.171–2)

Horatio articulates not merely his own but also *our* sense of relief. After the creepiness of the night, we welcome the warmth of Claudius's lively court.

But despite the birth of a new day, the menace of the night does not disappear entirely. On the contrary, it is now personified in the black-clad prince who lurks resentfully on the periphery of Claudius's court. The point of opening with the ghost scene is not merely to hook the audience; it also provides us with a symbolic context for interpreting Hamlet's resentful posture, which is clearly irritating the king and queen. "How is it that the clouds still hang on you?" (1.2.66) is the king's first question to Hamlet. And the queen is not far behind: "Good Hamlet, cast thy nighted color off / And let thine eye look like a friend on Denmark" (1.2.68–9). Even more than the usual reasons trotted out for Hamlet's melancholy (that his father is dead, that Gertrude's marriage is overhasty, that the prince has been disinherited), it is this symbolic contrast between night and day, between periphery and centre, that defines Hamlet's opening stance. "To thine own self be true," Polonius instructs Laertes, "And it must follow, as the night the day, / Thou canst not then be false to any man" (1.3.78–80). These may indeed have been wise words, but Polonius does not see their irony. No one tries harder to be true to his own self than Hamlet. But consciousness of self is born in resentment. The self is defined by its difference from others; in particular, by its difference from the more central other, which is originally a god, the figure of centrality itself. In being true to this resentful vision of the self, by debasing life and idolizing his dead father, Hamlet gives himself over to a life of resentment. And from this perspective it is indeed true that night *always* follows day. The menacing nighttime scene with which the play begins is but a prelude to the long winter of Hamlet's discontent. Wilson Knight's image of Hamlet as the "ambassador of death" picks up on the contrast between life and death, day and night, health and sickness, centre and periphery, that pervades the play.[20]

Far from providing a much-needed lifeline to the prince, Horatio's news of the ghost is a curse. I do not think that it is insignificant that Horatio makes the decision to contact Hamlet immediately after he delivers his beautiful lines personifying the new dawn. The relief in his voice is palpable. The burden of the night will be passed from himself to Hamlet. In doing so, Horatio enacts the aesthetic solution to resentment – the "deferral of violence through representation," as Gans puts it. By observing resentment in others, we purge it from ourselves.

Horatio must not himself get caught up in the centre's violence. By passing news of the ghost along to Hamlet, he can continue to enjoy the centre's benefits without suffering any of its ill effects. This is how aesthetic or theatrical catharsis works.

Hamlet responds eagerly to Horatio's news of the ghost. But Shakespeare's repetition of the metaphor of the ear suggests that the story is really a curse:

> Season your admiration for a while
> *With an attent ear* till I may deliver
> Upon the witness of these gentlemen,
> This marvel to you. (1.2.193–6; my emphasis)

These lines look backward to Bernardo's desire to assail Horatio's ears and forward to Hamlet's letter to Horatio, "I have words to speak *in thine ear* will make thee dumb" (4.6.25; my emphasis). They also point us towards the play's central image of a king murdered by a "leprous distillment" poured into his ears. The latter image is repeated no less than three times in the play: by the ghost, by the players in the dumb-show, and again by the players in the Mousetrap play.

We are now in a position to address a central question of the play. Why is Hamlet alone able to make the ghost speak? Why are Hamlet's ears the only ones keen enough to hear what the ghost says? Hamlet, I hasten to add, is not entirely alone in this regard. We too are privy to what the ghost has to say. But we are also privy to what Hamlet has to say in soliloquy. Our ability to overhear Hamlet's private thoughts provides us with a clue to answering the question of why Hamlet is the ghost's privileged interlocutor.

Consider what the ghost says in his interview with Hamlet. He describes himself as "a radiant angel" (1.5.56); Claudius as "that incestuous, that adulterate beast" (1.5.43), "garbage" (1.5.58) and "a wretch whose natural gifts were poor / To those of mine" (1.5.52–3); Gertrude as "lust" (1.5.56) preying on "garbage" (1.5.58); and the "royal bed of Denmark" (1.5.83) as a "couch for luxury and damnèd incest" (1.5.84). The ghost also fixates on the seeming virtue of the queen, who goes from loving virtue (the ghost) to preying on garbage (Claudius). Oh, Hamlet, what a falling off was there!

If these allegations sound familiar, it is because we've heard them before. In his first soliloquy Hamlet had called his father Hyperion, Claudius a satyr, and Gertrude a beast. He characterized the marriage between Claudius and Gertrude as incestuous, and he fixated on the image of Gertrude as exceptionally submissive to her former husband. Each of these details is painstakingly repeated by the ghost. It is true, of course, that Hamlet was less fulsome in his description; he did not give so much detail. But the appetite grows by what it feeds on. What begins as a tiny mole of nature spreads like a cancer, eventually breaking down the pales and forts of reason.[21]

The one detail Hamlet neglects to mention in his first soliloquy, but which the ghost now inserts, is the fact of the murder itself. Except for this one key fact, all the circumstantial evidence is already firmly in place in Hamlet's soliloquy – which is why Hamlet is unsurprised to hear that Claudius is the serpent that stung his father's life. His prophetic soul predicted it. The ghost is a fuller, more vivid picture of the resentment evident in Hamlet's first stage appearance.

Am I saying that the ghost is a figment of Hamlet's imagination? But how can that be true? Has not the ghost been seen by no less than four different people? Does this not prove beyond all possible doubt the objectivity and honesty of the ghost?

But Shakespeare is rarely so obvious in his moral signposts. On one level, to be sure, the ghost is an honest ghost. He accurately discloses Claudius's villainy to the son, who is now obliged to carry out his filial duty and avenge the father. What follows is the stereotypical revenge plot. All the audience has to do is wait for the final thrust when Hamlet kills Claudius, and justice has been served. No wonder audiences have been puzzled by Hamlet's delay. If this is indeed a revenge play, it is not a very good one. T.S. Eliot discerned the contradiction implicit in this generic view of the play. His response was to declare the play a failure; the revenge plot was intractable when set beside Shakespeare's anterior interest in the protagonist's resentment.

When I teach *Hamlet*, I always ask why Hamlet is so resentful in the play's second scene. It is rare indeed that among the various responses I get (that his father is dead, his mother a slut, Claudius a usurper, and so on) I do not also hear, "Because Claudius murdered his father!" The response is certainly not stupid. On the contrary, it shows the acumen of a T.S. Eliot. For what this student senses is how disproportionate Hamlet's resentment in fact is. The only possible explanation can be murder most foul. All other explanations are merely *excuses*. This student makes the link Shakespeare wants us to make, the link between resentment and collective violence, between the private and public scenes of representation.

But Shakespeare does not stop there. Hamlet goes to his grave believing that Claudius murdered his father, but never once does he consider the ambivalence of the evidence before him. His masterwork is *The Mousetrap*, Claudius's response to which he regards as definitive proof of his uncle's guilt. But as W.W. Greg pointed out many years ago, *The Mousetrap* is itself profoundly ambivalent.[22] It reveals to the spectator whatever the spectator wants to believe: Hamlet believes that it betrays Claudius's guilt; Claudius believes that it betrays Hamlet's desire to assassinate him; Gertrude believes that it is aimed at her overhasty remarriage; and the rest of the court believes that it is a gross insult to the king and queen. The fact that the play pricks Claudius's conscience is a further irony. Hamlet believes that Claudius is seeking forgiveness, but he does not overhear Claudius's confession, because he would then realize that his quest for forgiveness is abortive. We alone have definitive evidence of Claudius's guilt, but not Hamlet.

Does this matter? From the point of view of the revenge plot, it does not. If Claudius killed Hamlet's father, Hamlet is obliged to avenge him. But as a study of resentment it matters a great deal. If resentment is anterior to revenge, then the revenge plot is itself an attempt to deal, however inadequately, with the problem of resentment. Resentment is itself generative of revenge. When you look at *Hamlet* from this perspective, as a study of resentment rather than revenge, things look infinitely more interesting.

Consider, for example, the old problem of Hamlet's delay. Why does the prince take such an infernally long time to get around to killing Claudius? And why is he himself so hyperconscious of his own inadequacy as a revenger? Is he overwhelmed by his task? Does he find it so terribly difficult to screw up his courage and confront his uncle man-to-man? Is Hamlet squeamish about violence?

Goethe believed he was.[23] Like Eliot, but more subtly I think, Goethe grasped the resentful condition in which we first see Hamlet. The prince was not particularly ambitious. He did not covet the throne. But now that he sees his uncle on it, he is *scandalized*. In one crippling blow, he has gone from being the heir apparent to no better than a private nobleman. Indeed it is much worse because the private nobleman has no expectations of becoming a monarch, whereas Hamlet did. To him the idea of being deprived of the centre must be truly devastating. It is akin to nothingness. For the first time, the prince, Goethe says, is "constrained to consider the difference which separates a sovereign from a subject," and he feels "needy and degraded."[24]

Why then does Hamlet not rejoice at the prospect of avenging his father after he learns of the foul play from the ghost? Does not the revenge offer him the perfect alibi he needs for regaining his former condition? Here Goethe is less convincing. He explains Hamlet's incapacity to live up to his filial obligation as a failure of nerve: "A lovely, pure, noble, and most moral nature, without the strength of nerve which forms a hero, sinks beneath a burden which it cannot bear and must not cast away."[25] Hamlet doesn't have the guts to kill Claudius.

The problem with this explanation, as A.C. Bradley pointed out, is that Hamlet can be quite violent and bloodthirsty when he wants to be.[26] After all, we are talking about the same man who showed no hesitation in stabbing Polonius, or boarding the pirate ship, or sending his erstwhile friends Rosencrantz and Guildenstern to their highly unpleasant deaths. Plus, it must be admitted that when he finally kills Claudius, he does it in truly spectacular fashion, stabbing him with the poisoned sword and then, for good measure, forcing him to drink from the poisoned cup, and all this quite publicly in front of the king's shocked audience.

Bradley is scornful of Goethe's theory, which he calls "sentimental."[27] But despite its inadequacies as a reading of Hamlet's character, it nonetheless succeeds in pointing out the peculiarity of Hamlet's resentment at the beginning. Nor do Bradley's own explanations of Hamlet's resentment fare any better. Certainly Bradley is more attentive to the facts of the text *after* Hamlet's first stage appearance, but he is also more inclined than Goethe to accept uncritically Hamlet's point of view. Thus, where Goethe sees Hamlet's resentment as rooted in his displacement from the throne, Bradley sees only a melancholy prince wholly justified in his eccentric behaviour. Bradley is quite happy to accept Hamlet's own explanation of his behaviour in the first soliloquy. What could be more disgusting to a loving and loyal son than to see his mother's "coarse sensuality, 'rank and gross,' speeding post-haste to its horrible delight" as she engages in "incestuous" sex with her husband's brother?[28] The thought is just too hideous and repulsive for Bradley, who instinctively sympathizes with Hamlet's vehement disgust of his mother and idolatry of his father. But who is being sentimental now? Why is Bradley so keen to identify with Hamlet's self-pitying representation of himself as the victimized party in all this?

It is the sentimentality of Hamlet's *own* self-representation that Bradley misses but that Goethe, the celebrated author of the highly sentimental *The Sorrows of the Young Werther* and the rather more ironic

Wilhelm Meister's Apprenticeship, immediately sees. In exaggerating the injustice of his mother's behaviour, Hamlet inevitably makes us feel sorry for him. The representation is sentimental precisely because it is so obviously contrived. It is no accident that Hamlet's first speech of any length is a vehement defence of his sincerity,[29] which he believes his mother has just questioned:

> Seems, madam? Nay, it is. I know not "seems."
> 'Tis not alone my inky cloak, good mother,
> Nor customary suits of solemn black,
> Nor windy suspiration of forced breath,
> No, nor the fruitful river in the eye,
> Nor the dejected havior of the visage,
> Together with all forms, moods, shapes of grief,
> That can denote me truly. These indeed seem,
> For they are actions that a man might play.
> But I have that within which passes show;
> These but the trappings and the suits of woe. (1.2.76–86)

The gentleman doth protest too much, methinks. Gertrude has touched a real nerve with her son. How would Hamlet have responded if she has said, "Why *is* it so particular with thee?" What sets Hamlet off is an extremely subtle semantic difference between two words. Gertrude might have used "is" but she quite innocently said "seems." For most of us, saying "Why do you seem so sad?" is not much different from saying, "Why are you so sad?" But there is a difference, albeit a very subtle one. "Seems" suggests a degree of uncertainty or tentativeness. We tend to use it when we don't wish to appear overbearing or presumptive. In the case at hand, it is a more tactful way of inquiring into someone's feelings. "You seem sad, is there something wrong?" is a less direct and therefore less intrusive way of saying, "Why are you sad?" The first question does not assume you are correct in your assessment. It leaves open the possibility that you may be wrong. The second phrasing provides no such face-saving escape route. Either you are right or you are wrong. And if you are wrong, the hearer can only respond by denying your statement, which may be a troublingly combative thing to do. ("Why are you sad?" – "I'm *not* sad!") In other words, it is always less conflictive to use "seems" rather than "is."

Hamlet manages to take Gertrude's polite and conciliatory inquiry in exactly the opposite manner she intended. He interprets it as an attack on his sincerity. By using "seems" rather than "is," she must be accusing him of insincerity. How dare she question his authenticity! Can't she see how authentic he is? He isn't just wearing black to *look* sad. He is sad inside too. In fact, there isn't enough black in the entire world that could possibly denote him truly. What does a man have to do to show how upset he is?

Now only someone who doubts his own authenticity could overreact in the way Hamlet does. Such defensiveness is not at all uncommon. On the contrary, it happens all the time. People thrive on flattery and they are defensive when it is not forthcoming. But flattery should not be self-directed. We are automatically suspicious of people who praise themselves. We assume that such a person lacks confidence and that is why he constantly needs to reassure himself. This is what makes Bradley so uncomfortable when he reads this outburst of Hamlet's. The speech, Bradley says, "sounds very strange and almost boastful."[30] Hamlet is flattering himself, but Bradley believes that a real hero, one with some genuine nobility, doesn't do that sort of thing. That is why Bradley breathes a huge sigh of relief when he reads the soliloquy a few lines later. Of course, Hamlet was not talking about himself, he was talking about Gertrude! Hamlet's undignified outburst towards his mother, Bradley says, "is not, in effect about Hamlet himself at all; it is about his mother."[31] Hamlet is trying to get Gertrude to reflect on her own inadequacy when it comes to demonstrating her grief for her dead husband.

Goethe is less certain of the inherent nobility of the hero. Instead he sees him as "needy [*bedürftig*] and degraded [*herabgesunken*]." The phrase is perfect. Hamlet's neediness is indeed quite shocking in this scene. He is simply dying for some attention. But when he gets it he is super-defensive. He projects onto others the same sense of scandal he experiences when the attention is turned on them. So Goethe is justified in detecting an indelible strain of sentimentality in Hamlet. Hamlet does not even believe in himself, let alone in Gertrude or Claudius. In fact, it is precisely his distrust of himself that leads to his distrust of others. "To thine own self be true," Polonius says to his son. "If only I could" would be Hamlet's laconic and bitter reply.

Hamlet's sentimentality, his *lack* of authenticity, is a natural consequence of the neoclassical protagonist's distance from the centre. Goethe's description of Hamlet as "needy and degraded" captures this "re-sentiment of dispossession,"[32] or *ressentiment*, that lies at the heart of the neoclassical aesthetic. Since the Greeks, the lesson of tragedy has always been to avoid centrality.[33] But whereas the classical protagonist treats the centre as his natural birthright, the neoclassical protagonist is aware of his dispossession from it – hence the irony and sentimentality of his longing for it. The centre can never truly be his because he depends upon it, rather than the other way around. The centre preexists him. It is a curse defining his whole existence. The more clearly he understands his predicament, the more hopeless his desire appears to be, and the more virulent his resentment becomes.

This is what happens in *Hamlet*. Aware of his own marginality, Hamlet tries various dramatic tactics to refigure the centre for himself. This intention is evident not merely in the play Hamlet stages for the king, but also in Hamlet's very first stage appearance, which is a fairly obvious attempt to undermine the natural or given hierarchy between the king and his subjects. All eyes are on the king, which is where they are supposed to be. But this natural focus on the central figure is upstaged by the eccentric strategy of the prince. His peculiar dress and snarling asides suggest that all is not as it appears in Denmark. When the scene closes with Claudius and his court exiting the stage, we sense that the real play is just about to begin. What has this rather peculiar and eccentric figure got to say for himself? Hamlet's first soliloquy upstages the king's magnificent public address. It takes our attention away from the public scene represented by the king and his court and moves it towards the resentful imaginings of Hamlet's private scene of representation.

Earlier I suggested that Horatio has no wish to get too close to the ghost. He wisely decides to pass this task on to Hamlet. The lines Shakespeare gives first to Horatio, about the cock announcing the "god of day" (1.1.158) who chases away all the evil spirits, and then to Marcellus, about the association between the dawn and the birth of Christ, are clearly intended to show us that no good can come of this ghost. We do not have to be orthodox or practising Christians, whether Protestant or Catholic, to understand that the ghost is bad news.[34] Readers are often puzzled by the fact that Hamlet is surprised to see Horatio, despite the fact that Horatio states he was present at the old king's funeral, which must have taken place some months, or at least one month, before the moment when the two friends meet for the first time since Wittenberg.[35] This is indeed a puzzling fact. Equally puzzling is Horatio's absence from the opening court scene. Surely as a guest of the king, Horatio's presence would be expected on such a grand occasion. But though these are interesting questions to ask, they are the wrong way to approach

Shakespeare's overall design. Horatio is not just a realistic character, with a precise and consistent background and history. He also performs a symbolic function vis-à-vis the protagonist. More specifically, he represents our complicity in shaping the tragedy to come.

Shakespeare's plays are full of such mediating figures. They thematize the aesthetic scene's dependence on the spectator, the centre's dependence on the periphery. It clearly was a theme Shakespeare gave much thought to. Iago is probably the most famous example of such a figure. In *Othello*, the mediating figure becomes in effect the central figure, the real protagonist of the play. Prospero is a more salutary and less tragic example. But even in a play like *Julius Caesar*, our complicity in the sacrifice of the central protagonist is emblematized by Shakespeare. Not only is there the obvious aesthetic self-referentiality of Brutus and Cassius when they describe the murder of Caesar as an event that will be reproduced on the stage for future generations of playgoers; there is also the more subtle suggestion that in shunning Portia and embracing Ligarius, Brutus is fulfilling our own "sick" desire for violence onstage. This is not to imply, as Girard does, that Shakespeare's theatre is an exercise in bad faith. On the contrary, these self-referential gestures suggest an awareness that the theatre performs an important role in constraining or sublimating potentially dangerous resentments. In Shakespeare's hands, the theatre becomes an "anthropological discovery procedure," an exploration of the originary scene of representation.

It is this function that defines Horatio more precisely than his surface dramatic role as Hamlet's best friend. In fact, I think that Horatio's friendship with Hamlet *depends* upon his position as our confidant. Horatio is Hamlet's passport to a good name, as Hamlet realizes when he persuades Horatio to tell his story to the as yet unknowing world. It is no accident that Othello, who is far less aware of his audience than Hamlet, also considers Iago to be his closest friend and ally. Indeed, Othello's case is interesting precisely because the relationship between protagonist and confidant is inverted. Othello's tragedy is that he fails to grasp the degree to which his centrality is controlled by the periphery. In this, he is closer to someone like Julius Caesar than Hamlet. The periphery controls the centre. This lesson, unavailable to the classical protagonist, is the guiding principle for the neoclassical protagonist. In *Hamlet*, we meet a protagonist who manages to maintain his control of the centre until the very last moment, at which point he usurps it and dies.

Among Shakespeare's tragic protagonists, Hamlet stands out for his awareness of the centre's ambivalent aesthetic power over all those who approach it. The centre is both a blessing and a curse. It is a blessing because it confers significance on the protagonist's otherwise insignificant life. But it is a curse because this significance is won at the cost of the protagonist's demise. Hamlet's preoccupation with death is conditioned by an awareness of this predicament. His reflections on suicide become increasingly obsessed, not merely with death, but with violent death. In his first soliloquy Hamlet imagines death rather vaguely as flesh resolving itself into a dew. In his most famous soliloquy, however, death is associated more explicitly with violence:

> To be, or not to be, that is the question:
> Whether 'tis nobler in the mind to suffer
> The slings and arrows of outrageous fortune,
> Or to take arms against a sea of troubles
> And by opposing end them. (3.1.57–61)

Here Hamlet grasps the essential paradox. "To be" means to live. But to live means to suffer in the mind rather than in reality. "Not to be" is to die, but death is here conceived as not only an abstract end to life, but also as violent action (taking arms against a sea of troubles). But "to be" also means to be in the centre, for that is where desire tends. It follows that "not to be" means to remain on the periphery, imagining the fulfilment of desire but not carrying it out. The paradox is that "to be" in the first sense (to live) is the same as "not to be" in the second sense (to live on the periphery, to exist merely "in the mind"). Likewise, "not to be" in the first sense (to die) is "to be" in the second (to take arms against the more central other).[36]

To this point, Hamlet has resisted the centre's violence. He has contemplated murder rather than attempted to carry it out. But this imaginary or aesthetic contemplation of violence also describes the experience of the audience. We contemplate violence, but do not suffer any of its negative consequences. In other words, we remain in the condition of Hamlet *before* he takes arms against a sea of troubles. The fact that Hamlet's first murder takes place almost by accident, when he impulsively stabs the wrong man, only reinforces the disjunction between the aesthetic idea of revenge and the brute fact of violence. When Hamlet kills Polonius, he had but moments earlier deliberately declined to kill

Claudius at prayer. The opportunity struck Hamlet as wholly unaesthetic, so he imagines a more fitting moment:

> When he is drunk asleep, or in his rage,
> Or in th'incestuous pleasure of his bed,
> At game, a-swearing, or about some act
> That has no relish of salvation in't. (3.3.89–92)

Hamlet has from the beginning been fixated on the image of Claudius's drunkenness and lechery. When he stumbles across the king at prayer, he is unprepared for the image that greets him. His mind quickly works to produce an alternative scenario, one more fitting to the level of resentment he now experiences after the Mousetrap play has "proven" the ghost's story. Hamlet doesn't ever really imagine Claudius alone and vulnerable, let alone kneeling in a position of remorse and guilt. This is why he is incapable of killing Claudius at this moment. He had never imagined such a scenario. Why would he? Contrition and guilt are not something villains should be capable of, and Hamlet has firmly resolved that Claudius is a villain. This is indeed the lesson he has been repeating to himself since his interview with the ghost – that one may smile and smile *and* be a villain. But here he sees the king not merely not smiling but in a state of anguished guilt and repentance.

Bradley regards Hamlet's failure to kill the king at prayer to be the turning point of the play.[37] If Hamlet had done the deed, the lives of Polonius, Ophelia, Rosencrantz, Guildenstern, Laertes, Gertrude, and Hamlet might have been spared. Why then did Hamlet not kill the king when he had the opportunity? Bradley is on the right track when he observes that Hamlet's speech here follows the same pattern as his previous soliloquies:

> Now might I do it pat, now 'a is a-praying;
> And now I'll do't. And so 'a goes to heaven,
> And so am I revenged. That would be scanned. (3.3.73–5)

There is a paradoxical movement back and forth between the action and the representation of the action. What would it look like *if* I were to do it now? Hamlet, once again, reflects on the *representation* of the murder. As in the previous soliloquies, Hamlet is imagining the object of his resentment. What differentiates this soliloquy from his previous soliloquies, however, is that he is now closer than before to the anticipated murder. This speech is Hamlet's equivalent to Macbeth's dagger soliloquy. But unlike Macbeth, who has to imagine the dagger, Hamlet does not need to imagine Claudius, who is kneeling before him. But even in this situation, where he has his victim helpless at his feet, Hamlet refuses to give up on the primacy of his imaginary object. He refuses to allow his representation to become a reality.

Is there an ethical dimension to this refusal of Hamlet's? Many critics have insisted there is. Harold Goddard, for example, argues that "in his heart Hamlet does not believe in blood revenge in any circumstances."[38] The fact that he refuses to kill Claudius here is an unconscious moral act for which Hamlet gives a conscious (and reprehensible) reason; he will devise a more terrible death for Claudius later, when he is about some act that has no relish of salvation in it.

The paradox that sees Hamlet defer violence only by imagining a more terrible occasion for it is the central paradox of representation. Indeed, it is the basis of Hamlet's resentment, which in the originary hypothesis emerges in the gap between the sign and its object. The sign defers mimetic conflict by situating the object at the centre of a collective scene where it is not merely perceived but desired. But the flip side to desire is resentment. Desire turns into resentment when the sign is no longer felt to be an adequate compensation for the object. But the object without the sign is insignificant, so the subject returns to the sign by which alone the object's "perfection" can be imagined. In returning to the sign, resentment is once more deferred, but only by ramping up, so to speak, the intensity of the sign, which must now deliver a more satisfying representation of the object than was previously produced. This return to the sign is characteristic of all aesthetic experience. In *Hamlet* it structures the protagonist's relationship to his play more profoundly than in any of Shakespeare's other plays.

All Hamlet's major soliloquies are reflections on the central paradox of representation. By imagining a more perfect violence, Hamlet defers it for the time being. But this deferral only works by continually ratcheting up the expectations of the spectator, who accepts the protagonist's delay only on the condition that this delay will provide a more spectacular form of violence in the end. Hamlet is a man of violence only because he is in the first place a man of resentment. It is the buildup of resentment that causes Hamlet's violence. When he draws his sword over the prostrate Claudius, resentment has almost burst its representational constraints. Hamlet succeeds in deferring violence one more time only by imagining a more perfectly violent scenario.

But Hamlet's imagination is rapidly running out of representational reserves. How much longer can he up the ante of representation? How much longer can Shakespeare defer the audience's desire for violent gratification?

From this perspective, we can agree with both Bradley and Goddard. Bradley is correct to see in Hamlet's refusal to kill Claudius merely another excuse for the delay that characterizes his whole condition, and he is not wrong to say that Hamlet's hatred of Claudius is genuine and that Hamlet would have been quite happy to see Claudius damned in the horrifying manner he imagines. However, Goddard's notion that in the depths of his unconscious, Hamlet is morally incapable of revenge also makes sense. But rather than attribute Hamlet's moral instincts to a mysterious unconscious force inside the protagonist, we can refer to the originary hypothesis. What motivates Hamlet's delay is not his moral unconscious, but the deferral implicit in all representation. There is, to be sure, an ethical component to this deferral. The aesthetic oscillation between sign and referent permits resentment – and therefore violence – to be deferred. But the downside to this deferral is that it ups the ante on representation. Hamlet is trapped in a cycle he cannot control. Try as he might, each successive deferral merely draws him closer to the tragic denouement. Hamlet moves through progressively more violent representations as he seeks to purge his resentment of Claudius. The ghost, the player's Pyrrhus speech, and the Mousetrap play are all attempts to remain a spectator of *somebody else's violence*.

And here lies the germ of truth in the Freudian reading of the play. Ernest Jones says that Hamlet delays his revenge because he sees in Claudius the mirror image of his own desire to unseat his father and marry his mother.[39] What is perceptive in this reading is the notion that Hamlet uses Claudius as a proxy for indulging his own interdicted desires. This idea strikes me as a keen observation. It is surely a crucial aspect of the play Hamlet stages for Claudius. Most auditors and readers assume that Hamlet is simply testing the ghost's word. But Hamlet declares that he also testing himself:

> If his occulted guilt
> Do not itself unkennel in one speech,
> It is a damnèd ghost that we have seen,
> And *my imaginations are as foul*
> *As Vulcan's stithy.* (3.2.79–83; my emphasis)

If Hamlet wanted merely to test the ghost's word, why would he make reference to his own foul imagination? Earlier he had expressed concern that the ghost "May be the devil" (2.2.600) and he conceives of the Mousetrap play as a means to seek "grounds / More relative than this" (2.2.604–5). Hamlet is concerned that the ghost is a figment of his filthy imagination. It is not that Hamlet wants to relieve himself of the charge of having foul thoughts. There is no way around that. As we have seen, his very first soliloquy is already suffused with the same prurient and sensational language used later by the ghost. Moreover, if Claudius does blench, this does not then relieve Hamlet of sharing in the same guilt. Rather, what Hamlet wants to test is the fact that Claudius's imagination *is as foul as his own*. This desire is no doubt what accounts for his extreme jubilation after *The Mousetrap* has been performed. He is ecstatic because his hypothesis has proven true. Claudius is as dirty minded as he is! The fact that this successful test provides him with firm grounds for revenge is really an afterthought. Hamlet behaves more like a playwright than a character in a revenge tragedy. He has successfully staged a spectacle for his audience. He has got his revenge upon his audience member by getting him to admit to his own filthy imagination. The ensuing scene in which Hamlet stands behind the kneeling Claudius, with his sword raised to strike, is Shakespeare's deliberate test of *our* "filthy imagination." It is a mirror image of the Mousetrap play that preceded it, but this time the scene of violence is directed at us rather than Claudius. How far are we willing to go in our identification with Hamlet's resentment? Can we condone the hero's violence?

The onstage image takes us back to an earlier image of revenge, Pyrrhus's sword suspended above Priam's "milky head" (2.2.478). The "hideous crash" (2.2.476) of Ilium falling to the ground takes "prisoner Pyrrhus' ear" (2.2.477) and so causes him to freeze and do "nothing" (2.2.482). This brief "pause" (2.2.487) in Pyrrhus's violent action is expanded considerably in Shakespeare's play. Hamlet thinks about violence much more than he enacts it. And he thinks about violence because he is in the first place a man of resentment. The resentment precedes the violence. Hamlet's fascination with the gruesome image of the blackened Pyrrhus, "horribly tricked / With blood of fathers, mothers, daughters, sons" (2.2.457–8), anticipates the image of Macbeth bathed in blood unseaming Macdonwald from the nave to the chops. How much blood would the audience like to see? Hamlet's delay depends on the promise of more violence to come, just as Pyrrhus's pause provides a moment of suspense before the climactic action of Pyrrhus's revenge.

In the end, what pulls Hamlet abruptly back into the vortex of revenge is an event he could not have predicted. He kills Polonius, whom he wrongly assumes to be the king. Moments earlier, at the height of Hamlet's triumph as the director of the Mousetrap play, Polonius had explained to Hamlet that he too liked acting; he had played Caesar and was killed by Brutus in the Capital. Hamlet responds with his usual lightning wit: "It was a brute part of him to kill so capital a calf" (3.2.103–4). For Hamlet, the assassination of Caesar is a joke, to be played on the stage in sport, just as *The Mousetrap* is about to be performed for the Danish court. Kings will bleed, but only in sport. But there is a layer of irony in this reference to Julius Caesar that exceeds even Hamlet's grasp.[40] The next time Hamlet and Polonius are in the same room together, Hamlet kills Polonius. Without knowing it, he puts himself into the position of the assassin in *Julius Caesar*. This event is the real turning point of the play. Hamlet is now embroiled in a revenge play he cannot control. With Polonius dead, he is now the target of someone else's revenge plot. As Girard points out, it is really the return of Laertes that arouses Hamlet to action.[41] The change in Hamlet that many critics have noted is a symptom of Hamlet's changed situation.[42] No longer a director or mediator of the other's desire, he himself is being directed or mediated. The most immediate source of this mediation is Laertes, whom he attempts to outface in Ophelia's grave. But the ultimate mediator is the playwright himself, who must draw his play to a satisfying conclusion.

We can draw a useful parallel between the situation at the end of *Hamlet* and the situation just before the assassination of Caesar. In the previous chapter, I suggested that Brutus was presented with the opportunity to back out of the assassination when he was approached by his wife Portia; but he ignores his better conscience and listens to the voice of envy represented by the sick conspirator Ligarius. Portia's subsequent behaviour, as she nervously oscillates between hope and fear, between desire for Brutus's success and fear of the violence his enterprise provokes, mirrors the experience of the spectator or reader of *Julius Caesar*. After Brutus kills Caesar we never hear of Portia again until the news of her suicide reaches Brutus at Philippi. Why does Portia fade so abruptly into the background? It is not simply that Brutus has dismissed her from his mind. We have too. If Brutus were to ignore Cassius and the conspiracy, there would be no play. There would be no mediation of *our* desire. We require a protagonist and Shakespeare obliges us, but not without first ironically acknowledging our own culpability in the desire for a sacrificial victim.

In *Hamlet* there is a similar emphasis on the audience's culpability in the tragedy. What could have prevented the tragedy from occurring? The answer is obvious. Hamlet's resentment should not have been encouraged. The ghost is the worst possible thing for Hamlet. Whether we decide that the ghost is a hallucination or an objective reality hardly matters.[43] What does matter, however, is that the ghost mirrors and amplifies Hamlet's resentment. But the solution to resentment is not more resentment, but love. Ophelia is the light that could have guided Hamlet away from his murderous hatred of Claudius. Critics have generally been stumped by Hamlet's treatment of Ophelia. Why is he so extremely hostile towards her? The vituperation that he showers upon her in the nunnery scene is truly extraordinary. Even more than Hamlet's hostility to Gertrude, his attack on Ophelia is completely disproportionate. The poor girl has done nothing to deserve this harsh treatment. It is misogyny of the most transparent and unpleasant kind.

Is Hamlet a misogynist? Is the noble prince little better than a wife beater? All attempts to justify Hamlet's resentment of Ophelia are merely a posteriori rationalizations made along the same lines as those that seek to justify his resentment of Gertrude. Hamlet's resentment precedes all the internal facts of the play. Why then does it reach such heights when it comes to Ophelia? In his brilliant heterodox reading of what he calls "the Shakespearean ethic," John Vyvyan argues that Shakespeare intended Ophelia to be "an allegorical figure representing a quality in Hamlet's soul … Everything that happens to Ophelia is an allegory for what is taking place in Hamlet."[44] The point is *not* that Shakespeare is seeking to reproduce verbatim the didactic effect of a moral allegory. On the contrary, as we have seen, *Hamlet*'s moral message is highly equivocal, a far cry from the transparent opposition between good and evil that characterizes the morality and mystery plays. Nonetheless Vyvyan argues that there is an ethical pattern to be discerned in Shakespeare's drama. Cassius is tempting Brutus, just as the ghost is tempting Hamlet. These figures are mediators of the protagonist's resentment. In this sense, they are mirror images of the protagonist's role vis-à-vis the audience. Just as the ghost provides the perfect context for Hamlet's resentment to flourish, so *Hamlet* provides the perfect context for us to indulge *our* resentment. We get to feel indignant with Brutus against Julius Caesar, or with Hamlet against Claudius. And when we are finished with our feelings of indignation, we do not have to suffer for indulging these violent emotions. Instead the protagonist himself is offered as a sacrifice. He pays for the crime of our resentment.

But he is not the only character to suffer, as Shakespeare makes clear. Portia and Ophelia suffer too, though in each case suffering is only indirectly related to the protagonist's violent actions. It is in this indirectness that we find a clue to their suffering. Ophelia, as Vyvyan argues, is an allegory of Hamlet's state of mind. To maintain his resentment, symbolized by his oath to the ghost, he must shun love, represented by his oath to Ophelia. We know that Hamlet has sworn his love to Ophelia from the letter he wrote to her before he saw the ghost: "But that I love thee best, O most best, believe it. Adieu" (2.2.121–2). When the ghost departs, he says,

> Now to my word
> It is "Adieu, adieu! Remember me."
> I have sworn it. (1.5.111–13)

How is Hamlet to reconcile his oath to love with his oath to death? He cannot, and this is precisely the cause of his inner torment. After he sees the ghost, Hamlet bursts in upon Ophelia "As if he had been loosèd out of hell / To speak of horrors" (2.1.85–6). He takes Ophelia by the wrists, studies her face hard, and, after minutes have elapsed, moves his head up and down and walks backward through the doorway without taking his eyes off her. Naturally the poor girl is terrified.

As Brutus rejected Portia, so too Hamlet rejects Ophelia. Laertes's words to his sister are prophetic:

> Perhaps he loves you now,
> And now no soil nor cautel doth besmirch
> The virtue of his will; but you must fear,
> His greatness weighed, his will is not his own. (1.3.14–17)

Laertes is referring to Hamlet's status as a prince. But Shakespeare, through Laertes, is also referring to Hamlet's status as a tragic hero. Hamlet's will is not his own because he is destined to play the role of the tragic victim. His fate cries out. From this point onward, he is lost to Ophelia. There is no place for love in the protagonist's devotion to resentment.

If Hamlet really loved Ophelia, why does he never mention her in any of his soliloquies? Bradley asks this question, and it is a very good one.[45] Except for the letter, which was written before the play begins, the only time Hamlet declares his love for Ophelia is when she is dead. But this declaration of love is pure sentimentality, an attempt to profit from the rhetoric of love. It is love in quotation marks, love ironized, love that can only be expressed resentfully, which of course is no love at all. As such, it is an exercise in self-love. Hamlet is finally able to declare his enormous love for Ophelia precisely because she is not present to make him feel ashamed of his huge hypocrisy. He has nothing to lose and everything to gain by thundering to the world how much he loved her. Hamlet's protestations of love for Ophelia are very much like his earlier protestations of love for his father. Both are pure romantic sentimentality.

> I loved Ophelia. Forty thousand brothers
> Could not with all their quantity of love
> Make up my sum. What wilt thou do for her?
> . . . .
> 'Swounds, show me what thou'lt do.
> Woo't weep? Woo't fight? Woo't fast? Woo't tear thyself?
> Woo't drink up eisel? Eat a crocodile?
> I'll do't. Dost thou come here to whine?
> To outface me with leaping in her grave?
> Be buried quick with her, and so will I.
> And if thou prate of mountains, let them throw
> Millions of acres on us, till our ground,
> Singeing his pate against the burning zone,
> Make Ossa like a wart! Nay, an thou'lt mouth,
> I'll rant as well as thou. (5.1.271–3, 277–87)

Hamlet is provoked into this exaggerated posturing by Laertes, whose own hyperbolic declarations of affection are too much for Hamlet to bear. Laertes, one senses, has irked Hamlet's sense of pride. Is he not the unquestioned super-mourner of this play?[46] Remember that Hamlet and Horatio have concealed themselves to observe the funeral proceedings. When Laertes leaps into Ophelia's grave and demands to be buried with her, Hamlet cannot contain himself any longer:

> What is he whose grief
> Bears such an emphasis, whose phrase of sorrow

> Conjures the wandering stars, and makes them stand
> Like wonder-wounded hearers? This is I,
> Hamlet the Dane. (5.1.254–8)

Hamlet announces himself, for the first time, as a competitor for the centre. He is not merely Hamlet, but Hamlet *the* Dane, ruler of Denmark. Hamlet has finally been coaxed from his position on the periphery to challenge publicly his competitors for the centre. His challenge is aimed not only at Laertes, but also at the king himself.

The larger symbolic significance of Laertes and Hamlet grasping each other by the throat in Ophelia's grave is not lost upon Vyvyan. "A soul that makes itself the grave of love," he writes, "inevitably becomes the womb of hate."[47] When hate flourishes, love dies. Laertes's return to Denmark represents the triumph of hatred over love in Hamlet. Anticipating Girard's reading of the play, Vyvyan says that Laertes is "Hamlet's deadly twin."[48] And indeed, when you stop to consider it, the symmetry is quite startling. The king gives Laertes leave to return to his studies in France, but forbids Hamlet from returning to Wittenberg to pursue his. Meanwhile the ghost appears to Hamlet and tells him of the king's foul play, and Hamlet vacillates in his duty until, in an impulsive move, he kills the wrong man. Now Laertes storms back to Denmark demanding vengeance for his father's death. Why do the rabble cry, "Laertes shall be king!" (4.5.109)? It cannot be because Laertes is a legitimate contender for the throne. The explanation is symbolic rather than based on the rules of succession in Denmark. Shakespeare intends him as a synecdoche of Hamlet. He is the embodiment of an aspect in Hamlet that the ghost has unleashed, but that Hamlet has struggled mightily to contain through various aesthetic devices. Laertes is revenge personified:

> To hell, allegiance! Vows, to the blackest devil!
> Conscience and grace, to the profoundest pit!
> I dare damnation. (4.5.134–6)

Whereas Hamlet defers his usurpation of the centre, Laertes throws himself headlong into it. The return of Laertes coincides with Hamlet's final descent into death. The graveyard in which we find Hamlet is, Vyvyan says, "really a materialization of his new inner landscape."[49] Hamlet grimly identifies with death's triumph over even the mightiest of historical figures, including Alexander the Great and Julius Caesar. The overthrow of love and triumph of death explain why he now announces himself as "Hamlet the Dane." Shakespeare has made us wait until the final act before his protagonist emerges from the shadows of the periphery to challenge for the centre.

Could Hamlet have avoided his tragedy? Should he have remained on the periphery indefinitely deferring his desire for the centre? Such a question may appear impertinent. *Hamlet* is a tragedy. To consider it to be something else is merely idle speculation.

The question is certainly speculative, but it is very far from idle. Shakespeare wrote many more tragedies after *Hamlet*, but he also wrote the romances. These latter plays strike me as attempts to rethink the tragic pattern in terms of the avoidance of tragedy. It seems highly unlikely that Shakespeare would write romances without being influenced by the ethical problems he had encountered in his tragedies.

I have already suggested that Hamlet's salvation lay in Ophelia. It is no accident that the nunnery scene, in which Hamlet vents his full hostility upon Ophelia, follows Hamlet's celebrated soliloquy on death, the "To be or not to be" speech. As Vyvyan perceptively observes, the speech, which is an abstract reflection on life and death, is followed by its "embodied" version when Hamlet sees Ophelia.[50] Death ("not to be") means more than just suicide. It is means violent death; and it is personified in the play by the ghost and its fatal command of revenge. Hamlet remains undecided about what course he will pursue – life or death – but when Hamlet sees Ophelia the abstract debate of the soliloquy is replayed in embodied and allegorical form. Ophelia represents life and she challenges the ghost, or death, which is also an aspect of Hamlet's soul. She serves as a reminder to Hamlet of why life is worth living. And this is precisely why Hamlet is so hostile to her. The same heightened emotions that he displayed in his encounter with the ghost now resurface in his encounter with Ophelia. Hamlet is a man torn between two irreconcilable paths: the path of life and the path of death. When she offers to return his tokens of love, she is not throwing them back in his face in an attempt to jilt him.[51] She is hoping to remind him of his former self. If there ever was a moment for spiritual regeneration, this would be it. But Hamlet rejects the offer: "I never gave you aught" (3.1.97), "I loved you not" (3.1.120). These are his rebuffs to her love. And then he launches violently into his tirade, "Get thee to a nunnery," which may be taken in both its literal and derogatory senses. In truth, what Hamlet says to Ophelia applies much better to himself: "God hath given you one face, and you make yourselves another" (3.1.145–6). It is

Hamlet, not Ophelia, who is two-faced. "What should such fellows as I do crawling between earth and heaven?" (3.1.128–30). Hamlet is caught between two worlds. Though he has sworn his oath to death, he cannot forget his oath to life and love.

What purpose does this deathward spiral serve? A clue to answering this question is provided by Shakespeare in the scene following the performance of *The Mousetrap*. Hamlet is jubilant that he has successfully trapped the king. He imagines himself in the role of the king's killer. It is the very witching hour of night. Hamlet reaffirms his allegiance to darkness:

> Now could I drink hot blood
> And do such bitter business as the day
> Would quake to look on. (3.2.389–91)

The light within is about to be extinguished. Hamlet's paean to the night marks the final descent. It is the same overthrow of the soul we saw in Brutus when he uttered his ode to the conspiracy. But just as Hamlet is sinking ever lower, Shakespeare chooses to show us the king at his most regenerative. Claudius is on his knees praying for forgiveness:

> Bow stubborn knees, and heart with strings of steel,
> Be soft as sinews as the newborn babe! (3.3.70–1)

The contrast could not be more vivid – on the one hand the king on his knees seeking repentance; on the other, Hamlet hoping to damn him forever. "My fate cries out," Hamlet had said upon seeing the ghost,

> And makes each petty artery in this body
> As hardy as the Nemean lion's nerve. (1.4.81–3)

But where has his fate led him? Whom do we admire more, the man attempting to remake himself as soft as the sinews of the newborn bade, or the man poised taut and ready to spring on his victim like the Nemean lion?

What prompts Claudius to seek salvation? It cannot be the fact that he realizes Hamlet is on to him. When Claudius prays, he has no idea his executioner stands behind him. Nonetheless, from the audience's point of view the image possesses an iconic significance. It suggests the medieval *memento mori*, in which death is personified standing directly next to the living. Claudius has indeed had his brush with death, and this has brought him to his current repentant state. But death has not been represented to him pictorially in a medieval *memento mori*. It has been staged for him dramatically.

Here we may suspect Shakespeare's hand subtly resisting the inexorable death march of the tragedy. Something has triggered a faint glimmer of hope in the king, and it has momentarily wiped the duplicitous smile off his face. Claudius has just finished viewing *The Murder of Gonzago*, and it has affected him deeply, but not in the way Hamlet imagines. Claudius sees himself mirrored not in the assassin but in the assassin's victim. He identifies with the dead Gonzago. Nor is his reaction simply defensive or indignant, as must be the case for the members of the court, who see in the play a thinly veiled death threat aimed at the king. On the contrary, it is precisely because he is himself an assassin that he now identifies with the victim of Lucianus's violence. He sees himself in the previous king's shoes – old, near violent death, and in danger of losing the love of the woman he adores. His entire life passes before his eyes. He imagines himself deprived of his queen, his crown, and his life. This is surely why Claudius doesn't react to the dumbshow.[52] Though it very graphically depicts the peculiar murder method Claudius is reported to have used (pouring poison into the ear), it does not generate any sympathy for the victim, who remains dumb and lifeless, like the iconic representations of death of the medieval *memento mori*, or the miserable dumbshows Hamlet had excoriated earlier. But when the spoken play begins, Claudius sees not only images but also hears the words that accompany the images. His ears are being assailed, just as Horatio's were in the play's first scene, and as Hamlet's were by Horatio and then by the ghost. Now Claudius hears the player king's speech on the passing of life and the inevitable decay of passion. The entire scene comes vividly to life, and he sees himself reflected in both the murderer and the man he murdered. Like Hamlet, he becomes a man to double business bound, both a murderer and a victim, an object of revenge and a revenger himself. This paradoxical doubling back and forth between the aesthetic sign and its object is characteristic of words or symbols, and this is precisely why the dumbshow does not succeed while the spoken play does.[53] No wonder Claudius's response is to stand up and cry, "Give me some light" (3.2.267). His cry is echoed by Polonius, "Lights, lights, lights!" (3.2.268). The light Claudius craves is not merely external and material, an *index* of what can be perceived by the eye. It is also a *symbol* of something beyond itself; in this case, of a soul struggling to move upward.[54]

So the Mousetrap play produces two contrasting effects. It causes Hamlet to sink lower in his deathward spiral, but it causes Claudius to rise upward in his search for grace. To be sure, Claudius's regeneration is abortive. His words fly up, but his thoughts remain below. Moments later he is back to his old habits, plotting Hamlet's death with Laertes. The play is a tragedy, and Shakespeare never intended it to be otherwise. But that Shakespeare did write regenerative conclusions to his tragedies is indisputable. As John Vyvyan has convincingly demonstrated, *Measure for Measure* picks up exactly where *Hamlet* leaves off.[55] And the same may be said for *The Winter's Tale* and *The Tempest*. These are tragedies that turn out well, which is to say, they end not with the protagonist's death, but with his spiritual rebirth after a carefully staged encounter with death.

Shakespeare's big men are aware that the scene of central significance precedes them. Unlike their classical precursors, whose mere appearance on stage is sufficient guarantee of their centrality, Shakespeare's heroes must demonstrate to their audiences why they deserve the spectator's attention. In his speech to the conspirators, Brutus presented the murder of Caesar as a beautiful aesthetic object that could be possessed equally by all within the individual's internal scene of representation. Brutus imagined sacrifice to be free of resentment; ritual violence is divorced from the evil intent that precedes it. Though he is haunted by the evil of what he is about to do, Brutus never experiences guilt. When he is visited by Caesar's ghost, he experiences fear but not remorse. Resentment is overt but remains unthematized.

In *Hamlet* resentment is thematized by the protagonist himself. Hamlet's celebrated inwardness or self-consciousness reflects the protagonist's greater awareness of resentment. Brutus was irked by Caesar's preeminence, but his personal resentment of Caesar is never presented as the basis of a rival centre of interest that could turn the periphery in his favour. On the contrary, Brutus refuses to admit that resentment has anything to do with the assassination, which he would rather conceive in public and wholly sacrificial terms. The private scene of internal reflection remains contained by the public scene of Roman politics. In contrast, the private scene in *Hamlet* becomes so pronounced it risks swallowing the public scene altogether. The power of Wilson Knight's analysis of the play derives from this difference. By focusing on the good qualities of Claudius's monarchy, Knight restores a sense of balance to the opposition between private and public that Hamlet has, over the centuries, swayed heavily in favour of the former. No doubt our post-romantic sensibilities make it more difficult for us to appreciate the level of suspicion that would have attended Hamlet in his very first stage appearance in the Elizabethan playhouse. But the transformation of this suspicion into identification is the very point of the play. Hamlet's resentment is something we identify with – so much so that today we tend to privilege Hamlet's personal scene as the ontological condition of the play. Whereas Brutus's private scene lasts only for a few brief soliloquies at the beginning of the second act, Hamlet's private anxiety becomes the focus of the play, until the final act when he finally accepts the traditional role of revenger. But what is most revelatory about *Hamlet* is not the final act of revenge but the preceding four acts in which revenge is traced back to resentment. The violent *sparagmos* of the play's final scene has its origin in Hamlet's resentful imagination.

In Shakespeare's next tragedy, the audience's complicity in the protagonist's resentment will be more explicitly thematized. Othello is inseparable from Iago. The presence of the latter continually forces us to reassess our opinion of the former. The centre is constantly subject to an ironic attack by the periphery. Every move Othello makes is subject to a countermove by Iago. But this is not a battle between two antagonists competing for the centre, as Brutus and Mark Antony do, or even Hamlet and Claudius. On the contrary, Othello has no clue that he is being undermined by "honest" Iago. Hence the classical agon takes on an explicitly ironic structure. The protagonist's downfall, given by the structure of classical tragedy, is thematized by the play itself. Iago personifies neoclassical resentment. His resentment of Othello is a condition of the play. In this he is like the audience member whose paradoxical identification with and alienation from the protagonist generates the formal structure of tragedy. We are Iago's co-conspirators.

5 Iago, Our Co-Conspirator

Let us retrace the general outline of the argument so far. The neoclassical protagonist is aware of his distance from the centre. Unlike the classical protagonist, whose mere presence on stage is sufficient to guarantee his centrality, the neoclassical protagonist must demonstrate his worthiness to occupy the centre, which precedes and therefore threatens his being – hence the neoclassical aesthetic's focus on resentment, which is a consequence of lateness with respect to the centre. Yet the violent centre, necessary for the protagonist's self-definition, cannot be refused. Consequently it is both desired and resented. In *Hamlet*, this ambivalence is reproduced in the protagonist's soliloquies, most notably in the "To be or not to be" speech. On the one hand, the centre is figured as a place of absolute transcendence, "a consummation / Devoutly to be wished" (3.1.64–5). On the other, it is a reminder of the peripheral self's insignificance. Hamlet's resentful vision of the self, as an object burdened by life's ills and destined to "grunt and sweat under a weary life" (3.1.78), reflects the self's recognition of its peripherality. This same paradox is reproduced in Hamlet's experience of the ghost, which is figured as both benevolent and terrifying, attractive and repulsive, an object of pity and of fear. "My fate cries out" (1.4.81), Hamlet exclaims as he looks longingly at the ghost's beckoning figure. But once the ghost has divulged the crimes of the king, Hamlet's desiring identification gives way to resentment: "Oh cursèd spite / That ever I was born to set it right!" (1.5.197–8). Goethe saw in these lines the crux of Hamlet's tragedy. The needy and degraded prince is unable to carry out the violent task demanded of him.

What Goethe put his finger on was the conflict between the private and public scenes of representation, a conflict that lies at the basis of all language and that is the source of the aesthetic oscillation between the central sacred object and the peripheral human sign by which alone the centre is known. Privately Hamlet has no qualms about what he must do. In his mind's eye, he can sweep to his revenge "with wings as swift as meditation or the thoughts of love" (1.5.30–1). The ghost would be inconceivable were Hamlet not already defined by his resentment of the centre. Attempts to justify this resentment in the light of the play's internal events confuse the form of tragedy with its content. Bradley's determination to see in the prince a noble soul who is momentarily unbalanced by the unusual conditions he finds himself in is doubtless the most sophisticated example of this type of psychological criticism. But, as we have seen, Hamlet's resentment is not adequately explained by the play's content. This was the intuition behind Eliot's celebrated claim that Hamlet's resentment was "in excess of the facts." Hamlet's resentment is excessive because resentment is the *sine qua non* of the play. The fact that the ghost appears first to us rather than the prince indicates that resentment is a precondition of aesthetic representation. The play's very first scene is a literal *mise en scène,* a miniature version of the more celebrated "play within a play" of the third act. We may choose, like the guard Francisco, to abandon the scene. But then we must abandon the aesthetic spectacle Shakespeare has prepared for us. Shakespeare's play, like the ghost itself, functions as a temporary aesthetic purge – a deferral – of the resentment without which there would be no motivation for paying attention to the play, or the ghost, in the first place.

In *Othello,* Shakespeare pushes the focus on the periphery's resentment of the centre to its limit. Iago is not merely a stereotypical villain, a descendent of the Vice of the medieval stage.[1] He is a mediator of the spectator's desire. Like Cassius seducing Brutus into sharing his resentment of Caesar, Iago seduces Othello into sharing his vengeful fantasy. But this seduction involves much more than Iago holding the mirror up to Othello. Through Iago, Shakespeare holds the mirror up to *us.* Othello's jealousy depends upon Iago's resentment, and Iago's resentment depends upon our identification not with Othello but with Iago. We are the willing conspirators in Othello's tragedy. It is we who willingly follow Iago through to his violent and vengeful conclusion. When his masterpiece is finished, Iago has nothing more to say. His play ends at exactly the point Shakespeare's does.[2]

If critics have generally been content to accept without irony Hamlet's resentment of Claudius, Iago's resentment of Othello has presented the opposite problem. After reading Iago's first soliloquy, Coleridge famously described it as "the motive-hunting of motiveless malignity."[3] Looking beyond Iago's own motive hunting, Hazlitt explained Iago's resentment as motivated by a mundane "love of power."[4] Hazlitt does not mean that Iago is an ambitious man who seeks worldly power. Iago's desire for power is instead abstract and intellectual. Rather than using brute force, he prefers psychological coercion. In this he is rather like the poet or playwright who controls his characters' thoughts. Hazlitt goes on to say that Iago is "an amateur of tragedy in real life." Swinburne refined this idea when he suggested that Iago is not simply a poet but an "inarticulate poet."[5] Insufficiently talented to purge his resentment by purely aesthetic means, Iago takes it out on those around him. But he is not like the thickheaded bully who simply beats you up. Rather, he vents his frustration by playing with your mind. Physical violence not being his forte, he messes with your head instead. Finally Bradley takes the psychological criticism of Coleridge, Hazlitt, and Swinburne, and draws the logical conclusion. *Othello* is Iago's tragedy too. Here is an ordinary man, not without some talent, including a certain inventiveness and intellectuality. Bradley says he is "not by nature malignant," and he imagines that before Iago embarked upon his crimes he had probably led a guiltless and decent if also rather selfish life – "enjoying the excitement of war and of casual pleasures," as Bradley puts it.[6] In short, Bradley imagines Iago to be rather like you and me – a thoroughly bourgeois and insignificant individual. His inflated and fragile ego makes him sensitive to perceived slights, but the inevitable resentment he experiences from these slights is not fatal as long as his career continues to *progress upward* in the ordinary and predictable manner that we have come to expect in our professional and personal lives. We live in a world in which things are supposed to get better.[7]

What then precipitated the disastrous events of the play? The key to understanding Iago, Bradley says, lies in his "absolute egoism."[8] He has an extremely high opinion of himself. This inflated egoism, when combined with an extreme coldness or lack of fellow feeling, is potentially very dangerous. His feelings of superiority and contempt of others make him notably sensitive to perceived slights or injuries, which he is unlikely to forget. They remain in his consciousness, where they serve as unpleasant reminders of the injustices he has experienced. Now ordinarily Iago would be able to get on with his life without allowing these injuries to upset him unduly. "Under ordinary circumstances," Bradley writes, "he was restrained, chiefly by self-interest, in some slight degree perhaps by the faint pulsations of conscience or humanity."[9] Bradley has the emphasis right here, I think. As long as Iago's self-interest can be satisfied, he remains relatively harmless. Indeed he is quite ordinary. Iago is surely not exceptional in either his selfishness or his talent for deception. The fact that Bradley concedes that Iago is not totally devoid of a moral conscience is also worth remarking. One might say that it is an inevitable consequence of Bradley's view that this is Iago's tragedy too. The problem, however, is that Iago's career *is* thwarted, and in a way that Iago cannot allow himself to overlook or forget. When Othello denies him the lieutenancy, Iago is incensed at the injustice of the "system." From this seemingly insignificant seed the entire tragedy grows.

Bradley's reading, which is ultimately a more detailed and rigorous elaboration of Hazlitt's, emphasizes two things. First, it stresses the utterly mundane or ordinary nature of Iago's resentment. Second, it points to the artistic means whereby Iago seeks to vent his frustration. Related to both points is Bradley's stress on the total absence of passion in Iago's actions. His resentment remains, from beginning to end, cold and mean. There is nothing grand or imposing about it. Bradley compares it negatively to Macbeth's ambition and Shylock's hatred. Macbeth's ambition is "a volcano in eruption," while Iago's is "a flameless fire of coke." Shylock's hatred manifests itself in "a consuming desire to hack and hew your enemy's flesh," while Iago's is evident "in the resentful wish, only too familiar in common life, to inflict pain in return for a slight."[10] These points are well taken, but I am surprised Bradley doesn't extend the comparison to its most obvious target: Othello. Othello's jealousy is truly magnificent. It burns rapidly and brightly across the stage like a comet and then dies with a climactic show of violence, when he strangles Desdemona and stabs himself. Iago's jealousy is by contrast a weak, paltry, sneaking thing, hinted at repeatedly in the soliloquies but never represented vividly on the stage in glorious, life-sized, three-dimensional reality. It lacks the ocular proof. Is this why Iago insists that Othello kill Desdemona with his bare hands? Real jealousy must explode on the stage with brutal violence. When Othello suggests poison, this irks Iago's sense of what counts as a genuine tragic spectacle.

What I find interesting about Bradley's interpretation is that it emphasizes exactly what I stressed in the preceding chapters on *Julius Caesar* and *Hamlet*. Iago seems to be a distillation of Shakespeare's thoughts on tragedy as the playwright becomes increasingly interested in the link between resentment and aesthetic form. This development can be traced in Shakespeare's protagonists. Brutus's existence is supplemental to Caesar's; he goes to his death attempting to imitate his more famous predecessor. Never once does Brutus recognize the role of resentment in his desire to usurp the centre. Shakespeare's next tragic protagonist, Hamlet, is far more aware of the centre's ambivalence. He sees both the desire and the resentment; hence his refusal to usurp the centre until the final act. The next protagonist in this series, Iago, shows absolutely no interest in usurping the centre. Of all Shakespeare's protagonists, he is by far the most ironic. He is defined entirely by what he is not – "I am not what I am" (1.1.67). Iago is most definitely not a typical tragic hero.

This last remark invites an obvious objection. Isn't Othello the hero of this play? Indeed he is, and that is exactly the point. Shakespeare can't call the play *Iago* because Iago is too ironic to be a tragic hero. His resentment is so pronounced it outgrows even the irony of the neoclassical stage, which is defined by its ironic stance towards the classical hero's unselfconscious centrality. It would make even less sense to rename *Othello* after Iago than to rename *Julius Caesar* after Brutus. The comparison is nonetheless illuminating because it points out the difference between the two tragedies. Othello and Caesar are similar in the sense that they remain wholly ignorant of the danger they face. Likewise, Brutus and Iago are comparable in the sense that they control the fate of their less knowing but socially superior antagonists, after whom the plays are named. Yet there is an important difference. Iago far outmatches Brutus in his skill at handling the conspiracy against the protagonist. The origin of this skill has nothing to do with intellectual temperament. No doubt Iago is more intelligent and more devious than Brutus; but his superiority over his victims comes not from a finer intellect but rather from his more clear-sighted awareness that occupation of the centre is a *moral crime*. Iago must be the first literary character to glean the power of victimary rhetoric. His animosity towards the Moor, as his opening speech makes clear, is motivated by the moral scandal of Cassio's promotion to the lieutenancy. As a spokesman for the excluded other, Iago is truly ahead of his time. Nobody in the play really cares about Iago's complaint, certainly not the rather dull Roderigo. But today there would be a human rights tribunal to ensure that no injustice had occurred. His superior control of the victimary centre comes from his highly advanced and thoroughly modern sense of moral injustice. He knows that centrality is not determined by social rank, and he is not afraid to cry foul when asymmetries appear, as they inevitably must.[11]

This is not to say that Iago is a romantic revolutionary. On the contrary, Iago would never dream of challenging Othello on his own turf. He knows he is destined for a life of service. His innovation is to turn the existing social hierarchy into a source of inner strength. He knows that that this hierarchy is purely symbolic and possesses no intrinsic connection to individual *moral* worth. This is why he is so resentful. He is scandalized by any hint of moral injustice, particularly when it affects his own ability to succeed, which is the point of his remarks on service. He follows Othello to serve his turn upon him. Only fellows like himself – that is, those who believe in themselves despite their inferior status in the social hierarchy – have "some soul" (1.1.56).

Iago's intellectual detachment has been often remarked, but what has been less frequently noticed is the connection between his intellectual detachment and the stage. In this regard, Iago can be fruitfully compared to Horatio. Before Hamlet stages the Mousetrap play, he takes Horatio aside and says these extraordinary words:

> Since my dear soul was mistress of her choice
> And could of men distinguish her election
> Sh' hath sealed thee for herself, for thou hast been
> As one, in suffering all, that suffers nothing,
> A man that fortune's buffets and rewards
> Hast ta'en with equal thanks; and blest are those
> Whose blood and judgment are so well commeddled
> That they are not a pipe for fortune's finger
> To sound what stop she please. Give me that man
> That is not passion's slave, and I will wear him
> In my heart's core, ay, in my heart of heart,
> As I do thee. (3.2.62–73)

As we have seen, Horatio occupies a curious position in the play. His presence in the first scene is critical. He correctly identifies the ghost and gives us a detailed account of the old king's warlike history. When the ghost disappears, he decides that Hamlet must be told. I have described Horatio as a mediator of our aesthetic attention. He mediates our desire for significance, directing us towards the ghost, whose martial and warlike form suggests the "firstness" of the classical hero or "big man."[12] He may be usefully contrasted with Francisco, who abandons the scene and is never heard of again. But Horatio very quickly passes the burden of mediating the audience's desire to Hamlet. Having relinquished control of our scenic imaginations, he remains content to play the role of straight man beside the more engaging figure of the prince. But in the middle of the third act, just before Hamlet plans to "play on" the king, we get this tribute to Horatio. The tribute is all the more remarkable because Hamlet makes it just before he enlists Horatio's help in observing Claudius. The point of the Mousetrap play, Hamlet explains, is to spy on the king. Horatio may not be passion's slave, but Hamlet certainly hopes that Claudius will be. The passions about to be performed on the inner stage will so provoke the king that he will betray himself. Later, after the Mousetrap play has been performed, Hamlet indignantly accuses Guildenstern, whom he suspects of being a spy for the king, of attempting to play on *him* like a pipe. Hamlet does not see the irony of this accusation. His obsession with subterfuge and spying betrays his own perverse attachment to the scene he affects to despise. If Hamlet so hates Denmark, why does he stick around to play these ridiculous spy games with the king?

The same question could be asked of Iago, who has even less reason than Hamlet to remain attached to the scene he so vociferously claims to despise. Roderigo clearly doesn't understand why Iago continues to serve the Moor: "I would not follow him then" (1.1.42), he says flatly, after Iago has explained to him for the umpteenth time why he despises Othello. But Roderigo is not a very perceptive man. If he were, he would remove himself as fast as possible from all association with Iago, and seat himself comfortably beside the spectator in the playhouse. At least there he could participate in all the intrigue without suffering any of its horrible consequences. Of course, such disrespect for the boundary between stage and audience, centre and periphery, is not to be tolerated. But this does not mean that Shakespeare cannot thematize from within the play itself our complicity in the violence that unfolds on the stage before us. Iago's dispassionate manipulation of the characters in the play figures our dispassionate attachment to the very same scene.

In *Othello* the counterpart to Hamlet's Mousetrap is the temptation scene in which Iago untunes the pegs of Othello's music. This raises a rather interesting question. Is Iago the man Hamlet wishes to emulate when he pays his tribute to Horatio? One can't find a much better example of someone who is not passion's slave. Hamlet's notion of a man who in suffering all suffers nothing is most brilliantly illustrated by Iago. The idea suggests the aesthetic experience of the spectator, who gets to experience the centre's violence but does not have to suffer any of its violent consequences. Iago seems to be a more fully worked out embodiment of Horatio. It is as though Shakespeare, when writing *Othello*, saw Hamlet as split between two contradictory moments of the aesthetic scene. On the one hand, he is clearly allied to Horatio, the detached spectator of the unfolding tragedy and the only person to survive proximity to the prince. All the others, including the king, the queen, Polonius, Ophelia, Laertes, Rosencrantz, and Guildenstern, suffer for being a "little more than kin and less than kind." Horatio of course only narrowly avoids death at the last minute. But unlike the others, he had volunteered to imitate his mentor. It is only because Hamlet persuades him not to drink from the poisoned cup that he lives to tell the prince's story. On the other hand, Hamlet has one foot in Claudius's camp. He may be constantly criticizing the centre his uncle occupies, but he is nevertheless fascinated by it. The power of Ernest Jones's Freudian reading of the play relies on this fact. Hamlet cannot kill Claudius because he is fascinated by the latter's usurpation of the centre. It is something he had imagined to himself many times before, and this parricidal thought keeps him rooted to the spot, a secret admirer of his more audacious rival. The contest between these two Hamlets, represented on the one side by Horatio and on the other by Claudius, is ultimately split into two separate characters in *Othello*. Hamlet/Claudius becomes Othello and Hamlet/Horatio becomes Iago.

In a characteristic comment, Bradley notes that were Othello and Hamlet to swap places, there would be no tragedy in either Denmark or Cyprus.[13] Othello would have run Claudius through in a trice, and Hamlet would have spotted Iago's deception immediately. The suggestion accurately captures the psychological differences between Hamlet and Othello, but I think a more interesting question to ask is, what if Hamlet and Iago were to swap places? In a sense, we don't really need to imagine such a transposition, because Shakespeare has already done it for us. Iago is to Othello as Hamlet is to Claudius. Iago is Hamlet taken to the next level, so to speak. I don't mean to imply that their characters are highly similar, though Bradley recognizes that there are important similarities between the two men. What I mean is that Iago is Hamlet denuded of all centrality. Goethe was certainly right to characterize Hamlet as "needy and degraded." Yet despite his uncle's usurpation, Hamlet is still a prince, and Claudius is quite adamant he behave like one. When Hamlet turns to Horatio and expresses his admiration for the man who is not passion's slave or a pipe for fortune's finger, he is articulating a desire to be divested of the burdens of the public scene represented by Claudius and his court. His emphasis on Horatio's status as a private man lies at the heart of his tribute:

> Nay, do not think I flatter,
> For what advancement may I hope from thee
> That no revenue hast but thy good spirits
> To feed and clothe thee? (3.2.55–8)

Hamlet's desire to escape the public scene remains but a dream. After *The Mousetrap* is performed, Hamlet kills Polonius. This fatal act draws him irresistibly into the centre's violence. When he returns to face the man whose father he has murdered, he announces himself as "Hamlet the Dane." The assumption of the royal title signifies the prince's usurpation of the tragic centre, the violent passions of which he has now become a slave to. As Girard points out, the passionate and vengeful Laertes provides Hamlet with the perfect model to imitate.[14]

In contrast, Iago would never dream of announcing himself in such a fashion, and not simply because Iago is a common soldier rather than a prince. Desire for nobility is not what motivates Iago. For him, the centre has become a wholly negative locus, something to be held in permanent suspicion rather than revered or aspired to. Were Iago to have had a realistic shot at the lieutenancy, one suspects he would find a way to sabotage it. Consider how Iago might have acted were he in Hamlet's shoes. I think he would have laughed in the ghost's face: "How quaint! Thank you, but I really can get along just fine without *your* instructions." No doubt Iago would have applauded Claudius's victory over his unsuspecting brother. That is how you serve your turn on those insufferable fools who think they're better than you.

Bradley's idea of Iago as a basically decent man who goes off the rails when he discovers he has been denied the lieutenancy misses this point. I agree with the notion that Iago's resentment is unexceptional and commonplace. (*That* is very much the point.) But I disagree that Iago is particularly bothered by his failure to win the promotion. Interestingly, Bradley is somewhat inconsistent on this point. He suggests, rightly, that Iago is a kind of artist; the early soliloquies are brain-storming sessions, as Iago tries to sort out his revenge plot. It is therefore rather pointless to take any of his soliloquies as evidence of what Iago truly believes. They are merely heuristic devices to think his plot through. The point may be put more generally by observing that the soliloquies occupy a privileged metatheatrical position in the play. They reveal

Iago's plan to victimize the other characters. Psychologically, they demonstrate his obsession with power and control. I can think of only two instances in all of Hamlet's soliloquies that have a similar effect. The first is when Hamlet hits upon the idea of using the play to "catch the conscience of the king" (2.2.606); and the second is when Hamlet, on the point of killing the king, "scans" his action and decides to await a more "horrid hent" (3.3.88). The second example in particular captures something of Iago's spirit. Hamlet has the king at his mercy and wishes to prolong this tremendous feeling of power over his victim.

Bradley notes that in the soliloquies Iago at times seems to approximate Hamlet, and he observes that just as we cannot always trust Hamlet's soliloquizing (particularly in the matter of his delay), so too we cannot trust Iago's.[15] But after making this very useful point, Bradley contradicts himself, arguing that the kerfuffle over the promotion is devastating to Iago. But why should we take Iago seriously when he tells Roderigo (and not for the first time) why he hates Othello? What is to distinguish the authenticity of this story from the inauthenticity of the others? Bradley even admits that much of the story about the failed promotion is invented. So why believe any of it?

Iago's resentment of the centre precedes any explanation of it, including those ventured by Iago himself. As with Hamlet's resentment, Iago's is a precondition of the play. And just as we are encouraged to identify with Hamlet's resentment, so too we identify with Iago's. This is the point of the play's opening scene, in which Iago explains to Roderigo why he has never wavered in his hatred:

> RODERIGO: Tush, never tell me! I take it much unkindly
> That thou, Iago, who has had my purse
> As if the strings were thine, shouldst know of this.
> IAGO: 'Sblood, but you'll not hear me.
> If ever I did dream of such a matter,
> Abhor me.
> RODERIGO: Thou told'st me thou didst hold him in thy hate.
> IAGO: Despise me
> If I do not. (1.1.1–9)

Nothing could be more typical or commonplace. Two men are arguing about money. One man feels he has been conned by the other and expresses his indignation. The other is exasperated at the accusation, but rather than seeking to deny it outright he conditionally affirms the other man's resentment. You would (Iago implies) be justified in your resentment if I did indeed intentionally conceal Othello's courtship of Desdemona from you. Furthermore, you would be right to despise me if I do not indeed hate Othello as much as I did when I first agreed to help you win Desdemona. Iago takes care not to deny or dampen or otherwise contradict the bare fact of Roderigo's resentment, which he regards as a precious resource to be cultivated and exploited. Resentment is Iago's means to "put money in his purse." But resentment is a tricky emotion to handle or trade in, even for so skilled and enterprising a monger of resentment as Iago.[16] It must be handled with the greatest of care, for there is always a chance that in exploiting it you may yourself become the target of it. This risk is what concerns Iago in the opening scene. Resentment is "in the air." The two men are, after all, arguing about money, the most liquid form of value available. The way money changes hands so rapidly without any respect for the inherent value of things can be quite disconcerting. But Iago is a master of the fluid situation. What is more, his exchanges in this volatile market are made openly and in good faith. It is well known how *honest* he is. No man could be more frank in his commitment to your private grievances.

The question, then, at the outset of the play is how resentment will be managed. Iago's skill as an envy monger is immediately demonstrated when he easily realigns Roderigo's resentment towards a more fitting object: the Moor.[17] He invents a story to explain why he hates Othello. Roderigo already knows that Iago hates Othello because Iago has divulged this fact to him in the past. We are meant to suppose Iago's motive for supporting Roderigo's suit is in large part due to his longstanding hatred of Othello, who is a rival for Desdemona and whom Iago would not wish to see succeed. But now Roderigo suspects Iago's motives. If Iago really hated Othello, how could he stand by passively without at least informing Roderigo of Othello's intentions with respect to Desdemona?

Iago ignores all this. Instead he redirects Roderigo's resentment by (once more) encouraging him to identify with his – Iago's – hatred of the Moor. Like Cassius whispering into Brutus's ear, Iago channels Roderigo's resentment onto its proper object. His personification or embodiment of resentment serves as a model for Roderigo. Iago explains the most recent indignity he has suffered at the Moor's hands:

> Three great ones of the city,
> In personal suit to make me his lieutenant,
> Off-capped to him; and by the faith of man,

I know my price, I am worth no worse a place.
But he, as loving his own pride and purposes,
Evades them with a bombast circumstance
Horribly stuffed with epithets of war,
And, in conclusion,
Nonsuits my mediators. For, "Certes," says he,
"I have already chose my officer."
And what was he?
Forsooth, a great arithmetician,
One Michael Cassio, a Florentine,
A fellow almost damned in a fair wife,
That never set a squadron in the field
Nor the division of a battle knows
More than a spinster – unless the bookish theoric,
Wherein the togaed consuls can propose
As masterly as he. Mere prattle without practice
Is all his soldiership. But he, sir, had th'election;
And I, of whom his eyes had seen the proof
At Rhodes, at Cyprus, and on other grounds
Christian and heathen, must be beleed and calmed
By debitor and creditor. This countercaster,
He, in good time, must his lieutenant be,
And I – God bless the mark! – his Moorship's ancient. (1.1.9–34)

How much of this speech is true? Did Iago really employ three great ones of the city to advocate for him? Did Othello purposely obscure their advocacy by using military doublespeak? Did Othello then render the whole question nugatory by stating that he had already filled the position? Is it true that Cassio has no experience in the field?

Bradley, who recognizes that much of what Iago says is bullshit, nevertheless maintains that Iago's failure to achieve the lieutenancy is a fact that precipitates the whole tragedy. But I don't think we need to cling even to this fact.[18] Iago's speech, like Cassius's diatribe against Caesar, or Hamlet's first soliloquy against the king and queen, is not meant to be assessed on strictly logical grounds. As in those previous examples, its main function is to steer our resentment towards the play's central figure. Roderigo's response, "By heaven, I rather would have been his hangman" (1.1.35), shows that Iago's story has been successful, at least with respect to Roderigo, who identifies with Iago's sense of injury sufficiently to want to hang Othello. The fact that Othello is never referred to by name in the first scene, but rather by various derogatory epithets ("the Moor," "the thick-lips," "an old black ram," "a Barbary horse"), underscores the abstractness of resentment at this point. No doubt resentment must have an object, but the experience of scandal at the self's insignificance is anterior to the focus of resentment on any particular object. The opening lines of Hamlet's first soliloquy are not concerned with imagining the particular sins of the king and queen (drunkenness, sensuality, incest). Rather, they express the prince's general lassitude, weariness, and disgust. Resentment begins with this experience of exclusion from the centre. The task of imagining the fulfilment of desire is necessarily resentful because the desirable centre cannot be imagined independently of the prohibition of the centre implicit in the use of the sign. Without the sign, the centre could neither be imagined nor resented. It would remain a mere object of appetite. Frustration at its denial would then be mere animal frustration, the obstruction of a need rather than the (sacred) prohibition of a desire. The ambivalence of desire is apparent in Roderigo's reaction to Iago's story. On the one hand, he wants to be Othello's executioner; on the other, he admires and envies the "full fortune" (1.1.68) Othello seems to possess. As is often pointed out, this ambivalence is reflected in Othello himself. On the one hand, he is black, an outsider, and a "Turk." On the other, he is a highly respected general in the Venetian army who is to be employed in defending Cyprus against the Turkish infidel. Like Oedipus, who is always referred to as *tyrannos* (king by successful coup) rather than *basileus* (king by inheritance), Othello is the paradigmatic example of the hero "you love to hate."[19]

More clearly than either Cassius or Hamlet, Iago articulates the resentment of the excluded other. Bradley's caution that we cannot take Iago's words at face value, though certainly true, does not refute this point, for the same warning applies with equal force to Cassius and Hamlet. The reason why Bradley feels he has to remind us of this fact with respect to Iago is because his own interpretation relies so heavily upon identifying with the expressed motivations of the characters. Both Hamlet and Iago therefore present a peculiar problem for Bradley. They seem extraordinarily conscious of themselves as characters in a play. "I have that within which passes shows," says Hamlet. "I am not what I am," says Iago. But whereas Bradley identifies with Hamlet, he is not nearly so generous with Iago. Iago is a villain, and he must be treated like one if we are to maintain the moral integrity of the tragedy.

If Iago represents the voice of the excluded other, why is Roderigo his first victim? Roderigo is a warm-up exercise for Iago, an appetizer to prepare us for the much grander dish to follow, the temptation of Othello. Like all fools, Roderigo's foolishness comes from an inflated belief in his own merit, and this makes him easy prey. When Roderigo asks why Iago continues to serve the man he hates, Iago's reply contains a clever double entendre that Roderigo is too stupid to notice:

> You shall mark
> Many a duteous and knee-crooking knave
> That, doting on his own obsequious bondage,
> Wears out his time, much like his master's ass,
> For naught but provender, and when he's old, cashiered.
> Whip me such honest knaves. Others there are
> Who, trimmed in forms and visages of duty,
> Keep yet their hearts attending on themselves,
> And, throwing but shows of service on their lords,
> Do well thrive by them, and when they have lined their coats,
> Do themselves homage. These fellows have some soul,
> And such a one do I profess myself. For, sir,
> It is as sure as you are Roderigo,
> Were I the Moor I would not be Iago.
> In following him, I follow but myself. (1.1.46–60)

If Roderigo were in the least bit attentive, he would immediately see that Iago's account of deception is a red flag. Why should he trust a man who admits he is not to be trusted? In the final lines of the speech, Iago says that Roderigo is exactly as he appears to be, whereas he, Iago, is not. The lines present a puzzle that deserves to be examined more closely.

When Iago says, "Were I the Moor, I would not be Iago," he is not merely stating a logical tautology (A is not B), or a differential structural principle (*cat* is not *bat*). He is also articulating a version of the fundamental originary paradox of human origin. One might paraphrase Iago's statement as follows. If I were in the centre like the protagonist of this play ("the Moor of Venice," as he is referred to in the play's subtitle), I would not be able to enjoy the glorious spectacle of his downfall. The centre depends upon its designation by the periphery. Central significance is generated by the collective sign – the "joint attention" of the scene's peripheral human designators. Take away the human periphery, and there is no tragic centre, no victimary scene or violent spectacle, to observe. Put Iago in the centre, make *him* the Moor, and there is no play, because there is no secondary ironic figure to designate the centre. Iago is necessary for our experience of tragic suffering. He allegorizes the passage of desire from periphery to centre, from the human sign user to the central sacrificial victim. In Kenneth Burke's terminology, he helps to point the "arrows of our expectation" towards the denouement, the fulfilment of desire in a scene of central suffering.[20]

Iago is thus the high priest of tragic spectacle. As many commentators have pointed out, he personifies negation.[21] But negation here is not merely logical negation. It is the negation – or, more precisely, the prohibition – of a highly desirable and therefore highly dangerous object. The object is too desirable to remain unguarded by sacred or cultural prohibition. In the originary scene, the emission of the sign converts animal appetite into human desire. The central object is now not merely an object of instinctual need. It is desired for its collective or symbolic significance. The sign thus negates appetite by shifting attention away from the object and onto the sign. But this return to the sign is paradoxical because the sign points us back to the object. The latter now seems all the more desirable because of the mediation provided by the sign. But the object without the sign is insignificant. So we return to the sign to remind ourselves of its general significance at the centre of the scene.

Why does Shakespeare begin with Iago rather than Othello? The answer ought now to be obvious. Iago is responsible for directing our attention towards the central figure. He is the mediator of our desire for significance. In Burke's phrase, he is the "impresario" who furnishes us with the means for the "filthy purgation" of tragedy.[22] *Othello* is hardly unique in delaying our encounter with the protagonist. Only very rarely does Shakespeare begin a tragedy with his protagonist. Richard of Gloucester's opening soliloquy in *Richard III* springs to mind, but precisely in this case Richard is *not* (yet) the king; his opening lines are an attack on the centre from which he feels unfairly excluded. Generally speaking, however, our approach to the tragic protagonist is mediated from the beginning by what others say about him before we see him on the stage.

What is unique about *Othello* in this respect is the degree to which Shakespeare foregrounds the mediating figure. Few characters in Shakespeare control the stage as completely as Iago. Prospero is his only real rival. It is impossible to think of Othello without first thinking of Iago. This is no accident. Compared to Hamlet, Othello spends remarkably little time alone on stage. His first soliloquy does not occur until almost the end of the third act, directly after Iago's first temptation of him. Othello and Iago are almost inseparable. Moments after Iago has incited first Roderigo's and then Brabantio's resentment of the Moor, Iago appears beside his general in Othello's first stage appearance. Notice that it is Iago, not Desdemona, who stands beside Othello on this, his wedding, night.

While it is very difficult to imagine Othello independently of Iago, it is relatively easy to think of him independently of Desdemona. The idea of Othello as a divided man split between good (Desdemona) and evil (Iago) is no doubt important for grasping the religious background of the tragedy, but the allegorical context of the moralities does not explain our aesthetic experience of the play. If it did, we would enjoy *Everyman* as much as we do *Othello*.[23] More important than the religious background is the aesthetic context. It is the latter rather than the former that helps us understand Iago's function as an impresario, a mediator of desire. It is certainly meaningful to say that Iago personifies resentment, but this is not because he is a Vice figure left over from the medieval stage, but because he represents an integral element of our aesthetic experience. His management of Roderigo's resentment is a miniature version of Shakespeare's management of ours. Roderigo represents the most elementary level of audience response. On the one hand, he is envious of the Moor's success and would like nothing better than to see him suffer – "I would rather have been his hangman" (1.1.35). On the other, he identifies with him precisely because he is successful: "What a full fortune does the thick-lips owe / If he can carry't thus!" (1.1.68–9). There is genuine admiration in these lines. How can this guy, who isn't even one of us (i.e., one of the "wealthy curlèd darlings of our nation" [1.2.69]), be so successful in wooing the beautiful Desdemona? Roderigo is in the position of the tragic spectator; in momentarily identifying with the tragic hero, he forgets that this man is also a usurper of the centre and therefore a target of his resentment.

Roderigo, however, doesn't pay very close attention to what Iago says, for if he did he would realize that Iago is merely serving his turn upon him. Like Cassius holding up the mirror to Brutus, Iago is holding up the mirror to Roderigo. But rather than inspect the beam of resentment in his own eye, Roderigo is content to project it onto someone else. In this he is like the naive playgoer, who effortlessly catches on to the spirit of resentment whipped up by Iago:

> Call up her father.
> Rouse him, make after him, poison his delight,
> Proclaim him in the streets; incense her kinsmen,
> And, though he in a fertile climate dwell,
> Plague him with flies. Though that his joy be joy,
> Yet throw such changes of vexation on't
> As it may lose some color. (1.1.69–75)

Iago successfully redirects Roderigo's resentment onto a substitute victim. Abstractly, the victim is "the Moor," but here it is concretized in what is most immediately to hand. "Here is her father's house," Roderigo says, "I'll call aloud" (1.1.76). As the unfortunate Cinna the poet in *Julius Caesar* discovered, resentment alights on whatever object is to hand. Iago urges Roderigo to spread resentment onto others, beginning with Desdemona's father:

> Do, with like timorous accent and dire yell
> As when, by night and negligence, the fire
> Is spied in populous cities. (1.1.77–9)

Harold Goddard remarks on these two speeches that this is the one time Iago seems to betray his true self to us. Here he mentions, in quick succession, his delight in the destructive spectacle of poison, plague, and fire. A less intellectual man, Goddard speculates, would have been a pyromaniac, for like the pyromaniac, Iago delights in observing the destruction he creates. It is the combination of intellect and hatred that make Iago so menacing. He is, Goddard says, a "moral pyromaniac."[24]

Roderigo is one more example of the playwright's manipulation of the audience's resentment. The latter is needed just to get his play off the ground. In *Julius Caesar,* we saw how first Cassius, then the conspirators, and finally Caius Ligarius performed this function. The recruitment of conspirators is necessary for the assassination to take place. Insofar as we desire to see the assassination of Caesar performed, we too need to be recruited to the "honourable" goals of the conspiracy. As Burke pointed out, we must sympathize with the "Brutus-principle." We must see the assassination as Brutus does: as a sacrifice, not a murder.

But Shakespeare does not let us get away with such an idealized picture. We are also guilty of desiring murder, even if it is only an imaginary one, and for this crime we stand in need of expiation. Hence we quickly turn against Brutus and the conspirators when we hear Antony speak movingly of Caesar's love for the people and the injustice of Brutus's butchery; for butchery is now how the assassination appears to us, at least while we are under Antony's spell.

The resentful imagination is obsessed with sexual deviance, which becomes another insult to hurl at the evil seductions of the centre. Hamlet's first soliloquy was an attack on the "incestuous" marriage of the king and queen. Now it is Iago's filthy imagination mediating our attention on the doomed couple: "Even now, now, very now, an old black ram / Is tupping your white ewe" (1.1.90–1); "you'll have your daughter covered with a Barbary horse" (1.1.114–15); "your daughter and the Moor are now making the beast with two backs" (1.1.118–20). Brabantio's reaction is typically Shakespearean:

> Strike on the tinder, ho!
> Give me a taper! Call up all my people!
> This accident is not unlike my dream.
> Belief of it oppresses me already.
> Light, I say, light! (1.1.144–8)

As we have seen, in Shakespeare the call for light is both literal and symbolic. The darkness of the night means that Brabantio needs a torch to find his way. But Iago's words are also poison in his ears, and he must needs find light within himself to prevent these noxious thoughts from poisoning his mind. Unfortunately, he totally fails in this second task. He allows Iago's poison to possess him completely. When he encounters Othello in the next scene, he shouts all kinds of abuse at him and tries to have him arrested. When he discovers, in the council scene, that Desdemona chose Othello of her own free will, he wallows in resentful self-pity. The damage to his reputation is so great that he dies in the next few days. Brabantio is the first victim of Iago's poison. His story is a miniature version of Othello's. Iago probably got his idea for ensnaring Othello's body and soul from the old man's last resentful words:

> Look to her Moor, if thou hast eyes to see.
> She has deceived her father and may thee. (1.3.295–6)

In the play's final scene, when Brabantio's brother Gratiano looks sorrowfully upon Desdemona's strangled body, he says that it's a good thing his brother is dead because this sight would cause him to "curse his better angel from his side / And fall to reprobance" (5.2.216). But Brabantio had already cursed his better angel from his side when he failed to heed the duke's words:

> If virtue no delighted beauty lack,
> Your son-in-law is far more fair than black. (1.3.292–3)

This sounds trite but the advice is good, for it is the antithesis of Iago's poison. The duke represents the better angel that Brabantio curses from his side when he condemns Desdemona's marriage to Othello.

We could summarize this point by observing that the first act is really a parody of the traditional comic ending. It begins with a marriage thwarted by a stubborn father. Then, after a brief confrontation, violence is averted and the obstacle removed. The act is a parody because the obstacle to the lovers' desire, represented by the stubborn father, is really a distraction. As Girard observes, Shakespeare has a habit of representing his stubborn fathers as "paper tigers."[25] Egeus in *A Midsummer Night's Dream* appears briefly at the beginning, and he indeed makes a big fuss about whom Hermia should marry. But just as quickly he vanishes, and the lovers are soon tripping over each other instead. As Girard convincingly shows, the lovers themselves are the real obstacles to the fulfilment of their desires. In the shenanigans of the midsummer night they obstruct one another far more effectively than did the ineffectual father. For Girard, the message is clear: if desire lacks an obstacle, it will produce one for itself.

The same rule applies to the first act of *Othello*. Brabantio is as magnificent as Egeus in his opposition to the marriage of his daughter. Indeed, he has even more reason to be upset than Egeus because Desdemona, who is as thoroughly modern and independent a woman as Hermia, has married Othello without even bothering to get her father's consent. No wonder Brabantio is so full of bluster and indignation. He fulminates against Othello's devious African practices. The only explanation for his daughter's incredible act of insubordination must be that the Moor has bewitched her by some dark magic unknown to civilized nations. But Othello is no impressionable adolescent like Lysander or Demetrius. He scoffs at the swords raised by Brabantio's officers, and calmly proposes that they resolve the matter nonviolently. Despite the late hour, Othello knows the duke is in council. He has himself just received an urgent request to join the duke in his council chambers. Why not go together and put the matter before the duke himself?

Poor Brabantio is doubly shocked. Not only has his daughter run off with Othello, but he now discovers that the duke is in council without him. The Turks are threatening Cyprus, and a military response is urgently needed. This is why Othello is so confident. He knows that the duke will favour him. The duke has no choice. He cannot abandon his best soldier when he needs him most. In Othello's world, the public always trumps the private. This failure to grasp the centre's dependency on the periphery is the cause of his downfall.

As in *Julius Caesar* and *Hamlet*, Shakespeare once again stresses the opposition between public and private, centre and periphery. We first see Othello outside the Sagittary talking to Iago. Where is Desdemona? Presumably she is within. Why then is Othello outside talking to Iago? Has Othello consummated his marriage, or is the consummation still to come?[26] Iago has already poisoned our minds with images of Othello's wedding night, but when we finally do encounter Othello we see him in his public guise, a calm and confident general, unperturbed by the abuse thrown at him by Brabantio and eager to get on with military affairs and the defence of the Venetian state.

Othello is defined by his career as a professional soldier. He knows his public services to the Venetian state will "out-tongue" (1.2.19) any complaints raised against him. And this gives him the confidence to face his detractors head-on:

> My parts, my title, and my perfect soul
> Shall manifest me rightly. (1.2.31–2)

The first act appears to be a resounding victory for Othello. He successfully averts the threat to his private life represented by the enraged Brabantio, and his status as Venice's top soldier is reaffirmed when he is selected to head the campaign against the Turks.

But more important than this victory is the manner in which it is achieved. Brabantio may be a paper tiger whose threats are not to be taken seriously but, as Girard points out, he is in fact the unwitting cause of his daughter's elopement.[27] This old man has a penchant for tales of adventure, and he eagerly invites Othello into his house so the soldier can regale him with marvellous stories of his exceedingly romantic life. Desdemona overhears Othello talking to her father and she is immediately hooked. She requests a private audience with the Moor and "with a greedy ear" devours his "discourse" (1.3.151–2). As Girard puts it, Othello is her Amadis of Gaul.[28] When Othello summarizes to the duke and his councillors the gist of his narrative, the duke is forced to concede that "this tale would win my daughter too" (1.3.173).

Girard's point is that Desdemona imitates her father's desire. The father becomes a model for the daughter to copy. Just as the father craves a mediator in the figure of the exotic Othello, so too does the daughter. Brabantio should therefore not be surprised when his daughter eventually falls in love with the Moor. His belated accusation of witchcraft is a case of protesting too much. What really upsets him is that she is a much more enthusiastic imitator of desire than he is.

Girard does not quite put it this way, but I think it is implicit in his notion of mimetic desire. Old Brabantio is content to remain a mere spectator of Othello's desire; he experiences Othello's violent world at a safe distance, consuming but not directly participating in Othello's stories. Desdemona, on the other hand, aspires to be not merely a passive spectator but a participant in the same romantic world as Othello. She demands to follow the Moor wherever he goes, including into the very jaws of battle. When Brabantio describes his daughter as modest and shy – a "maiden never bold" (1.3.96) – he is not lying. That is how she appeared to him. It therefore comes as a total shock when she falls in love "with what she feared to look on" (1.3.100). Nor is this fear a figment of Brabantio's imagination. He has himself experienced it when he listened to Othello's terrifying stories. Doubtless these same stories lie behind his premonition, which comes to him in a dream (1.1.146), that Desdemona has fallen in love with Othello. Othello himself emphasizes Desdemona's *aesthetic* reaction as the key moment in their courtship:

> My story being done,
> She gave me for my pains a world of sighs.
> She swore, in faith, 'twas strange, 'twas passing strange,
> 'Twas pitiful, 'twas wondrous pitiful.
> She wished she had not heard it, yet she wished
> That heaven had made her such a man. (1.3.160–5)

Desdemona's response includes both pity and fear. She pities Othello as the victim of violence, but she fears the violence that he both inflicts and has inflicted upon him. That is why she says she wished she had not heard him speak. The violence is almost too horrible to contemplate.

But in Desdemona's case, the pity outweighs the fear. She identifies so completely with Othello's victimhood that she throws herself wholeheartedly at him. Unfortunately this fatal decision to share the public centre with Othello leads to its inevitable tragic consequence. She is forced to suffer the same horrible violence that she had once feared to look on.

Othello's account of himself may entrance his onstage auditors, but our response to his glorious poetry is unavoidably tainted by Iago's cynical irony. Iago's relationship to Othello is analogous to the neoclassical protagonist's relationship to the centre of the scene he occupies. This is not to say that Othello himself resembles the protagonists of classical tragedy. On the contrary, his poetry is already tinged with a decadence and sentimentality that is by definition neoclassical.[29] What distinguishes Othello's sentimentality from Iago's irony, however, is the superior anthropological insight implicit in the latter. If Othello delivers to his audience a sentimental romance, Iago provides us with a genuine anthropological discovery procedure. For Iago's manipulation of the aesthetic scene relies not upon the stock figures of romance but upon a superior understanding of desire. Like Hamlet's cynical posture at Claudius's court, Iago's menacing figure surrounds and undermines Othello's romantic view of himself. No doubt Iago (who is not on stage while Othello recounts his story) has heard Othello's story a thousand times. Even if he hasn't, it is not difficult to imagine how he would respond. He would be amazed at the credulity of Othello's auditors. Why is everybody so easily taken in by the stories of this *professional killer*? Can't anybody see the bitterness and resentment seething in the breast of the desiring hero? All of this talk of heroism is merely a disguise for the monstrosity of the hero's desire.[30] Othello is projecting his own violence onto the horrible creatures he claims to have so triumphantly overcome. The concluding lines of Othello's story are particularly interesting in this regard:

> She thanked me,
> And bade me, if I had a friend that loved her,
> I should but teach him how to tell my story
> And that would woo her. (1.3.165–8)

If Desdemona can imitate her father as the consumer of Othello's story, Iago can imitate Othello as the producer of a rival story, one infinitely more ironic than Othello's. Unconsciously Othello provides Iago with the seed out of which the latter's counter-narrative will grow. Iago will transform this friend mentioned casually and innocently by Othello into the bitterly hated *rival*. It is precisely this rivalry that Othello's own narrative of the solitary romantic hero conveniently ignores or represses. All Iago has to do is point it out to Othello himself:

IAGO: My noble lord –
OTHELLO: What dost thou say, Iago?
IAGO: Did Michael Cassio, when you wooed my lady,
Know of your love? (3.3.101–4)

Othello does not regard his marriage to Desdemona as a private affair to be kept separate from his public and professional life. On the contrary, he feels he has earned his right to marry her because of his exceptional military service. When the state comes calling, Othello feels duty-bound to respond. But the flip side to his obligation to the state is the state's obligation to him, which includes publicly endorsing his marriage to Desdemona. It is a curious fact that when the legitimacy of the marriage is being questioned there is no mention of the priest who must have been responsible for conducting the sacrament. Nor do we generally worry about related details such as where and when Othello and Desdemona got married. It must have been in a church just prior to their arrival at the Sagittary, where the marriage is, presumably, to be consummated. But these questions seem irrelevant to our understanding of the play. What does seem relevant, however, is the fact that Othello insists that his marriage be publicly acknowledged in the context of his military service. It is as if this counts as the real marriage ceremony for him. When he is outside the Sagittary and Iago advises him to go inside rather than face the wrath of Brabantio and his armed officers, Othello insists on standing his ground: "I must be found" (1.2.30). One feels that Othello is positively willing the confrontation, not because he wants actual violence to break out, but because he wants to prove to Brabantio that he is deserving of his daughter. To the end Desdemona remains for him a symbol of his military reputation. To lose Desdemona is to lose his reputation. This is why he is so devastated by Iago's insinuations. It signifies the destruction of his military career and therefore of himself: "Farewell the plumèd troops and the big wars / That makes ambition virtue!" (3.3.365–6).

Othello's refusal to believe that he can be defined outside the public scene makes him peculiarly obtuse when it comes to matters we would regard as strictly private. It is this blinkered and exclusive focus on the public scene that Iago recognizes as a weakness and exploits.[31] Iago superimposes on Othello's view of the world an ironic vision that suggests that the public scene is not what it appears to be. It conceals a shadowy private world that opposes and undermines the surface reality complacently accepted by Othello.

Iago's temptation of Othello involves pointing out this conflict between the private and public scenes, between periphery and centre. Yes, Cassio is a good soldier but he is also charmer and a flirt who knows his way around a lady's bedchamber. Yes, Desdemona appears to love you passionately, but look how she deceived her father, who thought she was "a maiden never bold." Yes, you're highly respected in Venice, but what do you really know about Venetian women and their private lovers?

I agree with Bradley that Othello's jealously only comes fully to his consciousness well into the temptation scene.[32] Nonetheless, there must be a reason that accounts for the fact that many readers assume that Othello is jealous much earlier in this scene, almost from the moment Iago says, "Ha? I like not that" (3.3.35), as he draws Othello's attention to Cassio stealing "away so guiltylike" (3.3.40).

I think the reason readers are prone to making this assumption is that Shakespeare has prepared us for the temptation from a very early stage. The seed of jealousy has already been planted in our minds in the first act. In his first soliloquy, Iago says:

> I hate the Moor;
> And it is thought abroad, that 'twixt my sheets
> He's done my office. I know not if't be true;
> But I, for mere suspicion in that kind,
> Will do as if for surety. (1.3.387–91)

Has Othello really slept with Emilia? To ask the question is already to be taken in by the thought. We must imagine the scenario before we can reject it as a falsehood. There is, in fact, no evidence in the play to prove the claim either true or false. But even if we decide to reject the claim as a falsehood, the damage has been done. The thought has been sown in our minds where it remains to poison every subsequent thought.

> IAGO: But oh, what damned minutes tells he o'er
> Who dotes, yet doubts, suspects, yet fondly loves!
> OTHELLO: Oh misery! (3.3.182–4)

Othello's misery is particularly alarming because it seizes on an object that is, to put it delicately, constantly open to doubt. He cannot be 100 per cent sure of his wife's sexual habits *all the time*. As a man whose occupation means a lot of travel, no doubt this thought must have weighed a bit more heavily on his mind than is perhaps normal. Is this why he agrees to have Desdemona accompany him to Cyprus? It probably doesn't help that she is an exceedingly attractive woman who enjoys dancing and good company.

I should like to stress that Othello's doubt is based on an extremely common principle. The principle is implicit in all language use, and it is by no means necessary that it take such tremendously significant objects (such as one's wife's sexuality) as its main focus. The principle is simple. Before you can verify a proposition, you must understand it. This understanding takes place independently of any contact with the facts. In most cases, it is impossible to verify the facts right away, if indeed at all.

WIFE: Did you remember to lock the front door?
HUSBAND: Yes, I did – at least I think I did. Oh misery! Now I'm going to be worrying about it all through the flight.

Iago's temptation of Othello is a superb illustration of reverse psychology. It follows exactly the technique used by Mark Antony when he converts the crowd's love of Brutus into its very opposite. By referring repeatedly and ironically to Brutus's honour, Antony incites the crowd to transform the idea of honour into dishonour: I must not make you think of Caesar's love for you, I must not read the will, I must not stir you up, I am no orator like Brutus but just a plain, honest, and rather blunt man. And, naturally, all those things come to pass which must not. Iago pursues the same tactic. Beware, my lord, of jealousy. The green-eyed monster will set you on the rack. Don't think of it even for a minute! So, naturally, Othello dutifully thinks of all the things that *could* make him jealous:

'Tis not to make me jealous
To say my wife is fair, feeds well, loves company,
Is free of speech, sings, plays and dances well;
Where virtue is, these are more virtuous.
Nor from mine own weak merits will I draw
The smallest fear or doubt of her revolt,
For she had eyes, and chose me. (3.3.197–203)

Othello practically makes Iago's argument for him. He has an extremely attractive wife, who also happens to be a talented musician and dancer. And on top of all this, she loves good company. Naturally she is a much admired and sought-after guest, who instantly becomes the centre of attention at all the parties she loves to attend. It is truly a miracle that she chose Othello. Yet she did. Othello puts a lot of stress on this last point – "For she had eyes, and chose me."[33]

But such *forwardness* in a lady is to be suspected, is it not? Might she not, with equal forwardness, choose somebody else when the time comes? Her father never suspected her, and yet she managed to choose a man behind *his* back. The more Othello thinks about Desdemona's general desirability, the more jealous he becomes. How does he know that her love of company is not *too* liberal? How does he know that she has not yielded up her chaste treasure to other eager suitors? Once Othello begins to pursue this line of inquiry, he cannot stop. Soon he is demanding the "ocular proof." The thought alone is not enough. There must be some more tangible object that can confirm his suspicions. So Iago produces the handkerchief. But the object is self-confirming, its symbolic value a product of Othello's imagination. There is no question of fact here. Othello has produced his own version of reality out of nothing. And so has Shakespeare. He has carefully prepared us to believe in the protagonist's jealousy through his proxy Iago.

When Iago observes Cassio and Desdemona in conversation on the quayside as they await news of Othello's ship, Iago, in an aside to the audience, provides a running commentary that ironizes the scene before us. Moments later, Iago draws Roderigo into his ironic view of things:

> IAGO: Didst thou not see her paddle with the palm of his hand? Didst not mark that?
> RODERIGO: Yes, that I did; but that was but courtesy.
> IAGO: Lechery, by this hand. An index and obscure prologue to the history of lust and foul thoughts. (2.1.256–61)

Iago is incredulous at Roderigo's astonishing naiveté. When a gentleman opens the door for a lady, he is hoping she will open her legs for him. When a lady touches a man's naked hand, she wants to touch a lot more of his nakedness. "When these mutualities so marshal the way, hard at hand comes the master and main exercise, th'incorporate conclusion" (2.1.263–6). Even now, now, very now, Cassio is tupping Othello's good-looking young wife. The thought clearly excites Iago because moments later, in his second soliloquy, he is updating his wife's scorecard. Not only has "the lusty Moor" "leaped into his seat" (2.1.297–8), so has Cassio: "For I fear Cassio with my nightcap too" (2.1.309).

Again, we are not meant to suppose that what Iago says is true. How could we? Shakespeare has painstakingly demonstrated that Iago is not to be trusted. But truth is not our main objective here. What we are after is an aesthetic effect. Borrowing from Keats, we can describe this effect as the linguistic or symbolic capacity to sustain our interlocutor's attention "without any irritable reaching after fact."[34] Keats was thinking about Shakespeare when he said this, but the phrase could be applied equally well to Iago. Iago knows how to grab our attention, and he does not constrain himself unnecessarily by any irritable reaching after fact. Keats called this gift for loquacity unconstrained by facts "negative capability." A philosopher concerned only with truth might call it "bullshit."[35] Either way, it describes Iago's method pretty well. And in Iago's case, it certainly achieves its main purpose, which is to convince us of the naturalness of Othello's jealousy. Iago's offhand hints of his own jealousy serve as an "index and obscure prologue" to Othello's more spectacular jealousy. It is like the dumbshow in *The Murder of Gonzago*. The first murder (the dumbshow) is too briefly presented to really upset Claudius, but by the second time it is performed, with words to match the action, Claudius cannot ignore it.

But why should we pay so much attention to Iago? After all, he is not the protagonist. Am I not guilty of overemphasizing his influence? In his highly informative and rewarding study of *Othello*'s "interpretive traditions," Edward Pechter divides criticism of the play into two eras: the pre-Bradley era, and the post-Bradley era. In the pre-Bradley era, which includes Bradley himself, criticism was not all that interested in Iago. Instead, the focus was on the play's noble protagonist. The advantage of this way of looking at the play was that one got one's money's worth. Tragedy requires the downfall of a hero. To get the full tragic effect, one needs not just any old protagonist, one needs a hero, a charismatic and transcendent big man, whose suffering stirs pity and fear in the audience. The more heroic the protagonist, the greater the cathartic effect. The disadvantage of this approach, according to Pechter, is that by ignoring or marginalizing Iago's influence, Othello's downfall remains something of a mystery. How could so magnificent a hero be duped by such a resentful lowlife? In stressing the protagonist's heroism, one gets maximal catharsis, but only at the cost of logical consistency.

In the post-Bradley era, Pechter argues, the situation is reversed. By switching focus from Othello to Iago, one gains logical consistency but loses the cathartic effect. Taking Iago seriously, one sees the *inevitability* of Othello's downfall. But this logical coherence is won at the cost of the experience of catharsis. Once you identify with Iago, you no longer respect or admire Othello. This is very roughly Pechter's characterization of the current critical situation, which begins with T.S. Eliot and F.R. Leavis, who inaugurated the idea of a "feeble" Moor, and extends into the very latest postmodern dismantling of Othello's heroism: "By helping to account for precisely that sense of guilty complicity refused by the heroic reading, twentieth-century interpretation restores the voice that makes for *Othello*'s coherence."[36]

Pechter himself is ambivalent about the post-Bradleyan emphasis on Iago.[37] He cautions us against a too-easy dismissal of Othello, which merely negates the ambivalence of the text. Alienation assumes the prior experience of identification. If we don't admire Othello, then there is no point in being alienated from him, because the whole point of tragedy is to produce this fundamentally paradoxical effect. Identification is followed by alienation, but you can't have it the other way around. Alienation, like atheism, assumes the existence of something in which you (or your ancestors) once believed.

I agree with Pechter on this point, the logic of which is impeccable. However, Pechter draws a further conclusion that I find unwarranted. He argues that the ironic focus of recent criticism empties the play of its "tragic power."[38] The problem with this argument is that it conflates two related but nonetheless distinct experiences of the text. There is the theatrical experience, which comes to us in fully fleshed, embodied form, and there is the reader's experience, which is inevitably more detached. I think it is self-evident that criticism depends upon the possibility of disengaging from the immediacy of dramatic experience. Obviously we identify with Othello when we watch a performance, but reflection on the pattern of experience elicited by drama is always *at a distance* from theatrical engagement. Criticism is thus intrinsically ironic, in the sense that it theorizes the dramatic experience. I think the reason why recent criticism has been so interested in Iago is because he shares our sense of detachment from the fictional world. This sense of ironic detachment is the basis of criticism.

I also think that Pechter may have underestimated Bradley's capacity for ironic disengagement, particularly when it comes to estimating Iago's importance. Bradley ranked Iago as among the "most wonderful" and "most subtle" of Shakespeare's characters. Indeed, Bradley felt that only Hamlet could match Iago when it came to subtlety of character. Accordingly, Bradley expressed dismay at the "inadequacy" of previous interpretations of Iago, and no doubt this was why he felt compelled to devote an entire chapter to Iago alone.[39] Although Bradley found Iago's explanations of his revenge to be inadequate, he nonetheless credited them with some truth, particularly in the case of the failed promotion. What remained for Bradley to do as Iago's critic or psychotherapist, however, was to put this injury into the context of the man's character or psychological profile. Iago's immense egoism and contempt of others, together with his cold intellectuality and lack of fellow feeling, all combine to make him very dangerous, especially when he feels himself to be the victim of an injustice. Revenge is not something that erupts suddenly and passionately within him. Instead he waits patiently for his opportunity, delighting in the painstaking artistry of his revenge. For Bradley, the soliloquies are important because they show this artistry in action. They suggest a playwright in the process of composition. There is a "curious analogy," Bradley writes, "between the early stages of dramatic composition and those soliloquies in which Iago broods over his plot." So strong is this analogy that Bradley believes that "Shakespeare put a good deal of himself into Iago." But there is a fault in Iago's tragedy, which there never is in Shakespeare's. He misjudges Emilia, and this leads to his downfall. Iago, "the tragedian in real life," Bradley concludes, is "not the equal of the tragic poet."[40]

Doubtless none of Shakespeare's characters is the equal of the poet who gave birth to them. We need not argue with Bradley on this point. What seems rather more debatable is the reason Bradley gives for Iago's inferiority compared to Shakespeare. Bradley suggests that the flaw in Iago's tragedy is ultimately a moral flaw. Iago misjudges Emilia, who turns out to be loyal to Desdemona. Morally speaking, she elects to follow good rather than evil, and this upsets Iago's plan. In Emilia, Bradley sees an allegory for the play as a whole. Iago represents the "combination of unusual intellect and extreme evil," which is indeed a "terrifying" and "frightful" thing. But such an alliance will always fall short of Shakespeare's "*supreme* intellect." That is why Iago's frightful tragedy can never approach the truth of Shakespeare's: "the alliance of evil like Iago's with *supreme* intellect is an impossible fiction; and Shakespeare's fictions were truth."[41]

Bradley judges Iago's tragedy to fall short of Shakespeare's on purely moral grounds. Extreme evil simply cannot coexist with supreme poetry.

But this moral judgment lacks an anthropological foundation. On what basis can Bradley claim that supreme poetry and supreme evil are mutually exclusive? The claim remains for Bradley an unjustified premise of his humanist anthropology. It also distracts us from the otherwise very perceptive point Bradley makes about Iago as a kind of dramatic double of Shakespeare. The point is not to regard Iago as a rival poet over whom Shakespeare triumphs morally and intellectually. How could he not, since he invented Iago in the first place? The point is rather to notice the emphasis Shakespeare puts on the role of representation in deferring resentment.

Iago's resentment is, as we have seen, given by the play. This is the reason why critics repeatedly return to Coleridge's idea of "motiveless malignity." Iago's resentment is simply there. There is no point in denying its presence, or explaining it as motivated by something else. The real question is how it is to be managed. Nor can we pin the blame for this tragedy solely on Iago. His role is rather to hold the mirror up to Othello and, indeed, to the audience as well. Hence, the temptation occurs as an echoing of Othello's own thoughts, which allows Othello to draw his own conclusions rather than have Iago impose them on him.

IAGO: Did Michael Cassio, when you wooed my lady,
  Know of your love?
OTHELLO: He did, from first to last. Why dost thou ask?
IAGO: But for a satisfaction of my thought;
  No further harm.
OTHELLO: Why of thy thought, Iago?
IAGO: I did not think he had been acquainted with her.
OTHELLO: Oh, yes, and went between us very oft.
IAGO: Indeed?
OTHELLO: Indeed? Ay, indeed. Discern'st thou aught in that?
  Is he not honest?
IAGO: Honest, my lord?
OTHELLO: Honest. Ay, honest.
IAGO: My lord, for aught I know.
OTHELLO: What dost thou think?
IAGO: Think, my lord?
OTHELLO: "Think, my lord?" By heaven, thou echo'st me,
  As if there were some monster in thy thought
  Too hideous to be shown. (3.3.108–20)

But the monster is inside Othello, not Iago. Iago is merely providing an occasion for Othello to coax it out of himself. We saw how Cassius functioned as Brutus's mirror. He reflects back to Brutus the resentment that Brutus himself can never admit to. Iago does the same thing to Othello.

Why does Othello turn to Cassio for assistance in the courtship of Desdemona? Girard says it is because he lacks confidence in himself.[42] Othello believes he needs to acquire the necessary social graces, so he turns to a model whom he can imitate. Girard compares the situation to that in *Much Ado about Nothing*, in which the inexperienced Claudio seeks assistance from the more experienced Don Pedro. The latter "mediates" Claudio's desire. Don Pedro functions as a model for Claudio to imitate. Likewise Othello is unsure of how to behave in Venetian society, so he turns to Cassio, a gentleman soldier who is perfectly at home in aristocratic circles. Girard observes that it is all but inevitable that Othello's friend and model should eventually become his bitterly hated rival. Since the play is a tragedy, it tells the story of the tragic convergence of desire on a central "mimetic object." Of course comedy tells this story too, but it tends to conceal the violence generated by mimetic desire. Comedy ends happily by expelling violence from the community, usually by projecting it onto a marginalized figure who is not included in the final society that forms around the hero and heroine. Don John fulfils this role in *Much Ado*. But in tragedy the scapegoat is central to our imagination rather than peripheral. Violence is expelled, but the sense is that this time it has come rather too close for comfort. Othello is not a convenient scapegoat for the Venetians to expel whenever a mimetic crisis looms on the horizon. On the contrary, he is himself a highly valued member of this society. Expelling him is therefore not the easy option.

The paradox of Othello's status as ambivalently central and marginal within Venetian society contributes to the aesthetic effect generated by the play. We identify with this man who has usurped the centre from the outside. He is a romantic hero who successfully climbs to the very pinnacle of Venetian society. But in imagining Othello's successful usurpation of the centre, we are reminded of our own exclusion from it. Identification with the protagonist gives way to resentment of him. The play ends when the audience turns the universally admired object of desire into an object of hatred and vilification. Lodovico speaks for us all when he says,

> O thou Othello, that was once so good,
> Fall'n in the practice of a cursèd slave,
> What shall be said to thee? (5.2.299–301)

Othello is destroyed for having "loved not wisely but too well" (5.2.354). His failure to control his monstrous and excessive desire leads to his suffering and eventual suicide.

What is remarkable about the play is the emphasis it places on the byproduct of desire, which is resentment. In Iago's hands, Othello's entry upon the dramatic scene is presented in the context of an imaginary dispossession of central significance. Iago shows Othello that what he had imagined to be the crowning moment of his fabled career – his marriage to Desdemona – is in reality the exact opposite. This reversal or *peripeteia* occurs when Othello suddenly recognizes his essential vulnerability as the occupant of the centre. In one taut and justly celebrated scene, Othello goes from the serene and noble figure we saw in the first two acts to the envious and skulking figure that inhabits the final two. It is no accident that Shakespeare gives Othello his first soliloquy at this point in the play, midway through the temptation scene. The protagonist's sudden recognition of his distance from the centre causes him to withdraw into himself and question his whole being. His former self is now regarded with unendurable irony. Far from a triumph, his marriage is a curse:

> Oh, curse of marriage,
> That we can call these delicate creatures ours
> And not their appetites! I had rather be a toad
> And live upon the vapor of a dungeon
> Than keep a corner in the thing I love
> For others' uses. Yet, 'tis the plague of great ones;
> Prerogatived are they less than the base.
> 'Tis destiny unshunnable, like death. (3.3.284–91)

The last lines in particular illustrate Othello's newfound awareness that centrality is a curse imposed on him from a realm beyond his control. The soliloquy is the counterpart of Hamlet's recognition of the curse of centrality after his interview with the ghost: "Oh cursèd spite / That ever I was born to set it right!"

Iago's deception of Othello is a triumph of the stage. He is a panderer of the audience's desire for a victim. His victory over the Moor occurs when the latter realizes that he, too, is insignificant, merely another rival for the centre rather than its undisputed occupant. Othello's farewell speech to the "big wars" (3.3.365), "the neighing steed and the shrill trump" (3.3.367), the "Pride, pomp, and circumstance of glorious war" (3.3.370), signifies the end of his unselfconscious occupation of the centre. Divested of his former significance, Othello's resentment emerges as the driving force of the remainder of the play.

When Othello turns to Iago and violently demands satisfaction, "Villain, be sure thou prove my love a whore! / Be sure of it. Give me the ocular proof" (3.3.375–6), Iago offers him another story, this time of Cassio enacting in his sleep his filthy coupling with Desdemona. Othello's temper starts to boil: "Oh, monstrous! Monstrous!" (3.3.442), "I'll tear her all to pieces!" (3.3.446). Iago mentions the handkerchief: "Have you not sometimes seen a handkerchief / Spotted with strawberries in your wife's hand?" (3.3.449–50). Yes, Othello replies, "I gave her such a one. 'Twas my first gift" (3.3.451). Iago feigns disinterest in this last detail, "I know not that" (3.3.452), but it is in fact perfect. Othello's first gift! And now this gift is in general circulation, its sacrality profaned into common currency: "such a handkerchief – / I am sure it was your wife's – did I today / See Cassio wipe his beard with" (3.3.452–4). Now Othello has his "ocular proof." His gift – his wife! – is circulating shamelessly on the open market. The handkerchief is a metonymy of Desdemona, whom Othello imagines sharing herself with other men, nameless customers from the lowliest "pioneer" to the highest commander. It is the seed of the bordello scene. The thought is utterly repugnant to Othello, and yet he cannot tear his mind away from it. He finds himself horribly attracted to that which he fears to look on. The image, repulsive as it is, triumphs over him, overwhelming his better self, the self we saw at the beginning of the play. Like Hamlet erasing all trivial fond records from the table of his memory in order to make room for his oath to death, Othello must now shed his oath to love in order to swear allegiance to death:

Now do I see 'tis true. Look here, Iago,
All my fond love thus do I blow to heaven.
Tis gone.
Arise, black vengeance, from the hollow hell!
Yield up, O love, thy crown and hearted throne
To tyrannous hate! (3.3.459–64)

The scene ends with Iago and Othello kneeling together in a perversion of the marriage ceremony with which the play had implicitly begun:

OTHELLO. Now art thou my lieutenant.
IAGO: I am your own forever. (3.3.494–5)

The path is cleared for Othello's sacrifice of Desdemona, which reproduces in miniature Iago's sacrifice of Othello for *our* aesthetic satisfaction.

Iago's relationship to Othello thematizes the paradoxical relationship between centre and periphery. Iago's irony forces Othello to imagine himself as a spectator of his own desire. Iago puts Othello into the role of the voyeur. The temptation scene is the turning point of the play. From this moment on, Othello becomes the observer rather than the observed. The stage is now filled with plays within plays. Like Hamlet, Othello sees a conspiracy everywhere he looks. Every scene is read for a secondary, ironic meaning. He needles Desdemona for the handkerchief. He spies on Cassio and interprets the latter's jokes about his mistress as the triumphant boasting of a sexual rival. In the bordello scene, this dramatic irony is stretched to the limit. Desdemona becomes the "cunning whore of Venice" (4.2.93), and Emilia her bawd. He is not Othello, but another john in a long line of anonymous male customers. Othello's mind has turned to blackest pitch.

As in Cassius's temptation of Brutus, Iago's temptation of Othello involves turning the classical stage, with its unproblematic opposition between centre and periphery, inside out. Rather than the centre defining the periphery, it is the periphery that defines the centre. Iago persuades Othello to view himself from the outside as but another rival for the centre, an envious competitor for Desdemona. The extreme doubt and anxiety experienced by Othello reflect the neoclassical protagonist's awareness that the centre is an object of symmetrical and competing desires. Othello imagines the entire army, including the very the lowest "pioneers," as rivals for Desdemona's "sweet body" (3.3.362).

Girard argues that Iago's function as the villain of the play is to deflect towards himself "a great deal of the ugliness that should belong to Othello." In order for the audience to enjoy the play, Shakespeare cannot be too obvious about the hero's complicity in the violence he produces. Shakespeare needs to reserve a modicum of sympathy for the Moor, so he invents Iago as a "sacrificial substitute for the hero."[43]

This may indeed describe a naive playgoer's initial response to the play, but I think the idea that Shakespeare uses Iago as a way to sell more tickets is a bit too cynical. Iago is not simply a substitute victim for us to blame so we can sympathize more fully with Othello and therefore enjoy the play without destroying the illusion of Othello's big-man status. Iago is quite different from, for example, the rather wooden Don John in *Much Ado*. If we pay sufficiently close attention to Iago, we can see that Shakespeare uses his villain to show his audience that they are themselves guilty of the collective victimization of the Moor. We identify with Othello only because we first identify with Iago's resentment. Iago marks Othello from the beginning as a target of our hostility. By deftly channeling Roderigo's resentment onto the Moor, Iago shows us how to channel our own desultory and amorphous resentments.

Of course, there is plenty to *like* about Othello. Shakespeare's play will not achieve its goal if it does not also elevate the protagonist to a significant height. Pechter is right to defend Bradley's "noble" Othello. As Bradley says of Shakespeare's tragic protagonists, "they are not merely exceptional men, they are huge men; as it were, survivors of the heroic age living in a later and smaller world."[44] The ethical lesson implicit in Bradley's sense of the Shakespearean hero is that without transcendence, there can be no central suffering. But transcendence is not something intrinsic to the character; it is a consequence of the character's appearance on the aesthetic scene. Transcendence is inseparable from violent immolation. The classical aesthetic is the first aesthetic to demonstrate this paradoxical truth. Oedipus suffers for his crime of occupying the centre of our scenic imaginations. To be sure, we share in the hero's desire for centrality; but this identification with the hero is then shattered when we recognize that desire for centrality is a transgression against the centre itself. In Shakespeare, this oscillation between desiring identification and resentful alienation becomes not simply an effect but a central theme of the play. Iago is not merely a scapegoat to be blamed for Othello's suffering; he thematizes the periphery's complicity in bringing about the destruction of the central victim. In series of brilliant analyses, Harry Berger demonstrates the degree to which the peripheral characters contribute to the downfall of the central figure.[45] Berger's readings are testimony to the consistency of Shakespeare's anthropological imagination. What Berger calls the "complicity" of the peripheral characters in the immolation of the central figure is another way to describe the basic operation of Shakespeare's aesthetic, which explicitly thematizes the complicity between centre and periphery, transcendence and suffering, admiration and resentment, identification and alienation.

At the end of the play, Othello points to Iago and asks: "Will you, I pray, demand that demi-devil / Why he hath thus ensnared my soul and body?" (5.2.309–10). Iago refuses to answer the question: "What you know, you know. / From this time forth I never will speak word" (5.2.311–12). Bradley regarded Othello's question as *the* question about Iago, and he reckoned he had answered it in his analysis of Iago's character. But despite the sensitivity of Bradley's analysis, he never grasps Iago's function as a mediator of desire. This observation is less a criticism of Bradley's skill as a critic than a comment on his anthropology, which is firmly rooted in the romantic view of literature as a substitute for religion. Bradley lacked a critical anthropology that could explain his assertion that "Shakespeare put a good deal of himself into Iago."[46] The path from Bradley's psychological study of Iago to an anthropological reading of the play passes through the originary hypothesis. Iago is like Shakespeare because he exemplifies the fundamental human project of the deferral of violence through representation. Of course, Iago does not just defer resentment. He incites it. His resentment ultimately leads to a violence far worse than the petty bickering with which the play begins. But that too is a lesson of the originary hypothesis. To defer violence is not to end it. Words allow us to talk about things independently of the things themselves. This is most convenient. But eventually we need to get a hold of the things themselves, and when we do, we are always in danger of inciting the same old rivalry again. Words are cheap and easily reproduced; things are scarce and much more difficult to produce. But the answer is not to abandon the word, but to understand its power to defer rather than incite resentment. This lesson applies equally to the resentment that disguises itself as grief:

> The robbed that smiles steals something from the thief;
> He robs himself that spends a bootless grief. (1.3.211–12)

The duke says these words to Brabantio in an effort to cheer him up after he loses his daughter to Othello. Brabantio responds with mocking cynicism:

> But words are words. I never yet did hear
> That the bruisèd heart was pierced through the ear. (1.3.221–2)

Words are indeed but words, and yet the bruisèd heart is ever pierced through the ear. For what is *Othello* but the story of a man pierced in the heart through the ear? If Othello had at any point adopted the duke's faith rather than Brabantio's mocking cynicism, he would have been able to fend off Iago's aural assaults. But of course he failed to adopt the duke's advice. And why should he? We have paid good money to have our hearts piercèd through the ear. The difference is that we get to walk away from the scene, whereas Othello does not. Like Iago, we get to live another day, bleeding perhaps, but not killed.

Brutus, Hamlet, and Iago are one in their resentment of the centre. They exemplify the neoclassical representation of the classical scene as possessing both a centre and a periphery. Tragic identity is given by the peripheral status of the protagonist with respect to the centre he desires. Possession of the centre remains a resentful fantasy but it is never achieved. Brutus's assassination of Caesar leads to civil war and thence to Brutus's suicide. Hamlet's regicide culminates not in his possession of the throne but with his death. Iago is a permanent despiser of the centre whose story simply ends when he triumphs over the object of his resentment. In *Macbeth,* Shakespeare addresses the problem of resentment from the perspective of the successful usurper. After Macbeth murders Duncan, he becomes king. Yet the crown never sits comfortably upon Macbeth's head. As Bradley puts it, Macbeth was born to rule but not to reign.[47] After he is crowned, Macbeth's internal paranoia spreads to embrace the whole country. The protagonist's peripheral status with respect to the centre manifests itself not directly in resentment but in guilt for participating in the centre's destruction. No less than the other protagonists, Macbeth's usurpation reflects the basic problematic of resentment, the centre's dependency upon the resentful periphery. But Macbeth's resentment is far more decadent than the resentment of his precursors. *Macbeth* is Shakespeare's most concentrated study of the evil of the *sparagmos.*

6 Macbeth Unseamed

On the surface *Macbeth* seems to illustrate more clearly than *Julius Caesar*, *Hamlet*, or *Othello* the idea of the resented big man. In the earlier tragedies, resentment of the central figure is confined to a small segment of the periphery. Caesar is resented by a handful of patricians; meanwhile the plebeians, who are too low on the totem pole to be rivals of Caesar, remain under the sway of his godlike charisma, which becomes even more powerful after his death, as Antony's funeral speech demonstrates. In Claudius's Denmark, only Hamlet sees the king as an impostor; everyone else is happy with Claudius on the throne. Hamlet's main concern at the end seems to be that his regicide not be misconstrued as a botched grab for power, and this is why he begs Horatio to put aside the poisoned cup so he may live to tell Hamlet's story. As for Othello, he is loved by everyone except the one man in whom he puts all his trust. His final demand of Iago – "Why he hath thus ensnared my soul and body?" (5.2.310) – reflects the stunned incomprehension of both the onstage and offstage onlookers. Why indeed did this openhearted and generous man allow himself to be ensnared by evil? Compared to these other big men, Macbeth sticks out like a sore thumb. Universally reviled by his subjects, he alone deserves the reputation of a tyrant who draws the full animosity of the periphery upon him.

But this observation, though not incorrect, misses the larger point. Shakespeare's big men do not merely illustrate the tyranny of the centre. They dramatize its openness to all humanity. The Shakespearean big man exemplifies the historical opening of desire, at the dawn of the modern era, to the symmetrical and competing desires of the human periphery. The reification of desire into an ontological hierarchy between periphery and centre is an affront to desire itself, which demands satisfaction through repeated innovation. It is only because of the centre's openness to the periphery that one can subsequently regard the occupant of the centre as a tyrant or usurper. Hence the defining characteristic of the Shakespearean big man is not tyranny or even kingship, but resentment. In terms of their social status within the play, Caesar, Claudius, and Othello are more obviously central than Brutus, Hamlet, and Iago. But this is also why the latter are more interesting than the former. Brutus, Hamlet, and Iago are forced to internalize their opposition to the centre. Hamlet exemplifies the subjective experience of scandal that eventually persuades the big man to place himself at the centre rather than leave it in the hands of the immortal gods. It is only because Hamlet can imagine himself occupying the same position as Claudius that he can resent him. Ernest Jones's idea that Hamlet had inured himself to the sacred prohibition of the centre and is then outraged when Claudius scandalously appropriates the centre for himself makes a good deal of sense independently of the dogma of the Oedipus complex. Hamlet's slavish devotion to the memory of his father, whom he idolizes as Hyperion and contrasts bitterly with his satyr-like uncle, is a consequence of the sign's interdiction of the central appetitive object, an interdiction everyone else in the Danish court appears to have either forgotten or ignored. His brutal castigation of the flesh in the first soliloquy is not merely the hypocritical denunciation of a moral prude. It is inseparable from his belief in the superiority of the sign over the referent, of art over consumption. Hamlet objects to the "wicked speed" of Gertrude and Claudius; but he does not object to the representation of desire within his private imagination. On the contrary, the soliloquies contain little else. Hamlet is all too aware that his imagination is "foul / As Vulcan's stithy" (3.2.82–3). In this sense, he and Claudius are indeed partners in crime.

But Hamlet's attachment to the interdiction of the centre imposed by the sign cannot be maintained indefinitely. The emission of the sign makes possible the renunciation of appetite and the deferral of desire. But the longer this deferral is maintained, the greater the potential for resentment to accumulate and unleash itself in a final paroxysm of violence. Hamlet delays his usurpation of the centre, but not before leaving the stage littered with corpses. Tragedy reminds us that the convergence of desire on the object is but a hair's breadth away from the violent disorder of the mimetic crisis.

In the originary scene the aesthetic oscillation between the sign and its object is followed by the *sparagmos*, when the appetitive object is destroyed and divided among the members of the periphery. The resentment that is deferred during the aesthetic moment of the scene is unleashed in the violent destruction of the central object. The *sparagmos* is thus a return to violence within the bounds established by the sign. "The violence of the sparagmos," Gans writes, "is the originary example of evil."[1] This is the anthropological correlate of the biblical story of the Fall of Man. Humanity knows evil because it possesses the language by which to designate interdicted objects. The linguistic capacity for interdiction implies the possibility of transgression. If I say "Don't eat the apple!" you can imagine yourself disobeying the injunction and eating the apple. Perhaps you had no intention of eating the apple in the first place, but now the presence of an explicit prohibition makes the apple seem all the more attractive to you. Understanding the prohibition therefore implies the imagination of its transgression. Hence evil is always done knowingly. "The evil action of the sparagmos," Gans writes, "is preceded by evil intent. Each participant commits the crime of appropriation *in his imagination* at the very moment he renounces it in practice; the renunciation and the crime are inseparable [my italics]."[2]

Gans's description of evil as a crime of the imagination accurately describes the internal representation of desire by Shakespeare's tragic protagonists. In each case the protagonist imagines evil before undertaking it. Evil action is preceded by evil intent. This critical observation has been made by many Shakespeare scholars before me, but it has never been placed in the context of an anthropology. Gans's idea, as presented in his originary hypothesis, is that the renunciation of appetite is inseparable from the imagination of evil. This idea takes us beyond the analysis of literary content to an analysis of how form determines content. It takes us, in other words, from literary to originary analysis.

Why do we enjoy the spectacle of tragic suffering? The pleasure of aesthetic deferral yielded by attention to the protagonist's suffering passes through the originary violence of the *sparagmos*. Our attention to the protagonist comes with the prior knowledge that he will suffer for his crime of usurping the centre of our imaginations. Our renunciation of violence, which is a formal condition of our attention to the artwork, is inseparable from resentment of the protagonist. As Kenneth Burke puts it, "The audience *consents* to the sacrifice."[3] In Gans's words: "We may purchase a good conscience by imagining ourselves in the place of the tragic hero who is the object of our resentment rather than give this resentment free rein. But in the end, we are participants in his undoing."[4]

The Shakespearean tragic protagonist imagines evil before he commits it. We are complicit in this evil, for we have identified all along with the protagonist's evil intent. But our identification with the protagonist's evil is then paid for by the hero himself, who is sacrificed for his crime of usurping the centre. Unlike ourselves, the hero is doomed to bring his imagined crime to a fatal conclusion. The sacrifice of the hero is the moment our evil intent – our resentment – triumphs over the protagonist's.

Macbeth is unusual among Shakespeare's tragic heroes in the volume of resentment he attracts. Only Richard III rivals him in this regard. Does this make *Macbeth* more of a melodrama than a tragedy? Is the play too burdened by religious allegory to be considered a truly modern tragedy?

The question of Shakespeare's modernity cannot be settled by taking stock of the work's explicit or implicit references to the morality and mystery plays of the Christian tradition.[5] Nor can we use the stark contrast between good and evil in the play as a sign of Shakespeare's regressive moral tendencies when he wrote *Macbeth*. Evidently Shakespeare wanted to depict Macbeth as worse than he found him in his major source, Holinshed's *Chronicles*. But Macbeth's greater evil is accompanied by greater interiorization. As Bradley realized, it is this emphasis on the character's internal struggle that gives *Macbeth* a distinctly modern feel despite the weight of the moral allegory that seems to define the other characters. More precisely, it is the internalization of the classical aesthetic's unproblematic opposition between centre and periphery that defines the modernity of the Shakespearean protagonist. Macbeth does not merely possess the public centre; he desires it more profoundly than any of his rivals.

This desire is figured in the witches. Like the ghost in *Hamlet*, they are highly ambivalent figures attuned to the protagonist's characteristic weakness. This weakness is ultimately traceable to the periphery's desire for the centre. In Hamlet the weakness is idolization of the father. In Macbeth it is ambition for the throne. In both plays the connection between the apparition and the character's desire is made directly. Horatio announces that he will report the ghost to Hamlet. The witches announce they will meet Macbeth on the heath. But before the temptation scenes can occur, we are acquainted with the protagonist's character and his attendant weakness. Thus Hamlet is depicted, amidst the brightness of Claudius's court, obstinately mourning his dead father and, in the first soliloquy, longing for death. Macbeth too is described in his native element, the bloody battlefield, bathed in blood, as if to "memorize another Golgotha" (1.2.40), mercilessly taking the sword to the Norwegian invaders and the rebel Macdonwald, whom he unseams "from the nave to th' chops" (1.2.22). Once the protagonist's weakness has been established, the temptation scene follows. Hamlet's idolatry of his dead father is turned into a desire for vengeance. Macbeth's violence on the battlefield is turned into a bloody desire for the throne.

Here the similarities appear to end. Hamlet's desire for vengeance remains abortive until the murder of Polonius forces the king's hand and draws Laertes into the conflict. Up to this point Hamlet internalizes opposition to his uncle by playing out his resentment in various ironic postures. These range from the bitter and sardonic remarks on his uncle's sexuality and drinking habits to the more complex representations of the fictional revenge figures in the player's speech and Hamlet's Mousetrap play. In contrast Macbeth wastes no time carrying out the murder of Duncan. No sooner do the witches hail him as king than he sets about making the prophecy come true. If Hamlet has a problem of delay, Macbeth appears to have a problem of haste. "Whiles I threat, he lives," Macbeth says, "Words to the heat of deeds too cold breath gives" (2.1.61–2); and then the fatal bell rings signalling that Lady Macbeth has drugged the king's attendants and laid the daggers ready. Moments later Duncan is dead.

Yet all is not so simple. Though Hamlet and Macbeth are one in their obsession with the status quo represented by the big man's usurpation of the centre, they deal with this obsession in different ways. Hamlet resists usurpation for as long as possible by ramping up his astonishing linguistic virtuosity. He becomes an antic and a fool, a satiric commentator on the complacency of the Danish court, whose ignorance of the evil hanging over it becomes a source of bitter irony for the prince. Macbeth sees the evil as steadfastly as Hamlet; but instead of sublimating it in words he succumbs to it as, in Bradley's memorable phrase, "an appalling duty,"[6] hoping that this one murder "Might be the be-all and the end-all" and that he might catch "success" with its "surcease" (1.7.4–5). But the murder merely pulls him more aggressively into the violence of the *sparagmos*, and before he knows it he is "in blood / Stepped in so far" (3.4.137–8) that murder becomes a numbing habit. Macbeth's feverish energy is, Bradley says, motivated by the sense of guilt, and it is evident in his moodiness, sleeplessness, and solitary savageness.[7] "Oh, full of scorpions is my mind!" (3.2.39), Macbeth exclaims to his wife; and to purge himself of these scorpions, he immediately orders the murders of Banquo and Fleance.

In certain respects Macbeth resembles Claudius more than Hamlet, and it is perhaps with Claudius in mind that Shakespeare returned to the theme of regicide when he wrote *Macbeth*. In Claudius we notice the same guilt and the same feverish activity undertaken in a futile effort to purge himself of the sense of guilt. "For like the hectic in my blood he rages" (4.3.70), Claudius says after he has given orders for Hamlet's execution in England; and in those few moments of remorse we see the same dread of what he has done: "What if this cursèd hand / Were thicker than itself with brother's blood, / Is there not rain enough in the sweet heavens / To wash it white as snow?" (3.3.43–6). This speech anticipates Macbeth's greater horror:

> What hands are here? Ha! They pluck out mine eyes.
> Will all great Neptune's ocean wash this blood
> Clean from my hand? No, this my hand will rather
> The multitudinous seas incarnadine,
> Making the green one red. (2.2.63–7)

What persuaded Claudius to bend his "stubborn knees" and make his "heart with strings of steel, / Be soft as sinews of the newborn babe" (3.3.70–1)? It was the reproduction of the murder within his internal scene of representation. The Mousetrap play had restaged for him the originary significance of his crime and shocked him into a remorse so powerful it almost leads to repentance. Hamlet has persuaded his uncle to become, if only for a moment, the spectator of his own evil. For the first time, Claudius sees his crime not as a form of violence done in the service of the ethic of the big man, but as a moral crime before God. In his prayer Claudius attempts to extricate himself from the destructive pattern of resentment that motivated him to seek the throne in the first place. He sees the futility of the endless cycle of usurpations in which one big man is replaced by another younger and more powerful one. Years of participation in this brutal ethical system, passed down from father to son since the very first big man's usurpation, had inoculated him to its violence. Claudius himself had lectured Hamlet about the "common theme" of "death of fathers," "who still hath cried, / From the first corpse till he that died today, / 'This must be so'" (1.2.103–6). But now, as if by miracle, he recognizes the futility of the pattern and experiences guilt. He suddenly sees that the "common theme" of death passes through the originary violence of the *sparagmos*:

> Oh, my offense is rank! It smells to heaven.
> It hath the primal eldest curse upon't,
> A brother's murder. (3.3.36–8)

The "first corpse" referred to by Claudius in his lecture to Hamlet in 1.2 was Cain's murder of Abel. "It is of great anthropological interest," Gans writes, "that the expulsion from paradise is associated with the founding of agricultural society," and that the "very first episode that follows the expulsion, that of Cain and Abel, is the archetypal story of resentment."[8] The episode starkly illustrates the problem of resentment and, more precisely, the difficulty of controlling it in a society founded upon the status differences generated by the big man's praxis. What motivates Cain's resentment is God's apparent favouritism of Abel. God approves of Abel's sacrifice of the "firstborn of his flock" but rejects Cain's sacrifice of the "fruits of the soil."[9] The story is not meant to show the superiority of sheepherders over tillers of the soil, but rather the failure of ritual sacrifice to control the resentments generated by the big man's usurpation of the centre. The lesson Cain fails to grasp is that the apparent ethical superiority of Abel's sacrifice is insignificant next to the moral equality of all humanity before God. "If you do what is right, will you be not accepted?" God asks Cain.[10]

Like his biblical prototype, Claudius suffers the same confusion of the moral and the ethical. His resentment cannot divorce itself from attachment to "those effects" for which he did the murder, "My crown, mine own ambition, and my queen" (3.3.54–5). Like Hamlet, Claudius is condemned to desire the public spectacle of the Danish court. His attachment to the worldly effects of his crime prevents him from transforming originary guilt for his participation in the *sparagmos* into the clear conscience of the romantic protagonist, who has abandoned the public scene altogether to create a new one inside himself.

Claudius's guilt has the potential to be morally regenerative. Macbeth, however, experiences no similar moment of moral insight that might pull him from the brink. On the contrary, with each murder he becomes increasingly deaf to his conscience. His frenzied actions are undertaken in an effort to drown and thereby silence guilt. "There is a fever in his blood," Bradley writes, "which urges him to ceaseless action in the search for oblivion."[11] Menteith aptly describes Macbeth's state when he says, "all that is within him does condemn / Itself for being there" (5.2.24–5). The closest Macbeth comes to the kneeling Claudius occurs before he murders Duncan, in those moments when he intuits the moral evil of the anticipated crime. But the moral consequences of this intuition are never spelled out as clearly as they are in Claudius's soliloquy. Whereas Claudius's guilt stems from his revelatory recognition that the ethic of the big man fails to live up to the absoluteness of God's moral law, Macbeth's guilt emerges in vivid representations of horror. When he first conceives of the idea of the murder, after hearing the witches' prophecy on the heath, he reacts in terror to the unbidden images which take hold of his imagination. And as the dreaded moment approaches, his remorse surfaces in the image of pity "like a newborn babe" (1.7.21). The bloody dagger that leads him to Duncan and the ghostly image of Banquo's bloodstained head show us that Macbeth is a man haunted by vividly conceived images of evil. Lady Macbeth interprets her husband's extraordinary sensitivity to these images as childish fear. When he is too horrorstruck to return the bloody daggers to the scene of the crime, she scolds him: "'Tis the eye of childhood / That fears a painted devil" (2.2.58–9). But as Bradley observes, she has not herself the moral imagination to comprehend her husband, and she therefore misinterprets his terror as childish fear. And so do all those who see cowardice rather than terror in Macbeth's imagination.

Bradley explains Macbeth's experience of horror as the delayed or unconscious reaction of his poetic imagination. Externally Macbeth is a man of action driven by burning ambition, but internally he is "convulsed by conscience." His conscience, however, does not manifest itself in the "overt language of moral ideas, commands and prohibitions," but "in images which alarm and horrify." This leads Bradley to conclude that Macbeth's "imagination is thus the best of him" and that "if he had obeyed it he would have been safe."[12] I think this makes a good deal of sense, and it helps us to understand the underlying similarity between Claudius and Macbeth. In each case the experience of guilt is motivated by an intuition of the originary evil of the *sparagmos*. Claudius recognizes that the common theme of death passes through the "primal eldest curse," the first murder and archetype of resentment. He sees that he is guilty of a crime towards the sacred centre. Originary resentment is first directed not towards another human being but towards the sacred centre figured by the appetitive object. Crimes against humanity are in the first place crimes against God. But once the appetitive object is destroyed and ingested, the sacred centre can only be remembered by returning to the sign. God's immortality is also the immortality of the sign.

It is the distinctive role of the aesthetic in deferring the *sparagmos* that Bradley notices as a peculiar feature of Macbeth's character. His usual capacity for violent action is punctuated by bouts of internal reverie or rapt attention over which he seems to have little power. These occur without warning when his subconscious feelings of guilt rise to the surface and freeze action. These visions become progressively more powerful and terrifying as Macbeth draws nearer to accomplishing his purpose. On the heath after his heroics on the battlefield, he learns that he is Thane of Cawdor, and is immediately beset by "horrible imaginings" (1.3.139) as he contemplates the violence that seems to yield the crown to him. Banquo remarks twice on Macbeth's curious speechlessness. The first occasion is after the witches have hailed Macbeth as king: "Good sir, why do you start and seem to fear / Things that do sound so fair?" (1.3.51–2). The second occurs after Ross and Angus have delivered the news of Macbeth's new title: "Look how our partner's rapt" (1.3.144).

In the next scene Macbeth discovers that Duncan means to promote his son Malcolm to the throne. He responds by withdrawing further into himself: "Stars, hide your fires; / Let not light see my black and deep desires" (1.4.50–1). Later, when the king is a guest in his home, his conscience surfaces briefly again. He sees "Pity, like a newborn babe / Striding the blast" (1.7.21–2) and blowing the wicked deed into "every eye" (1.7.24). But Pity is confronted by Malice. Lady Macbeth enters, and when he attempts to call off the assassination, she attacks him where it hurts most. Is he a coward? What beast was it then that swore he would take the throne by force? Then follow the horrible lines about how she would not hesitate to pluck from her breast the nursing babe and dash its brains out if she had sworn to the deed as Macbeth had sworn to his. Macbeth is awed by her. "I am settled," he says, "and bend up / Each corporal agent to this terrible feat" (1.7.80–1).

But the internal struggle is not over. Macbeth's imagination continues to be haunted by horrifying images. On his way to kill Duncan he crosses the moonless courtyard and sees the suspended dagger dripping with blood. With noticeable effort, he dismisses the illusion: "There's no such thing. / It is the bloody business which informs / Thus to mine eyes" (2.1.48–50). But then the bell rings. It is the promised signal: "Hear it not, Duncan, for it is a knell / That summons thee to heaven or to hell" (2.1.64–5). But it is also a summons of Macbeth to a subjective hell of his own making. For no sooner has he murdered Duncan than a voice cries, "Macbeth shall sleep no more" (2.2.47). Every noise seems to broadcast his guilt to the world. "How is't with me, when every noise appalls me?" (2.2.62). There is a knocking at the gate, which Macbeth interprets as another appalling accusation: "Wake Duncan with thy knocking! I would thou couldst!" (2.2.78).

Why does Macbeth's increasingly feverish activity merely lead to a heightened sense of isolation and hopelessness? Macbeth attempts to enact what Hamlet longed for, the sweet oblivion of taking arms against a sea of troubles. But the originary violence of the *sparagmos* does not lead to oblivion, but to the isolation of each individual as he guiltily consumes his share of the interdicted appetitive object. In *Totem and Taboo* Freud attributed the origin of guilt to the remorse experienced by the brothers, who had killed their father because he would not share his wives. As Gans points out, all that is required to turn Freud's tendentious primal scene into a minimal originary hypothesis is the sign or word.[13] Independently of the Oedipus complex and the notion of the "primal father," the experience of guilt is implied in the linguistic designation of the central father/victim. The brothers can only experience guilt for the murder because they have previously imagined the transgression of the father's prohibition of the women. And this imagined transgression cannot take place without the prior origin of the word. For the father's prohibition to bring about the origin of religious interdiction (e.g., in the incest taboo), it requires more than the animal dominance system first noted by Darwin and alluded to by Freud. The word is universal in its application of the taboo. It can be understood collectively by the brothers. The animal dominance system, on the other hand, is incapable of enforcing prohibition other than by physical coercion. The alpha animal lets you know he is boss by inflicting pain upon you whenever you seek to appropriate something he doesn't want you to. Disputes over females or food are settled by one-on-one fights between the alpha and his challengers. Unlike the symbolic representations of human culture, the animal dominance system cannot constitute itself as a *collectively imagined scene*, with a centre and a periphery, in which all partake equally in the designation of the interdicted centre through the production of the word. The moment of guilt occurs after the *sparagmos* when the object to which the word refers has been destroyed and devoured. But what generates the experience of guilt is the awareness of the disparity between word and deed. The word refers to the undeformed object in its original totality; but once the object has been devoured, there is nothing left to figure the meaning of the word except the word itself. As Gans observes, only by returning to the word can the memory of the sacred object be reproduced:

> Guilt is the awareness inherent in the sign that its user is complicit in the destruction of the sacred object. The resentment previously focused on the object is now directed at the sacred itself as a being or force that interdicts the full possession of this object. Since the center is now empty, the resentment can only be renewed in the participant's "guilty" imagining of the remembered victim. The deliberate evocation of the object through representation arouses in the perceiver the oscillatory movement between the representation and its imaginary referent that we call the esthetic.[14]

This oscillatory movement between representation and its imaginary referent is strongly pronounced in Macbeth's imagination. It lies at the heart of those private reveries or hallucinations which intrude into Macbeth's consciousness and which he strives to ignore or repress through his increasingly desperate actions. It is also evident in Macbeth's peculiar fear of words: "Whiles I threat, he lives; / Words to the heat of deeds too cold breath gives" (2.1.61–2); "Strange things I have in head, that will to hand, / Which must be acted ere they may be scanned" (3.4.140–1); "From this moment / The very firstlings of my heart shall be / The firstlings of my hand" (4.1.146–8). Macbeth is constantly reminding himself to convert word into deed. He fears the originary deferral of the sign upon which all culture is built. This problem is the same one Hamlet had. But whereas Hamlet embraced the distraction provided by the word (and then castigated himself for being diverted by its pleasures), Macbeth fears it and strives to repress its hold on his imagination by plunging furiously into violent action.

This contrast between word and deed may be further sharpened by examining the temporality of the originary event. The word defers conflict by sacralizing the appetitive object. Possession of the object is now impossible without transgressing the taboo placed upon it by the word. But the word's interdiction generates desire for the object as well as resentment at not having it. Originary resentment can be partially controlled or sublimated by returning to the word in an effort to rethink the object in its apparent plenitude at the centre, untouched by the defiling hands of the periphery. Hamlet's more optimistic moments capture this experience of the centre's plenitude – for example, when he compares man to a god or angel. But Hamlet's optimism is undercut by the cynical awareness that this "paragon of animals" (2.2.308) is also a creature of appetite. The moment of imagined plenitude or perfect being gives way to the *sparagmos*, the unleashing of resentment in the destruction and division of the appetitive object among the members of the profane periphery. Once destroyed and devoured, the object is no longer figurable except by reproducing the word. The return to the word is the moment of originary guilt. Resentment towards the centre is renewed in the guilty reimagining of the destroyed object.

Hamlet's irony reflects his closer association with the sign rather than the object, with deferral rather than consumption. *Macbeth* emphasizes the other end of this narrative – namely, the violent *sparagmos*. This difference explains why resentment is so prominent in *Hamlet* but not in *Macbeth*. If Hamlet has a problem of resentment, Macbeth has a problem of guilt. Originary resentment precedes the *sparagmos*, whereas originary guilt occurs after the central object has been destroyed. But Macbeth's guilt manifests itself before he murders Duncan. His reaction to the witches in 1.3 clearly shows that he experiences guilt before the assassination. How can we explain this curious fact?

Macbeth's guilt arises from his poetic imagination. He imagines the crime before he commits it. This inward representation is not simply the rehearsal in the mind of a complex action, as when an athlete mentally visualizes an intricate manoeuvre before undertaking it. Macbeth's reflections on the pragmatic aspects of the crime, when they take place at all, are presented as afterthoughts, such as when he reacts with approval to Lady Macbeth's suggestion that they pin the blame for the murder on the king's attendants. The main characteristic of Macbeth's imagination is, as Bradley recognizes, horror. When the thought of murder comes to him, seemingly unbidden by the prophecy of the witches, he reacts with speechless terror. The debate about whether the witches sowed the idea of the assassination in Macbeth's mind or whether he had conceived of it beforehand is ultimately undecidable.[15] Let's just say that the idea of being king inspires in Macbeth feelings of guilt. Macbeth's first soliloquy, uttered as an aside while Banquo, Ross, and Angus confer with one another on the opposite side of the stage, illustrates the characteristic aesthetic oscillation between representation and its imaginary referent that produces the experience of guilt in Macbeth:

This supernatural soliciting
Cannot be ill, cannot be good. If ill,
Why hath it given me earnest of success

Commencing in a truth? I am Thane of Cawdor.
If good, why do I yield to that suggestion
Whose horrid image doth unfix my hair
And make my seated heart knock at my ribs,
Against the use of nature? Present fears
Are less than horrible imaginings.
My thought, whose murder yet is but fantastical,
Shakes so my single state of man
That function is smothered in surmise,
And nothing is but what is not. (1.3.131–43)

On the one hand, Macbeth imagines himself as sole possessor of the crown. On the other, he sees the centre as a locus of destruction, where "nothing is but what is not." The object upon which Macbeth focuses his mind – the crown – is both real and unreal, a source of both infinite desire and hideous violence. Macbeth's imagination grasps the fact that usurpation of the centre passes through the evil of the *sparagmos*.

These terrifying visions become progressively more powerful and vivid as Macbeth draws nearer to accomplishing his purpose. When he has the king at his mercy as a guest in his home, we get the second soliloquy in which Macbeth first imagines catching success in one final blow but is then appalled by the image of "Pity, like a newborn babe / Striding the blast" (1.7.21–2) and blowing the wicked deed into "every eye" (1.7.24). The horror almost saves him but then Lady Macbeth enters; she drowns the sense of guilt by calling him a coward and questioning his manhood. Night falls, and Macbeth is once more bent on committing the horrible deed. But still his mind interferes with the task at hand. He sees the vision of the dagger, which causes him to reach for his own:

I see thee yet, in form as palpable
As this which now I draw.
Thou marshall'st me the way that I was going,
And such an instrument I was to use. (2.1.41–4)

The unreal dagger points towards the real one. But now Macbeth sees that the illusory dagger is covered in blood: "I see thee still / And on thy blade and dudgeon gouts of blood, / Which was not so before" (2.1.46–8). Macbeth imagines the crime before committing it. The action of evil is preceded by evil intent, which is why guilt is present in Macbeth's mind before he commits the deed. He envisions murder so vividly that it is as if he had already accomplished it. It takes a significant effort for him to dispel the vision and return to the job at hand. But when the deed has been committed, the guilt returns at once. Macbeth's first fear is not that his crime will be discovered, but that he could not pronounce "Amen" in response to the prayers he has heard on his way to Duncan's chamber: "But wherefore could not I pronounce 'Amen'? / I had most need of blessing, and 'Amen,' / Stuck in my throat" (2.2.35–7). Macbeth's crime is, in the first place, a crime against the sacred centre. He has participated in the originary *sparagmos*. Like Claudius who cannot pray, Macbeth cannot say "Amen."

Macbeth's second murder is more cold-blooded. He procures, Iago-like, the services of two discontented men whose resentment he directs from himself onto Banquo. But despite this attempt to distance himself from the murder, he cannot extinguish the experience of guilt, which emerges in spectacular fashion during the banquet scene. Macbeth's hallucination of Banquo's ghost has been prepared for from the beginning by the witches, whose prophecy had explicitly represented Banquo as a fellow conspirator for the centre. As a party to the witches' prophecy, Banquo is implicated in Macbeth's murder of Duncan. Shakespeare is careful to show this. On the heath Banquo is, as Bradley suggests, initially contrasted to Macbeth.[16] He sounds the note of warning: "oftentimes to win us to our harm / The instruments of darkness tell us truths" (1.3.123–4). And again, just before Macbeth murders Duncan, a sleepless and restless Banquo expresses his sense of foreboding: "Merciful powers, / Restrain in me the cursèd thoughts that nature / Gives way to in repose" (2.1.7–9). But after the murder, Banquo is confronted with a clear choice. Does he abandon the scene like Donalbain and Malcolm (who will later be joined by Macduff), or does he side with Macbeth? Where will his allegiance fall? Banquo, Bradley argues, cannot resist the idea of what has been promised him by the witches, and this is why he sides with Macbeth.[17] Shakespeare leaves us in no doubt that despite suspecting foul play Banquo conveniently decides to overlook it:

> Thou hast it now – King, Cawdor, Glamis, all
> As the weird women promised, and I fear
> Thou play'st most foully for't. Yet it was said
> It should not stand in thy posterity,
> But that myself should be the root and father
> Of many kings. If there come truth from them –
> As upon thee, Macbeth, their speeches shine –

Why, by the verities on thee made good,
May they not be my oracles as well
And set me up in hope? (3.1.1–10)

Banquo's ambition is as great as Macbeth's and this is what keeps him rooted to the spot, unable to abandon the scene. It is this covert rivalry for the centre that Macbeth fears in his co-conspirator: "There is none but he / Whose being I do fear; and under him / My genius is rebuked" (3.1.55–7). Publicly Banquo is represented as "our chief guest" (3.1.11), whose absence at "our great feast" would be an "all-thing unbecoming" (3.1.12–13). But Macbeth's outward generosity hides his implacable resentment:

For Banquo's issue have I filed my mind;
For them the gracious Duncan have I murdered,
Put rancors in the vessel of my peace
Only for them, and mine eternal jewel
Given to the common enemy of man
To make them kings, the seeds of Banquo kings. (1.3.66–71)

And he immediately sets about plotting Banquo's murder in an attempt to put his restless mind at ease.

But after the murder has been accomplished there is no rest. Macbeth attempts to play the role of gracious host to his lords, but he finds no place for himself at the table. When Lennox points to the empty chair, Macbeth sees Banquo's ghost seated there. "Which of you has done this?" (3.4.49), he exclaims in horror when he sees the bloodstained apparition. Only by a tremendous force of will does he manage to dispel the illusion: "Hence, horrible shadow! / Unreal mockery, hence!" (3.4.107–8). The apparition expelled, he recollects his senses: "Why, so; being gone, / I am a man again" (3.4.108–9). Macbeth does not understand why he is visited by these horrible figures. But he aims to defeat them through the only method he knows. He plunges himself into violent action in an effort to annihilate the ghosts inside him: "My strange and self-abuse / Is the initiate fear that wants hard use. We are yet but young in deed" (3.4.143–5).

In *Julius Caesar*, after the murder of Caesar our identification with Brutus does an abrupt about-face. This reversal is reflected in the remarkable transformation of the crowd that goes from loving Brutus to hating him. One moment the plebeians are proclaiming Brutus to be another glorious Caesar; the next, they are shrieking for his blood. In *Macbeth* this same transformation takes place at the end of the third act, but it is done much more subtly. Our initial identification with Macbeth's evil intent is threaded through the witches, who identified Macbeth as the chief object of their conspiracy. After the temptation scene Macbeth's usurpation follows rapidly. Duncan is killed, and Macbeth crowned. But now Macbeth suspects Banquo, his tacit partner in crime. Like Claudius's suspicions of Hamlet, Banquo rages like the hectic in Macbeth's blood. Banquo's death is a tragedy in miniature, an instance of those "Bloody instructions, which, being taught, return / To plague th' inventor" (1.7.9–10). In refusing to abandon his desire for the violent centre, Banquo lifts the poisoned chalice to his own lips. As Bradley points out, Banquo's passive acquiescence in Macbeth's murder of Duncan makes him more obviously a victim of the witches than Macbeth.[18] Whereas Macbeth acts on his desire, Banquo remains a spectator of somebody else's violence, a violence that he hoped would some day bring him closer to the centre. In this respect Banquo is like Hamlet who spends the first three acts of his play ironically identifying with Claudius's usurpation. But unlike Hamlet, whose irony becomes the centrepiece of the play, Banquo's identification with Macbeth leads very quickly to his doom. Macbeth knows full well that Banquo suspects him, and so the two are drawn together. They are partners in crime because they have both been tempted by the witches. This conspiratorial relationship is also what makes Macbeth fear Banquo. Banquo's complicity in the conspiracy for the centre makes him a rival.

The third act ends with two rather curious scenes. The first features the return of the witches, but this time in the company of Hecate, goddess of witches who is evidently displeased by the antics of the weird sisters. Her displeasure appears to be motivated by jealousy. Macbeth has stolen her thunder. The spectacle of his evil is in danger of usurping her own. So Hecate plans her triumph: "This night I'll spend / Unto a dismal and a fatal end" (3.5.20–1). She will raise illusions that "Shall draw him on to his confusion" (3.5.29). The audience is being reminded of Macbeth's downfall. Hecate's curse, which reflects our expectation of tragic closure, will outlast Macbeth's.

The second scene features Lennox and an anonymous lord. Here too the sense of irony is strong. Lennox talks sardonically about the curious set of coincidences that have led to Macbeth's accession to the throne:

> The gracious Duncan
> Was pitied of Macbeth; marry, he was dead.
> And the right valiant Banquo walked too late,

Whom you may say, if't please you, Fleance killed,
For Fleance fled. Men must not walk too late.
Who cannot want the thought how monstrous
It was for Malcolm and Donalbain
To kill their gracious father? Damnèd fact!
How it did grieve Macbeth! Did he not straight
In pious rage the two delinquents tear
That were the slaves of drink and thralls to sleep?
Was not that nobly done? (3.6.3–14)

Clearly the irony of these two peculiar scenes is quite different. Hecate is a supernatural spirit whose prediction stands outside the play. In this sense she is closer to the audience member or reader who knows that Macbeth will suffer for his crimes. She thus functions as reminder of our complicity in Macbeth's evil, which we have, like Banquo, implicitly condoned. But she also reminds us of our formal relation to the protagonist, who is about to suffer for his usurpation of the centre. Lennox's irony, on the other hand, takes place within the formal constraints of the play. We know that Lennox is being ironic because we already know the devious means by which Macbeth attained the crown. Lennox's irony indicates the swelling tide of resentment against Macbeth from within the play. From this point forward Macbeth will become increasingly isolated. Content will conspire with form to focus resentment unambiguously on the central figure.[19]

The cauldron scene at the opening of the fourth act is an inversion of the ritual feast over which the big man historically presides. In egalitarian societies resentment is controlled by keeping desire strictly within the limits defined by collective ritual. No individual desire may exceed the bounds established by the sacred opposition between centre and periphery. The big man's usurpation of the sacred centre, however, produces a mature form of resentment that puts the ritual system under considerable strain. The repelling force of sacred interdiction is no longer sufficient to control desire for possession of the centre. Individual desire steadily erodes the mechanisms of ritual society. The scenes of feasting in *Macbeth* chart this erosion of the public and ritual centre.

As Wilson Knight observes, feasting is a prominent "life-theme" in *Macbeth*.[20] After Duncan has bestowed the title of Cawdor on Macbeth he announces that he will "bind us further to you" (1.4.43). Duncan indicates that he will ride to Inverness and feast in Macbeth's home. The king's absolute trust in his "worthiest cousin" (1.4.14) is stressed by the metaphor of the banquet: "in his commendations I am fed; / It is a banquet to me" (1.4.55–6). Macbeth responds politely to this honour but, as his aside makes plain, he was hoping for much more: "Stars, hide your fires; / Let not light see my black and deep desires" (1.4.50–1). It is surely not insignificant that we never again see Macbeth and Duncan onstage together, despite the fact that Macbeth hosts Duncan in his castle. Instead we get the soliloquies in which Macbeth struggles with his conscience.[21] When Duncan enters Macbeth's home, he asks for his host immediately: "Conduct me to mine host. We love him highly, / And shall continue our graces toward him" (1.6.29–30). The next scene, however, shows Macbeth alone. When Lady Macbeth enters she asks, "Why have you left the chamber?" to which Macbeth responds, guiltily, "Hath he asked for me?" (1.7.30–1). Then, on his way to kill Duncan, Macbeth encounters Banquo, who refers again to Duncan's generosity: "He hath been in unusual pleasure, / And sent forth great largess to your offices" (2.1.14–15). Banquo gives Macbeth the diamond, another gift from Duncan. But Duncan's generosity is repaid by treachery. Macbeth kills the man he has feasted and is duty-bound to protect.

The theme of inverted feasting is repeated in the banquet scene.[22] This time Macbeth is the central figure, the king as well as host of the feast. Macbeth announces the ritual order by which they are to sit: "You know your own degrees; sit down" (3.4.1). Then he says he will himself "play the humble host" and "mingle with society" (3.4.3–4). Everything appears set for the traditional feast. Macbeth notes that each man is seated according to his degree: "Both sides are even. Here I'll sit i'th' midst" (3.4.10). But before he can take his place in this hierarchically ordered microcosm of ritual society, he sees the first murderer at the door. His paranoia gets the better of him and he leaves the table to hear the murderer's report. The news is ambivalent: Banquo is dead, but Fleance lives. Macbeth's desire remains unsatisfied despite his possession of the throne:

> Then comes my fit again. I had else been perfect,
> Whole as the marble, founded as the rock,
> As broad and general as the casing air.
> But now I am cabined, cribbed, confined, bound in
> To saucy doubts and fears. (3.4.21–5)

Meanwhile the feast continues in Macbeth's absence. Lady Macbeth is forced to retrieve her husband from his position of conspicuous isolation.

But when he returns to the table he sees that it is full. His place has been usurped by Banquo's ghost. Macbeth stares in horror at the vision. "What is't that moves Your Highness?" (3.4.48), Lennox asks. The nobles rise in discomfort. Lady Macbeth strives to control the situation. She persuades everyone to reseat themselves and encourages them to ignore her husband's eccentric behaviour: "upon a thought / He will be well again" (3.4.55–6). And she hisses in his ear: "Oh, proper stuff! / This is the very painting of your fear. / This is the air-drawn dagger which, you said, / Led you to Duncan" (3.4.60–3). Again Macbeth retreats from the table, this time marvelling at how his guilt makes his victims "rise again" (3.4.81). Again his wife tries to draw him back: "My worthy lord, / Your noble friends do lack you" (3.4.84–5). But when he returns, the ghost reappears, and he again reacts in horror. The banquet is disrupted, and this time Lady Macbeth does not protest. She sees that her husband is not fit to play the host. Fearing that he may betray them both, she hurries the lords from the room, insisting that they pay no attention to the order and ceremony of leave-taking. Macbeth's guilt has undermined the ritual structure of the Scottish court.

What Shakespeare shows in these scenes of ritual feasting is the destruction of the public scene by resentment. Macbeth's desire dominates both scenes. In the first, Duncan's public feasting at Macbeth's home is never shown onstage. Instead we are presented with the soliloquies depicting Macbeth's resentful and guilty imagination. Macbeth's soliloquies in the first act bear the same relation to Duncan as Hamlet's soliloquies do to Claudius. They are internalizations of the fundamental opposition between sacred centre and profane periphery. Macbeth's horror at the idea of transgressing the prohibition of the centre stems from his incapacity to imagine himself independently of the ritual scene. The kingship remains for him an absolute manifestation of the sacred. Usurpation of the centre must therefore be an absolute desecration of it. The horror Macbeth experiences before committing the murder is a consequence of his resentful attachment to a scene he is powerless to resist.[23] On Shakespeare's stage, the public scene inherited from classical tragedy is shown to have both a centre and a periphery. There is, however, no alternative centre for the protagonist to focus his energy on. Unlike the romantic protagonist, who makes himself the source of a wholly personal aesthetic, the neoclassical protagonist remains attached to the public scene. The protagonist's imagination remains dependent upon the traditional figures of the ritual centre, which he is consequently condemned to usurp.

This dependency on the public scene explains why Macbeth's usurpation does not bring about the end of his resentment. He now imagines himself under attack by the same forces that propelled him to the centre. Banquo was present with Macbeth when the witches delivered their prophecies. He has heard everything. He had himself demanded of the witches to look "into the seeds of time" (1.3.58). And what had they said? That he was "Lesser than Macbeth, and greater," "Not so happy, yet much happier," and that he shall "get kings, though thou be none" (1.3.65–7). So Macbeth suspects Banquo, who has been his partner and close companion all this time. They fought bravely together against the rebels, and they are bound by the secret of the witches' prophecy. Banquo had not protested Macbeth's accession to the throne, which must have looked extremely suspicious to him. It is only a matter of time before Banquo becomes exactly like Macbeth. The same horror and guilt experienced by Macbeth starts to overwhelm Banquo. "Merciful powers," he exclaims on the eve of Duncan's murder, "Restrain in me the cursèd thoughts that nature / Gives way to in repose" (2.1.7–9); and when he meets Macbeth, he admits that he has been dreaming of the weird sisters. After Macbeth is crowned, Banquo imagines his own usurpation on the model of Macbeth's: "May they not be my oracles as well / And set me up in hope?" (3.1.9–10). For his illicit desires, Banquo must suffer; and so he is murdered by Macbeth. But during the ritual feast Banquo's ghost mocks Macbeth from the very position Macbeth has himself usurped. When Macbeth looks to the head of the table to find his place, he sees the bloody head of Banquo. The public centre has become a private hell. In his imagination, Macbeth sees his crime mirrored before him in the mocking figure of Banquo's ghost.

The cauldron scene illustrates the final perversion of the public scene. No food is consumed at this banquet. Instead it is a feast for Macbeth's resentful imagination. The food items thrown into the witches' cauldron are an ugly miscellany of plant, animal, and human parts, including "Root of hemlock" (4.1.25), "tongue of dog" (4.1.15), and "Liver of blaspheming Jew" (4.1.26). What this sinister cocktail produces are ambiguous representations of Macbeth's desire. Each of these representations, however, is subject to an irony that eludes Macbeth's grasp. The armed head is not Macduff's but his own after Macduff has severed it and set it on a pole. The bloody child is not one of Macduff's murdered children, but Macduff himself ripped untimely from his mother's womb. And the child bearing a tree signifies not the impossibility of Birnam Wood moving to high Dunsinane Hill, but the boughs cut down by

Malcolm's soldiers to disguise their numbers as they approach Macbeth's castle. These ironies are beyond Macbeth's grasp because in order to grasp them, Macbeth would have to transcend the play in which he is trapped. The final vision in which he sees Banquo smiling and pointing to the line of eight kings that stretches out before him illustrates the sterility of Macbeth's resentment. He will himself be usurped by Banquo's offspring despite all he has done to prevent such an end. What Macbeth learns is that desire is a curse – a curse that he is helpless to resist.

Macbeth is a rather bleak play. The main reason for this seems to be that the protagonist's fall occurs much earlier than it does in either *Hamlet* or *Othello*. The bulk of the tragedy is given over to the violence of Macbeth's occupation of the centre. This occupation is never represented as a healthy or normal state of affairs. There is no sense that the usurper will make a good king, as Claudius seems to be at the beginning of *Hamlet*. Macbeth's rule over Scotland is defined by the amount of blood he spills: "each new day a gash / Is added to her wounds" (4.3.41–2). The evil of the *sparagmos* hangs over the play like no other of Shakespeare's tragedies.[24] The light that emanated from characters like Lucius and Portia in *Julius Caesar*, or Ophelia in *Hamlet*, or Desdemona in *Othello*, is utterly extinguished. Lady Macbeth is, in the first act at any rate, even more terrifyingly committed to the *sparagmos* than her husband. The scene in which Macduff's wife and son are violently butchered underscores how the weak and innocent must fare in this world of brutal coercion, where the word is a sign of weakness and violence a sign of strength. "Why then, alas, / Do I put up that womanly defense / To say I have done no harm?" (4.2.78–80), Lady Macduff asks helplessly as the murderers enter to slay her and her children. Macduff is often interpreted as the saviour of Scotland, but he is himself complicit in Macbeth's violence. His exposure of his wife and children implies that they are necessary sacrifices for his country, victims offered on the altar of a tragedy obsessed with blood and violence.

In a penetrating analysis, Harry Berger argues against what he calls the orthodox view that understands Macbeth's guilt in isolation from the general theme of resentment.[25] On the contrary, Berger says, all the Scottish lords are guilty of Duncan's murder, because the sacrifice of the big man is intrinsic to the highly competitive ethical system that is ultimately responsible for renewing the kingship. Macbeth wins the throne by being the most successful warrior on the field of battle – a battle that, despite the inclusion of the various Irish and Norwegian factions, is traceable to an *internal* revolt among the Scottish thanes. Macdonwald and Cawdor are competitors for the Scottish throne; in defeating them, Macbeth clears for himself a more direct path to it. Berger shows how the opening scenes betray a general sense of unease on the part of Macbeth's peers. This unease is evident in the king himself, who must maintain his superiority over Macbeth if he is to survive the latter's implied challenge to his supremacy. Duncan's hasty transfer of the title of Cawdor to Macbeth betrays the fragile condition of the Scottish state. It is an example, Berger says, of the "honors only a king can bestow, honors by which the king may placate the thane and maintain his own edge of superiority."[26]

Berger's meticulous close analysis of the text is borne out by the historical context assumed by the play. The rules of succession in medieval Scotland did not stipulate that the eldest born son would succeed to the central position. The law of the *tanist*, which means literally "second in excellence," meant that the Scottish system relied on open competition between rival chiefs or thanes to decide on a successor.[27] The fact that Duncan feels compelled to announce Malcolm as his successor should be construed in this context as a defensive move designed to thwart Macbeth's sudden emergence as a competitor for the throne. Macbeth's obvious superiority on the battlefield clearly represents a greater threat to Duncan than does the risk of announcing Malcolm as his successor.[28]

Berger, in a second essay, expands on his reading of *Macbeth* by developing Girard's notion of the sacrificial tendencies of the theatre, which Berger opposes to the critical ironies available to the reader of Shakespeare's texts.[29] Where the theatre indulges the spectator's desire for victims, the text ironizes and thereby exposes the playgoer's complicity in the *form* of ritual sacrifice. I find myself in substantial agreement with Berger's overall argument. The only thing I would add is that rather than assuming that Shakespeare's text is the ultimate ground for this ethical reading, we formulate a hypothesis of anthropological origin. The difference between Shakespeare and an originary hypothesis is that the latter is open to modification whereas the former is not. The difference is by no means trivial. When Girard says that Shakespeare anticipated his theory of the scapegoat, we wish to debate the theory, not Girard's particular interpretation of Shakespeare. Of course, one way to dismiss the theory is to say that it has no relevance to Shakespeare. But this is less an argument than a refusal to engage in debate, it being taken as self-evident that whatever Shakespeare is, *he is not that*. But if he is not that, then he must be something else. In other words, a hypothesis ought to be formulated to make clear exactly what that something else is. It is a truism to say that Shakespeare's text transcends any particular interpretation of it. But the point is not to multiply our interpretations *ad infinitum*, which would be merely trivial. It is to explain the general significance of the interpretation we have in fact adopted. And in the final analysis, this significance must be anthropological. On this score, Girard at least can provide an answer. I will examine Girard's theory more closely in the final chapter of this book. For the moment, I would like to consider why Girard says virtually nothing about *Macbeth*, a play I have characterized as Shakespeare's most extended treatment of the *sparagmos*.

Girard regards *Julius Caesar* as the definitive example of sacrificial violence, but in many ways *Macbeth* would be a better example. It shows more lucidly the resentment that lies at the heart of the scenes of collective violence. In *Julius Caesar* resentment remains implicit rather than explicit. Brutus is encouraged to murder Caesar only after he has identified vicariously with Cassius's envy of Caesar. Brutus's soliloquies following Cassius's temptation of him are analogous to Macbeth's horrified contemplation of the murder of Duncan after he has been tempted by the witches. Alone in his orchard, Brutus cannot sleep: "Since Cassius first did whet me against Caesar, / I have not slept" (2.1.61–2). "The exhalations whizzing in the air" (2.1.44) reflect the usurpation taking place in his soul. Even the stars, symbols of permanence and light, are out of joint. Brutus is racked by the thought of the murder. It hangs over him like a "hideous dream" (2.1.65). The thought repels him, but he cannot put it from his mind. Like Macbeth, he feels a tremendous inversion of the soul in which the "state of man" suffers an "insurrection" (2.1.67–9). There is the same sense of impending darkness: "O conspiracy / Sham'st thou to show they dangerous brow by night, / When evils are most free?" (2.1.77–9). Just as Macbeth ponders his vaulting ambition, so too Brutus contemplates ambition's ladder. But Shakespeare's representation of Brutus's resentful interiority is not sustained. After the assassination, Brutus's guilt, like his resentment, remains almost wholly repressed or unconscious. It surfaces briefly when he is visited by Caesar's ghost, but there is nothing like the scenes of horror that haunt Macbeth.

What Shakespeare shows more clearly in *Macbeth* is that human violence originates in the resentful imagination. The mimetic conflagration of the *sparagmos* is preceded by the representation of it within the individual's internal scene of representation. Guilt is a necessary corollary of resentment. Resentment at being excluded from the centre leads to the imagination of the destruction and appropriation of the central object. But the destruction of the object means the destruction of the sacred, which the object appeared to incarnate. The return to the word in order to reconstruct the original sacrality of the object is accompanied by feelings of guilt for having participated, even if only imaginarily, in its destruction. Macbeth sees both the destruction and the reconstruction much more vividly than Brutus. Consequently, resentment and guilt are much more pronounced in him. In Brutus's case there is also the fact that guilt for the murder of Caesar is distributed among the conspirators. All participate in the murder, and this seems further to immunize Brutus against the experience of guilt. Where Macbeth is appalled by the blood on his hands and wonders whether there is enough water in the wide ocean to cleanse him of it, Brutus deliberately bathes his hands in Caesar's blood and marches through the streets of Rome crying, "Peace, freedom, and liberty!" (3.1.111).

Brutus's demagoguery is an instance of the forgetting of resentment through the collective action of the *sparagmos*. This public action is typical of Brutus, who frequently disguises his resentment of Caesar as a noble desire to uphold the ideals of the republic. In Shakespeare, subconscious guilt is accompanied by sleeplessness and bad dreams. Brutus cannot sleep on the eve of the battle of Philippi, and so he asks Lucius to play some soothing music for him. But the music lulls Lucius, not Brutus, to sleep, and it is exactly at this point that Brutus is visited by the ghost of Caesar. "Speak to me what thou art," Brutus asks the ghost. "Thy evil spirit," it replies (4.3.283–4). The exchange is brief compared to Hamlet's interview with his father's ghost, or Macbeth's with the witches. Brutus shows a curious deafness to the apparition. He is blind to the evil nature of the *sparagmos*. "Why com'st thou?" Brutus asks. "To tell thee thou shalt see me at Philippi," the ghost replies. "Why, I will see thee at Philippi, then," Brutus responds (4.3.84–6). And with that the ghost vanishes. What Brutus does not see is that resentment has unleashed civil war. The battle of Philippi is the natural endpoint of the resentment that Shakespeare has carefully traced back to Brutus's internal scene of representation.[30]

Whereas Brutus remains ignorant of his complicity in the evil of the *sparagmos*, Macbeth seeks to repress his guilt through furious action.

There is a connection to be made here to Bradley's remark that Macbeth exhibits an extraordinary sensitivity to the figures of his imagination. The force these images of horror exert on him seems to be immediately projected outward onto his surroundings. No other character in the play shows this tendency, and it clearly exceeds Brutus's imagination in *Julius Caesar*. Whereas Lady Macbeth hears only the sounds of the owl shrieking and crickets chirping, Macbeth hears a voice crying out to the entire house: "Sleep no more! / Macbeth does murder sleep" (2.2.39–40). When she looks at her bloody hands, she says, "A little water clears us of this deed" (2.2.71). When Macbeth does the same thing, he imagines the multitudinous seas turning blood red.

Like Hamlet and Othello before him, Macbeth illustrates the internalization of the opposition between centre and periphery inherited from the classical aesthetic. The tragic hero's entry onto the scene is self-consciously represented as a curse. The protagonist is aware of this curse, but he is powerless to resist it. The sense of powerlessness is most pronounced in Macbeth because in him the curse is strongest. Both Hamlet and Othello are, in their own ways, atypical representatives of the centre. Revenge is taken up only very reluctantly by Hamlet, and Othello's jealousy is overshadowed by Iago's resentment. But Macbeth's ambition is, in contrast, something huge and implacable. It is the "imperial theme" itself (1.3.130), and it completely consumes Macbeth, whose desire never slackens but rather increases with each wound he inflicts in his effort to secure the centre. The overall impression is one of reckless and violent speed. Macbeth's reign occupies at a minimum a few months in order for the events reported in the play to occur (e.g., Malcolm's flight to England, Donalbain's flight to Ireland, Macbeth's coronation, Macduff's flight to England, Malcolm's raising of the army, etc.).[31] But the impression Shakespeare gives us is much more compressed, which contributes to our sense of relentless pace. The moments of inner reflection that restrain Macbeth in the beginning disappear almost completely once he commits himself to the violent action of the *sparagmos*. He becomes obsessed with the notion that thought will paralyse action, and he moves with ever greater haste to transform thought into action. But this desire is itself paradoxical, for to imagine violent action, one must defer, if only for the briefest of moments, its implementation. There is no such thing as a violent action that is not also preceded by the representation or imagination of it. Macbeth longs for such a perfect congruence, but each attempt he makes demonstrates its impossibility. Thus, he is condemned to return to the resentful position on the periphery from which he first launched his assault on the centre.

Why does Macbeth return to interview the witches? Because he cannot abandon the scene that has tempted him from the beginning. The witches' curse cannot be explained as an instance of fate determining the protagonist's destiny. For what do we mean by fate? The curse is a metaphor for our desiring relation to the centre, which was established by the production of the word in the originary scene. The centre appears to possess a repelling force that prevents appropriation of the object. This force is what we mean by the sacred. But the sacred is available only because it is represented. We would not know God if we did not know the word through which he is known. Macbeth's desire to immerse himself in wordless action cannot transcend the word by which his tragic action is understood. The witches' cauldron does not produce food but rather images and words that must be interpreted and reflected upon. As it turns out, Macbeth is mistaken in his interpretations. He interprets the apparitions as evidence of his invincibility. But this belief in his invincibility does nothing to satisfy his desire, which is why he decides to make doubly sure of fate "just in case."

Suppose Macbeth had done nothing after his first encounter with the witches. Would the prophecy have come true? Would he have become king? The question is meaningless because the prophecy is but a manifestation of the periphery's desire for the centre. We are all subject to the illusory desire for centrality. But one can only conceive of desire as illusory from a position outside the scene in which desire is experienced. This is the irony of tragedy that the protagonist is by definition incapable of formulating. After Macbeth's head has been placed upon a stake by Macduff, we can go home satisfied in our awareness that Macbeth got what was coming to him, and chide him for his failure to realize that his desire was as illusory as the airy dagger that lured him to Duncan's bedside. But this does not explain our sympathetic identification with Macbeth's evil intent. This seems to be what Shakespeare, if not Macbeth, is driving at when his protagonist delivers the most famous lines of the play:

> Out, out, brief candle!
> Life's but a walking shadow, a poor player
> That struts and frets his hour upon the stage
> And then is heard no more. It is a tale
> Told by an idiot, full of sound and fury,
> Signifying nothing. (5.5.23–8)

Is life a tale told by an idiot, full of sound and fury signifying nothing? Macbeth's pessimistic view of existence, in which the brute fact of death proves the insignificance of life, expresses from a point inside the play the protagonist's disillusionment with fate. Viewed from the outside, however, the protagonist's predicament reflects not disillusionment but irony. More precisely, it reflects the irony of fate, which is the central irony of tragedy. The tragic hero's insatiable desire has led to the *sparagmos*. His whole existence has been defined by his failure to defer violence. But this ironic deconstruction of the formal barrier separating sign from referent, word from action, periphery from centre, is only formulable from a position that assumes the very distinction between sign and referent that the tragic protagonist's actions have undermined in the *sparagmos*. The theatrical metaphors in Macbeth's speech are a tribute to the theatre's capacity to defer violence through representation. The irony of Macbeth's fate can only be observed from the position of the ironically detached spectator. Our identification with the sound and fury of Macbeth's hour upon the stage is conducted from a position of perfectly nonviolent repose. Desire for centrality is from the beginning mediated by the peripheral sign.

As Bradley remarked, Macbeth and Othello incarnate the transcendence of the centre; their heroism separates them from the world of ordinary men and women. But this transcendence, which transpires as a temporary rather than permanent occupation of the centre, is revealed to be an illusion. Macbeth understands the riddles of the witches to represent his indestructibility when in fact they anticipate his demise. Despite this misinterpretation of the centre, Macbeth's guilt shows us that he sees more clearly than his peers the centre's morally ambivalent status.

In Shakespeare's last tragedy, we encounter a hero whose capacity for violence exceeds Macbeth's but for whom there is no equivalent experience of guilt. Coriolanus lacks the inner moral conflict we have come to associate with the Shakespearean protagonist. As we shall see, this perception of Coriolanus as morally opaque is not entirely accurate. Coriolanus does undergo a moral conflict; yet this conflict remains considerably muted compared to the conflicts experienced by Hamlet, Othello, and Macbeth. In Shakespeare's "pagan world," to borrow J.L. Simmons's phrase, the hero's conscience is overshadowed by the individual's attachment to the city and its public rituals. After being ignominiously passed back and forth between the patricians and plebeians, Coriolanus is abruptly ejected from the centre. The play dramatizes with startlingly clarity the sacrificial paradox lying at the heart of tragedy. *Coriolanus* is Shakespeare's most ironic experiment in tragic form. But tragedy cannot tolerate such relentless ironizing of the centre. After *Coriolanus*, Shakespeare turned from the tragic scene, in which the protagonist's monstrous desire for centrality is punished, to the romantic scene, in which desire becomes the occasion for the hero's redemption. While there is no redemption for Coriolanus, its possibility is suggested in the beautiful allegory of the reconciliation scene in act 5.

7 Coriolanus's Impotence

In returning to the world of ancient Rome in his last tragedy, Shakespeare sharpens the analysis of the conflict between individual and society. All tragedy deals with this conflict, but *Coriolanus* focuses on it to an unusual degree. No other Shakespearean hero is so obviously superior, and so obviously aware of his superiority. The fact that this superiority derives from the hero's unrelenting competitiveness on the battlefield merely heightens the difference between Coriolanus and the general citizenry, most of whom have neither the ability nor the inclination to compete, let alone win, in this particular arena. Nor can we ignore the play's historical setting, which further accentuates this difference. Surrounded by many hostile city states, the young Roman republic must either fight its enemies or be conquered by them. In this context the warrior's political authority is a good deal easier to accept. Coriolanus's belief in the inherent nobility of the warrior class (the patricians) reflects this geopolitical reality. It is grossly inaccurate to call Coriolanus a fascist. He has absolutely no inclination towards political demagoguery. On the contrary, he despises the tribunes precisely because they rely on words rather than deeds. A better analogy would be to the professional athlete, whose supremacy on the field of play is rarely a reliable indicator of eloquence or generosity towards the fans at the press conference afterward.[1]

Coriolanus's superiority on the battlefield makes him an obvious target for the resentment of those with less talent for swordplay and violence. What is most interesting about the play, however, is not that Coriolanus becomes the unfortunate victim of mass resentment, but that he willfully foments resentment by treating the Roman commoners with such unmitigated contempt. Coriolanus practically begs the people to sacrifice him. This is not quite the same thing as Hamlet's death-obsessed imagination, but it is an extroverted version of it. Coriolanus possesses none of Hamlet's self-consciousness of the sacrificial violence of the centre. But his bitter rivalry with the plebeians nonetheless illustrates with stark clarity the central moral problem of the neoclassical aesthetic.

This problem concerns the justification of the hero's centrality. Given the moral symmetry of all on the periphery, usurpation of the centre by the big man provokes resentment. As we have seen, the neoclassical solution to this problem is to put the entire scene, with its centre and periphery, on stage. The protagonist is not, as in classical tragedy, an unquestioned embodiment of superior being. Centrality is never a foregone conclusion for the Shakespearean hero. On the contrary, the tragic action unfolds as an ambivalent and dangerous quest to achieve it. The articulation of this paradox varies from play to play. Hamlet, the most lucidly self-conscious of Shakespeare's protagonists, explicitly understands centrality to be a curse. His first stage appearance dramatizes the awareness that from the point of view of the periphery centrality is a scandal. The ensuing action, which unfolds as a series of false starts towards the tragically centralizing duty of revenge, further demonstrates the paradox that centrality does not exist in itself but must be generated from the margins of the scene. As the romantics well understood, in creating this extraordinary character, Shakespeare risked destroying the very genre he had taken as his form.[2] Hamlet is so self-conscious of his tragic role that we sometimes wonder if the other characters are merely pawns in his play. All those associated with the centre, including not only the king but also Gertrude, Polonius, Ophelia, Laertes, Rosencrantz, and Guildenstern, suffer because of it. Occupation of the centre is a scandal. Those who trespass against it, whether they do so consciously or not, pay for their transgression with their lives.

Hamlet's resentful awareness of the crime of centrality puts him closer to the anti-hero Iago than to the big men of Shakespeare's later tragedies. Othello, Macbeth, and Coriolanus are, in their own ways, much more obvious incarnations of centrality. When they die, Bradley says, the world is noticeably diminished: "life has suddenly shrunk and dwindled and become a home for pygmies."[3] Bradley is speaking of the contrast between Coriolanus and his sacrificers, a group that includes not just the lowborn plebeians but the Roman and Volscian patricians too. All participate equally in the sacrifice of the central figure whose transgression is, in the final analysis, the crime of centrality itself. In *Hamlet* the opposition between the hero and his sacrificers is diluted by Hamlet's relentless irony. Hamlet ironizes the centre before he occupies it. When in the final moments of the play he usurps the centre, he does so with the full awareness that he, like the king he has just murdered, is dying.

Coriolanus is not given to reflecting Hamlet-like on the ambivalence of central suffering. Nonetheless his actions illustrate the same paradoxical relationship to the centre found in Shakespeare's previous tragedies. More aggressively than either Othello or Macbeth, Coriolanus competes for centrality. But just when he appears assured of achieving Rome's highest honour, he contemptuously throws it back in the faces of his electors. How can we explain this perverse action?

In deliberately provoking the plebeians, Coriolanus exemplifies not merely the tragic protagonist's insatiable desire for centrality, but more particularly the scandal of centrality itself. Nor should we limit our interpretation of this scandal to an analysis of the protagonist's character. To point to Coriolanus's pride and contempt is illuminating as a psychological description, but as an explanation of the play's tragic structure, it remains partial.[4] Volumnia is equally proud and equally contemptuous, yet she would have no difficulty smiling duplicitously to the plebeians in order to secure the power she covets. Nor is it plausible to suggest that Coriolanus is too immature to hide his feelings. Even a five-year-old child is able to disguise his intentions in order to get something he wants. In any case it is not true that Coriolanus is incapable of hiding his feelings. How else has he become so formidable a warrior if not by controlling the natural feeling of fear? When he comforts his distraught mother and silently weeping wife immediately after his banishment, he is setting aside his own feelings and thinking only of theirs. And the very fact that he is initially successful in obtaining the approval of the people, despite the humiliation of having to beg for their voices, shows that he is capable of a kind of diplomacy, however gracelessly or begrudgingly fulfilled. His subsequent violent outburst, which occurs only after he has been goaded by the devious and calculating tribunes, ruins everything. But this does not prove that he is incapable of hiding his feelings. It merely proves that his desire for centrality is matched by his resentment of those who stand in his way.

We arrive here at a key to the structure of the play, which unfolds as a series of dramatic turns or reversals in the conflict between individual and society. These reversals are themselves variations on the basic paradox structuring our relationship to the hero. Admiration of Coriolanus is inseparable from resentment of him. This paradoxical dynamic is evident from the start in the riot that begins the play. The first citizen foments resentment, calling Coriolanus "chief enemy to the people" (1.1.7–8). But the second citizen undercuts this resentment by reminding his fellows of the "services he has done for his country" (1.1.28–9).[5] Coriolanus is both the admired hero and the hated enemy. Which perspective you adopt depends upon the context in which you place him. Within the context of the famine in Rome, Coriolanus is the people's enemy because he is the most outspoken defender of social hierarchy.[6] Here it is well to remind ourselves of the close conceptual relationship between social hierarchy and food in agrarian societies.[7] Access to food is determined by proximity to the centre: those at the top get fed first. As one descends the hierarchy, the availability of food shrinks until, usually a good way before reaching the bottom, there is nothing left. In agrarian societies, food shortage is thus more or less a permanent condition of society, at least for those at the bottom, which of course includes massive segments of the population. (The hierarchy is a pyramid with a wide base, rather than a square with equal numbers above and below an imaginary "poverty line" running horizontally through the middle.) Crop failure because of drought or disease merely exacerbates an already precarious situation for those not at the peak, which is to say, more or less everyone.

This reference to the problem of food distribution should not be taken as endorsing a Marxist reading of the play, in which Coriolanus's defeat at the hands of the proletarian masses is imagined to be Shakespeare's revenge on a tiny minority of well-fed aristocratic warriors. The image of the fat aristocrat who eats candied fruit while the people starve in the streets clearly does not apply to Coriolanus.[8] The point of introducing the humorous Menenius is to show us that the people do not object in principle to fat patricians. Menenius can get away with being fat precisely because he flatters the people into believing that they are loved by their betters. In contrast, Coriolanus sets himself up as a target of the people's resentment because he insultingly reminds them of their insignificance. Hence the irony of Coriolanus's first stage appearance. After Menenius lavishes many "good words" on the people, Coriolanus enters the stage and addresses them with a searing barrage of invective:

> What's the matter, you dissentious rogues,
> That, rubbing the poor itch of your opinion,
> Make yourselves scabs? (1.1.163–5)

When the first citizen responds sarcastically ("We have ever your good word" [1.1.165]), Coriolanus replies with a line that not only undermines Menenius's attempt to patch up the relationship between the two classes, but also accuses any patrician who seeks to do so of craven flattery: "He that will give good words to thee will flatter / Beneath abhorring" (1.1.166–7). The contrast between the two strategies could not be more apparent. Menenius ingratiates himself with the people by claiming to love them, while Coriolanus insults them by reminding them of their social inferiority. Contrary to what some readers believe, there is nothing modest or self-effacing about Coriolanus.[9] He wears his superiority proudly on his sleeve, and this makes him an easy target of populist resentment.

But the picture changes considerably when the focus shifts from Rome's internal struggles to its external ones. As a fearless defender of the city, Coriolanus cannot but be admired. This perspective is adopted by the second citizen when he reminds his fellows of Coriolanus's services to his country.[10] The contrasting viewpoints of the first and second citizen are played out on the stage in the action that follows. Coriolanus insults the plebeians, thereby confirming the first citizen's view that he is chief enemy of the people. Then the news arrives of the Volscian attack. In the ensuing battle, which occupies the rest of the first act, Coriolanus defeats, virtually singlehandedly, an army of Volscians in their own city of Corioles before racing to help a struggling Cominius in the field, where his presence decisively turns the battle into a Roman victory. In this context Coriolanus's status as chief enemy of the people is swiftly forgotten. In the immediate aftermath of the war, Coriolanus becomes once more the darling of Rome. As the tribune Brutus sourly notes, the entire populace turns out to welcome him back to the city.

> Stalls, bulks, windows
> Are smothered up, leads filled and ridges horsed
> With variable complexions, all agreeing
> In earnestness to see him. (2.1.209–12)

The famine is forgotten, and the lynch mob of the opening scene turns into an adoring crowd. Yet the threat of violence remains. Coriolanus's "soaring insolence" (2.1.253) has not disappeared. As the tribunes accurately predict, sooner or later he will remind the people of their inferiority, and it will not require much effort or ingenuity on their part to stir the people's resentment into a "blaze" that, as Sicinius says, will "darken him forever" (2.1.257–8).

Sicinius's image of the people's resentment as "dry stubble" that Coriolanus's "fire" will ignite into a "blaze" is a powerful one (2.2.256–7), all the more so because it accurately describes a scene Sicinius himself fails to anticipate. For the people's resentment is nothing compared to Coriolanus's. Once the fire of his resentment is ablaze, Rome herself is in danger of being darkened forever. Surely the most memorable image of the play is the one Coriolanus has etched into his mind once he discovers that Rome has callously forgotten him. If, as Cominius says, "Rome must know / The value of her own" (1.9.20–1), what better way for Coriolanus to remind Rome of her mistake in exiling him than by burning her to the ground? Coriolanus personifies – and thereby exaggerates – the sense of injured merit that lurks in the hearts of all the characters in the play, including the plebeians, the tribunes, Aufidius, Volumnia, Menenius, and even, for a brief moment, Virgilia (when she vents her anger on the tribunes after her husband's banishment).[11] As resentment personified, he becomes an inhuman engine (5.4.19) or fire-breathing dragon (4.1.30, 4.7.23, 5.4.13):

> I tell you, he does sit in gold, his eye
> Red as 'twould burn Rome, and his injury
> The jailer to his pity. (5.1.65–7)

This image of Coriolanus, his eyes glowing red with the flame that will burn Rome, is a caricature of the resentful personality. Indeed, it is almost cartoon-like in its vividness. Shakespeare is pushing tragedy to its limits. A.P. Rossiter wonders if Shakespeare's emphasis on Coriolanus's resentment is too much. Has the play toppled from tragedy into irony?[12] But the point is clear enough. In fanning the flames of the people's resentment, the tribunes merely fan the flames of Coriolanus's. The difference is that Coriolanus's resentment is a thousand times more destructive than the people's. Rome will indeed learn the value of her own. Like the potlatch chief who flagrantly burns his worldly goods to prove his superiority over his competitors, Coriolanus will burn Rome to make the same point. There is no equal to the big man's desire, and there is no equal to his resentment. Coriolanus is Shakespeare's biggest big man. It is no surprise that his resentment should be equally huge.[13]

In a notorious argument Friedrich Nietzsche declared that only the slave is resentful because only the slave is impotent. Whereas the man of action, the warrior, takes what he wants by force and so expresses himself open-heartedly, fearlessly, and joyfully, the slave shrinks from the world, convinced that his actions are inadequate and the obstacles standing in his way are expressly designed to thwart and frustrate him. In resentful rage against this unfriendly and unyielding world, his thoughts turn inward, where they fester and steadily poison the soul. The slave's only source of release is to indulge in fantasies of revenge against the strong and noble, who daily remind him of his insignificance and inferiority. These revenges, however, are purely imaginary, and they therefore merely serve to underscore the humiliating reality of his weakness and impotence.[14]

Nietzsche's argument is a caricature. Nonetheless, it captures a truth about resentment that most philosophers have missed (when they do not ignore the subject altogether). Resentment is the impotent rage of the marginalized other. In the originary scene, it can be traced to the experience of dispossession from the centre produced by the emission of the linguistic sign on the periphery. It is therefore a universal experience. To experience resentment one must be a language user capable of interpreting the world in terms of a symbolic-aesthetic scene that exists in the first place in the individual's imagination. Nietzsche's anthropology would have us believe that resentment becomes productive as a historical category only with the inversion of values created by the rise of Christianity, which values the weak over the strong. But it seems clear that the origin of language precedes the origin of social hierarchy and Christianity's resentful moralizing against the aristocratic warrior ethic. In the beginning, all were inferior to the inaccessible centre because all were equal participants in the production of the sign. The origin of social hierarchy can be traced to this fundamental distinction between centre and periphery that defines the scene of human interaction. Human morality depends on the scenic awareness that centrality is a transgression against the prohibition of the linguistic sign. Nietzsche erred only in associating moral prohibition, and therefore resentment, exclusively with the slave. But without the moral prohibition implicit in all language use, there can be no human society and therefore no social hierarchy.[15]

But it is unnecessary to rely on recent anthropology to refute Nietzsche. One can also turn to Shakespeare, whose nobles are every bit as resentful as his slaves. Coriolanus is a case in point. Superficially, he appears to confirm Nietzsche's opposition between noble and slave. Coriolanus is all nobility. His contempt for the plebeians is an expression of his nobility, which is so huge that it barely registers the presence of the lowborn. They are to be swatted away like flies. At any rate, they are not worth taking seriously, especially when there is joyful, life-affirming business at hand, such as fighting other nobles like Aufidius. Meanwhile, the plebeians would seem to illustrate Nietzsche's category of the resentful slave. Impotent in the face of Coriolanus's manifest superiority, they resort to devious tricks and underhanded plots. They whine for representation and when they obtain it, they manipulate the system in their favour. Only by such roundabout and resentful means can they bring about the destruction of a superior being like Coriolanus.

Alas, this neat and tidy picture falls apart completely as soon as you examine the evidence with any care. For starters the noble Aufidius isn't quite so noble, and this undermines the image, expressed rather sentimentally by the hero himself, of Aufidius as the brilliant foil to his brighter star.

I sin in envying his nobility,
And were I anything but what I am
I would wish me only he. (1.1.231–3)

This romantic image of the noble Aufidius turns out to be completely false. When Aufidius suffers yet another humiliating defeat in his epic rivalry with Coriolanus, he decides that his only recourse is to craft and treachery:

Mine emulation
Hath not that honor in't it had; for where
I thought to crush him in an equal force,
True sword to sword, I'll potch at him some way
Or wrath or craft may get him (1.10.12–16)

This speech is merely the first of several in which the audience learns that Aufidius plans to kill Coriolanus dishonourably. Impotent in the face of Coriolanus's superiority on the battlefield, he resorts to the same treachery as the tribunes: "My valor's poisoned, / With only suff'ring stain by him" (1.10.17–18). Aufidius may be an aristocrat and accomplished swordsman, but he is no stranger to resentment.

We may feel that as a certified member of the Volscian tribe, Aufidius is justified in his treachery. All is fair in love and war. Certainly, we may feel it to be more justified than the same treachery unleashed on

Coriolanus by the Roman people and their cowardly tribunes. This sense of the matter is no doubt true to our emotional response to the play. The banishment scene comes as an appalling shock, whereas the scene of Coriolanus's death is all but expected, largely because we have been carefully prepared for it by Aufidius's resentful asides. But what we miss if we overemphasize the emotional contrast between these two scenes is the fact that the play scrupulously undermines the opposition between Rome and Antium. This is already apparent in Coriolanus's claim that were he not Coriolanus he would wish to be Aufidius. Curiously enough, it is also apparent in Coriolanus's name, which is taken from the Volscian city of Corioles. (Imagine an Arsenal fan naming his son Hotspur!) The odd little scene in act 4, when a Roman spy meets in secret with a Volscian spy, further undermines the distinction between the two cities. And, of course, this scene directly precedes the moment when Coriolanus secretly enters Antium to join forces with Aufidius.

The precariousness of the Rome-Antium opposition is explained by the fact that it functions as a pretext for a much more fundamental conflict. This conflict is that of the dramatic scene itself, which in tragedy involves the opposition between the hero at the centre and the social order on the periphery.[16] As Shakespeare makes clear, the latter includes both Rome and Antium. Everyone, whether noble or base, Roman or Volscian, participates in Coriolanus's destruction. Banished from Rome by the people, he storms back to the city with a terrible army at his back. But he is repelled once again, this time not by the impotent plebs and their calculating tribunes, but by three unarmed women and a boy. Aufidius's sarcastic insult that Coriolanus gave up Rome for "certain drops of salt" (5.6.97) is unfair, but it at least has the virtue of accurately capturing the irony of Coriolanus's image of himself as a fearless warrior. Shakespeare's most Nietzschean big man is repulsed by the impotent periphery – by slaves, three women, and a child. Nietzsche would doubtless have appreciated this irony, even if Bradley does not.[17]

It may be objected that by presenting Coriolanus's tragedy in these coldly theoretical terms, I have undermined the aesthetic experience of the play. Why would Shakespeare risk undermining the audience's sympathy for the hero by emphasizing the irony of his sacrifice? I will discuss the theoretical implications of Shakespeare's irony more directly in the next chapter. At this point, I will focus on what I take to be the uniqueness of *Coriolanus* as an ethical discovery procedure. As I hope will become evident, this is another way of answering the question about Shakespeare's use of irony.

Aufidius is very far from being noble in the sense that either Nietzsche or Coriolanus imagines. What about Coriolanus's patrician friends? Do they behave with the same honour and nobleness to which Coriolanus aspires? We have already seen that Menenius, for one, does not. By presenting himself as a friend of the people, he participates in exactly the kind of political doublespeak that Coriolanus despises. In a perceptive comment, Kenneth Burke notes that Menenius is a comic inversion of Coriolanus. Burke cites Menenius's line, "What I think, I utter, and spend my malice in my breath" (2.1.53–4), which suggests that Menenius is (unconsciously) parodying Coriolanus.[18] Menenius is an older, fatter version of Coriolanus, but unlike his young protégé he has a sense of irony. Despite believing in the inferiority of the plebeians and their tribunes, Menenius's sense of humour enables him to get along with them. The plebeians laugh at his jokes, even when he tells them what he thinks of them, as when he calls the first citizen the "great toe of this assembly" (1.1.154). Menenius has mastered the art of deferring violence through (comic) representation. He is above all a great talker and storyteller. His love of words stands in obvious contrast to Coriolanus's fear of them.[19]

How can we explain this fear? Why is Coriolanus so aggressively resentful of all attempts to praise him? Coriolanus's fear of words dramatizes the paradox of the neoclassical aesthetic. This paradox concerns the representation of the hero's centrality, which cannot fail to generate resentment. The neoclassical solution is to thematize this paradox, which in classical tragedy remains hidden. Identification with the centre is shown to be inseparable from resentful alienation. This paradoxical oscillation between desiring identification and resentful alienation underlies Coriolanus's eccentric attitude towards praise. The patricians doggedly seek to centralize Coriolanus by praising him, but each of their efforts is met by Coriolanus's equally stubborn refusal to accept the praise. This tug-of-war between Coriolanus and the patricians is a version of the more overtly combative struggles between Coriolanus and Aufidius, on the one hand, and Coriolanus and the plebeians, on the other. Aufidius both loves and hates Coriolanus; he embraces him like a lover in the fourth act, but then resentfully stabs him in the back in the fifth. Likewise the people both admire and resent their hero. They turn out in droves to rejoice in his victory; but moments later they resentfully whoop him out of the city. It is easy to overemphasize the significance of this last reversal because it comes as the climax to the action of the first three acts. But the banishment has been anticipated from the beginning by Coriolanus's eccentric relationship not just to the plebeians, but to every single character in the play, including Volumnia and Virgilia. When Cominius praises Coriolanus for his valiant deeds in the immediate aftermath of the battle of Corioles, Coriolanus stubbornly rejects both the praise and the award of a tenth of the spoils. Later, in the senate when Cominius rises to give an account of Coriolanus's worthiness, Coriolanus walks out rather than staying to "hear my nothings monstered" (2.2.77). It is hopeless to attempt to explain these bizarre actions solely in terms of Coriolanus's character. Bradley admits as much when he describes Coriolanus as "what we call an impossible person."[20] No doubt Coriolanus is impossible, but his peculiar character, as Kenneth Burke sees, is derived from the form of tragedy, and the form cannot be explained by resorting to such notions as an "impossible person." Coriolanus is impossible because his actions reflect the paradoxical experience of identification with and alienation from the tragic centre.

Let us consider the most obviously centralizing act in the play: Coriolanus's election to the supreme office of consul. At first he is successful. But then he deliberately undermines this success. By aggravating the plebeians, Coriolanus sabotages the hopes of his patrician friends. Much has been made of Coriolanus's obedience to his mother. Apparently, she is the only person Coriolanus will obey.[21] I beg to differ. Coriolanus's relationship to his mother might be described as passive-aggressive. She browbeats him into returning, cap in hand, to the plebeians, but instead of responding mildly to the plebeians, as he had promised, he explodes in unmitigated fury. This doesn't strike me as obedience. Rather, it looks like a deliberately roundabout strategy for undermining his mother's wish. Coriolanus, let us not forget, never expressed a desire to become consul. On the contrary, he explicitly objected to the idea. It is the patricians, and in particular his mother, who push it upon him.[22] Given the pattern of obstinate resistance to the desires of others that we have observed in Coriolanus from the beginning, it is hardly surprising that Coriolanus should throw the consulship back in the face of, not the plebeians, who never wanted him to become consul, but his mother, who very much did. What this defiant gesture shows is Coriolanus's determination to accept centrality on nobody's terms but his own. This is consistent with his resistance to praise, for in praising another, you inevitably dilute the other's significance. You imply that this person deserves attention only because you have pointed it out in the first place. In other words, you are undermining the very centrality you wish to point out. This irony is beautifully captured by an image used by Volumnia. As she attempts to persuade her recalcitrant son to return to the marketplace so he can rescue what he has lost, she paints a portrait of him as humble and meek, inviting him to mould himself to this new image. He is to appear bonnet in hand, knee bussing the stone, and "humble as the ripest mulberry / That will not hold the handling" (3.2.81–2). The image is paradoxical. Ostensibly, its purpose is to impress upon Coriolanus that he must appear as soft and pliant as an overripe berry. But the brilliantly vivid addition – "That will not hold the handling" – gives the image a rather more sinister meaning. Overripe berries cannot be easily picked without inadvertently squishing them. This is exactly what happens to Coriolanus. He is the overripe berry that will not hold the handling. He is passed back and forth between patricians and plebeians until he is, ignominiously and unceremoniously, squashed. It is a deeply ironic image of Coriolanus. Yet it accurately describes what comes to pass.

Coriolanus is not sufficiently self-aware to be able to extricate himself from this paradox. If he were, the play would not be a tragedy. Nonetheless, there are some more buoyant moments in what is otherwise a rather depressing and pessimistic play. The most clearly hopeful moment occurs in the immediate aftermath of his banishment. It is not difficult to see the reasons for Coriolanus's buoyancy, which given his normally grim and humourless behaviour might otherwise seem out of character.[23] Suddenly a huge weight has been lifted from his shoulders. Not since he was a child has life appeared so free. Released from his servitude to his mother's desire, he is at last free to build his own career. In a single stroke he has shed the burden of the centre. This burden began at a very early age; "when youth with comeliness plucked all gaze his way" (1.3.7–8), Volumnia, fearing that her son would grow "soft as the parasite's silk" (1.9.45), sent him to a cruel war at the age of sixteen. Her chilling image of the beauty of the soldier's forehead spouting blood vividly captures the weight of Coriolanus's violent burden. When he returned, his brow bound with oak, his career is set. The clock stops here for Coriolanus. He becomes an adolescent frozen in time, a creature of his mother's warlike and honour-craving fantasy. Thus prevented from reaching full maturity, he is condemned to play the same grimly violent role over and over again. No wonder he breathes a huge sigh of relief when he is banished. At last he is free to do things his own way.[24]

This major reversal in the brilliant career of Caius Marcius Coriolanus is anticipated in the first scene of act 2. Menenius is in conversation with the tribunes. As is his wont, he is engaging in a little spontaneous publicity for Coriolanus, prepping the tribunes for the moment when Coriolanus will have to run the gauntlet of the plebeians in the marketplace.

> MENENIUS: The augurer tells me we shall have news tonight.
> BRUTUS: Good or bad?
> MENENIUS: Not according to the prayer of the people, for they love not Marcius.
> SICINIUS: Nature teaches beasts to know their friends.
> MENENIUS: Pray you, who does the wolf love?
> SICINIUS: The lamb.
> MENENIUS: Ay, to devour him, as the hungry plebeians would the noble Marcius.
> BRUTUS: He's a lamb indeed, that baas like a bear.
> MENENIUS: He's a bear indeed, that lives like a lamb. (2.1.1–12)

The dialogue unfolds as a vertiginous attempt to lock onto its object (Coriolanus). There is to be news. Will it be good or bad? That depends upon your perspective (patrician or plebeian?). Good news for Rome (Coriolanus's victory) means bad news for the plebeians (his election to the consulship). Hence the apparent paradox that in hating Coriolanus the people are merely undermining their own interests. Sicinius counters that the people have every reason to hate Coriolanus, for he treats them contemptuously (even beasts know the difference between friend and foe). Ah, Menenius replies, but the wolf *loves* the lamb, just as the people would love to devour Coriolanus. Brutus scoffs: Coriolanus is no lamb, he is a bear and not even wolves dare to attack bears. Yes, Menenius says, on the battlefield Coriolanus is a bear, but off it he is a perfect lamb.

The exchange illustrates Shakespeare's thematization of the paradoxical relationship between centre and periphery. The centre is defined not by the protagonist at the centre, but by the onlookers on the periphery. There is no such thing as the intrinsic being of the hero. His centrality is not given by his existence; it is created by others.[25] Like all of Shakespeare's protagonists, Coriolanus struggles to free himself from the burden placed upon him by the tragic scene. Though he possesses none of Hamlet's self-consciousness of the centre's dependence on the periphery, his stubborn refusal to cooperate with others illustrates the neoclassical protagonist's ambivalent relationship to the centre.

No doubt next to Hamlet, Coriolanus comes across as inarticulate.[26] But he is by no means dumb. On the contrary, he is never more eloquent than when venting his spleen on the plebeians. Why this is so is not hard to understand. He has been brought up to respect his patrician elders, and above all his mother. But these are the very same people who, through their oppressive claims on his person, deny him his autonomy. Caught between his sense of filial duty and an inarticulate dissatisfaction for the warlike caricature he has become, he turns all his pent-up hatred on the plebeians, whose lowborn status seems to legitimize and explain his otherwise inexplicable feelings of discontented frustration. In Rome, they are the only outlet he has, and he takes every opportunity to vent himself upon them.

One of the great ironies of the play is that Coriolanus's tragedy has been anticipated not only by the plebeians ("First, you know Caius Marcius is chief enemy to the people" [1.1.7–8]), or the tribunes ("their blaze / Shall darken him forever" [2.1.257–8]), or even Aufidius ("I'll potch at him some way / Or wrath or craft may get him" [1.10.15–16]). Coriolanus has been created by his mother, and she is the one who eventually destroys him. Aufidius's role in the play is totally subordinate to this fact, and for this reason many playgoers and readers find the real climax to span the period between the twin rejections of Coriolanus in Rome. This is the period of his exile, which begins when he is rejected by the plebeians and ends when he is repulsed from Rome a second time, this time by his mother. Both scenes illustrate the pattern of frustrated desire that is the hallmark of tragedy. In the first, the frustration of desire is provoked by Coriolanus himself, as he deliberately undermines the wishes of his mother. In the second, it is Volumnia who functions as the obstacle to Coriolanus's desire. But in the latter case, the scene does not unfold simply as a contest of external wills (Coriolanus versus Volumnia). It is also an allegory of the inner moral transformation of the protagonist. The public scene of tragedy is internalized within the hero himself. Let us examine what occurs in the period of Coriolanus's exile.

We have already explained the reasons for Coriolanus's optimistic mood at the beginning of act 4. Relieved of the burden of the centre, he looks forward to a life of freedom and adventure outside Rome. Exile appears to afford him the best of both worlds. He will be sufficiently distant from Rome to be able to shape his own career, but he will not be so far removed as to be totally anonymous. He shall be loved when he is lacked. Reports of the high deeds of Coriolanus will flow into the city, and the people will marvel at the hero who had the audacity to turn his back on them:

> though I go alone,
> Like to a lonely dragon that his fen
> Make feared and talked of more than seen, your son
> Will or exceed the common or be caught
> With cautelous baits and practice. (4.1.29–33)

It is a breathtakingly romantic image. Notice how the dreamy mistiness of the picture is emphasized by the notion that the dragon is "talked of more than seen." Like some mythical figure Coriolanus will inhabit the people's imaginations even if they never actually see him. How can they when he is absent? All that remains is the idea of him, which is to say, the aesthetic scene in which his centrality is imagined. Bradley observes that, when we compare Coriolanus to Othello and Macbeth, we find none of the magnificent poetry that inhabits the speeches of these other protagonists.[27] Othello and Macbeth have soaring imaginations; Coriolanus does not. On the whole, I agree with this observation. But I would make an exception in this one instance. Coriolanus's description of himself as a lonely dragon is brief, but it rivals anything Othello says about himself, even if it falls short of Macbeth's imaginative terror at the prospect of usurping the centre.

In a fascinating discussion of Shakespeare's "new mimesis," A.D. Nuttall suggests that Coriolanus is caught halfway between Homeric shame culture and "the introverted form given to it by Stoicism."[28] This is an interesting idea, but it neglects the greater influence of Christian anthropology on Shakespeare's conception of the hero. What Coriolanus's particular predicament suggests is the moral awareness that centrality is problematic. No longer accepted as given, as in the classical aesthetic, centrality must be generated from within the scene itself. Nuttall implicitly recognizes this when he writes that Coriolanus "is a kind of nothing and acquires what positive nature he possesses by adventitious role-adoption."[29] Nuttall traces this process of role-adoption to Pico della Mirandola, who pictured man as caught in a dynamic historical struggle between God above and the devil below. Like all Renaissance artists, Shakespeare was strongly influenced by this moral picture. In *Coriolanus*, however, the protagonist's moral struggle is often submerged, and perhaps this is why Nuttall felt drawn to the idea of Coriolanus as a Stoic. Nonetheless, Coriolanus's inner moral struggle emerges from time to time in the play, and never more prominently than in the period of his exile. The buoyancy of his mood in 4.1 is a sign of his potential for *moral* growth, in the specifically Christian sense of the word. This is not Stoicism. On the contrary, it is something much more radical, which is why I do not think it is historically inaccurate to describe it as romantic.[30]

The difficulty is that Coriolanus fails to sustain the romantic self-image. What Coriolanus discovers when he abandons Rome is that there is no world elsewhere.[31] As the length of his exile increases, his romantic hope for a better, more rewarding life shrinks to nothingness. Meanwhile, life in Rome continues as before. Unburdened of the poisonous mood created by Coriolanus, a tentative peace settles on the city. Even Menenius admits that Rome is no worse off – and possibly a good deal better off – in the wake of Coriolanus's banishment. When the tribunes ask if he has heard any news of his friend, he merely shrugs his shoulders. He has heard nothing, and neither have Coriolanus's mother and wife. Coriolanus's romantic vision of himself is brutally falsified. His exile confirms the humiliating reality of his anonymity. This is why he makes his way to Antium. Unable to achieve the dragon-like recognition he craves, his resentment of his banishers grows to become a burning obsession. He turns to his former enemies to annihilate the very scene he had declared unnecessary to his existence.

The scene in which Coriolanus appears before Aufidius has to be one of the funniest in all of Shakespeare. I do not mean that it is designed to send the audience into fits of belly-aching laughter, like the duel between Viola and Sir Andrew in *Twelfth Night*. The recognition scene – or unrecognition scene, to put it more precisely – is funny in a much darker, much more ironic sense. The scene should be compared to two prior scenes: first, the moment when Coriolanus, after strenuously objecting to the praise bestowed on him by Cominius, forgets the name of the man he wished to save in Corioles; and second, the moment when Coriolanus goes before the plebeians and succeeds in getting their approval, despite his graceless performance. Both scenes illustrate the lesson of the scandal of centrality that Coriolanus does not grasp until he is forced to experience for himself the painful reality of life on the margins. In other words, Coriolanus undergoes a moral awakening. The journey between Rome and Antium is Coriolanus's road to Damascus. When he returns to Rome, it is with a new appreciation for the morally inspired resentment of the impotent.

This impotence is evident in the soliloquy he utters as he stands outside Antium, gazing at the city walls:

> A goodly city is this Antium. City,
> 'Tis I that made thy widows. Many an heir
> Of these fair edifices 'fore my wars
> Have I heard groan and drop. Then know me not,
> Lest that thy wives with spits and boys with stones
> In puny battle slay me. (4.4.1–6)

Even if we assume that he is being ironic when he says that wives and boys may slay him (and how can we not?), this irony is trumped by the far greater irony that Coriolanus has become, by this point in the play, invisible both to his former admirers in Rome and his enemies in Antium. The soliloquy is a desperate effort to cheer himself up, to tell himself that he is still the great man he once was.

This irony is heightened by the events that unfold next. After being mistaken for a beggar by the servants in Aufidius's household (How the mighty have fallen!), Coriolanus places all his hope in Aufidius. Surely he, of all people, will recognize him. What happens next is extraordinarily difficult to perform on the stage because it is danger of veering into pure comedy. Aufidius asks Coriolanus for his name six times over the space of thirteen lines, so it is clear that Aufidius hasn't a clue who his interlocutor is. The apparent implausibility of this situation forces directors and actors to invent ways to explain Aufidius's failure to recognize his sworn rival. Coriolanus must be hooded, his face is turned away, the light is poor, he hasn't shaved in a while, his clothes are torn and dirty. But none of these extratextual details satisfactorily explains the irony in the text. Nor is it sufficient to appeal to the stage direction at the beginning of the scene ("*Enter Coriolanus in mean apparel, disguised and muffled*"). Evidently Coriolanus feels the need to disguise himself when he enters the city of his enemies, but once he gains access to Aufidius, it is clear that he sheds the disguise.

So why doesn't Aufidius recognize him? Shakespeare, I'm certain, wanted to draw our attention to the irony of the encounter. What better way to drive home the point that Coriolanus depends on the very scene he believes unnecessary to his existence? Not only is Coriolanus forced to name himself; he must also account for the significance of his existence by providing a narrative of his accomplishments and the indignity of his banishment. With no one to praise him, the great man must speak for himself.[32]

The speech Coriolanus utters to Aufidius is by far his longest. In naming himself, Coriolanus illustrates a truth he has thus far strenuously denied or repressed. He depends, as much as the next person, on the community. Furthermore, this community precedes his existence – indeed, defines his existence. In tragedy the protagonist's refusal of this truth leads to his downfall. No one, not even the most godlike or superhuman of heroes, exists outside of the minimal community given by language. And the most obvious proof of this, as Shakespeare makes singularly clear in this scene, is that without a name, membership in the community is impossible. Names are not simply a matter of convenience; they are necessary for our very concept of selfhood. The name is not a mere indexical marker, like the colour of one's eyes, or the prints left by one's fingers. It is an expression of one's being, a gift bestowed on the individual by the community, without which the individual could not exist as a human being. This is the moral lesson Coriolanus learns in the period of his long and humiliating exile.

Coriolanus's moral awakening occurs as a maturing of the protagonist's understanding of his desiring relation to the centre. Before his exile, centrality was unproblematic; he understood it to be self-evident or synonymous with his being. Whatever he desired was noble; whatever he hated, base – whence his contempt of the plebeians, which simply reinforces his nobility. His resistance to the consulship can be explained as motivated by this unproblematic understanding of centrality. As A.P. Rossiter perceptively notes, Coriolanus fears the dialectical centre-periphery relationship that defines the political scene.[33] This dialectical relationship is epitomized by the election, which undercuts Coriolanus's unproblematic conception of centrality as something created exclusively by himself. The sense that many playgoers and readers have that Coriolanus is a spoiled child who never grows up derives from this elementary or immature understanding of significance. Indoctrinated by his mother to believe that significance exists on the battlefield alone, Coriolanus is incapable of adapting to the political context. His fear of this scene is everywhere evident, but it looms especially during the election. In the senate Coriolanus says, "When blows had made me stay, I fled from words" (2.2.72). The line is directed at the tribune Brutus, who had moments earlier goaded Coriolanus by observing, quite accurately, that his track record with the people is unlikely to win him any favours. When one of the senators asks Cominius to rise and recount Coriolanus's worthy deeds, Coriolanus's irritation is visible and he makes to leave the room. Seeing this, Brutus takes the opportunity to irritate him further: "Sir, I hope / My words disbenched you not?" (2.2.70–1). In fact, Coriolanus is not disbenched by Brutus's sarcastic jabs. He is disbenched by the prospect of Cominius's praise. The reason for this should by now be plain. In praising Coriolanus with fair words, Cominius is trading promiscuously on Coriolanus's nonlinguistic deeds. The speech may be intended to ennoble Coriolanus, but for the duration of its utterance the audience is under the speaker's, not Coriolanus's, power. This is why Coriolanus abandons the scene. It is not modesty that causes him to excuse himself from the senate. It is the scandal of another's usurpation of a scene he believes to be exclusively his own.[34]

During his exile Coriolanus is unable to sustain this immature conception of the scene of significance as coeval with his being. His isolation robs him of the very audience he requires for self-definition. With no one to affirm his significance, he is forced to reflect on his new condition. Either he is truly nothing, or the world is badly mistaken. And if it is mistaken, it must be punished. What had begun as unproblematic contempt towards the merely inferior turns into an implacable resentment of the scene from which he feels unjustly excluded. The sense of injury overwhelms him, until it crystallizes into a single vengeful thought. Rome must burn for her treachery. His sense of loyalty to mother, wife, and son are dwarfed by his resentment. All are guilty of rejecting him, and all must be condemned to the flames.

This transformation can be described as moral because it forces upon the protagonist the awareness that his desire is not primary but in conflict with the desires of others. Before his exile, Coriolanus imagined his desire to be unproblematically identical with the general good of Rome. What was good for Coriolanus was good for Rome. This belief is why Coriolanus can never accept the plebeians as legitimate members of the city. If he despises them, how can they be? As far as Coriolanus is concerned, Rome is better off without them.[35] What his banishment ignominiously suggests, however, is that Rome might be better off without him. This humiliating possibility is not easy to contemplate, and it is unsurprising that Coriolanus refuses to consider it. Instead he focuses on the injustice of his banishment. But this is already an advance over his unreflective contempt of the lowborn. As Nietzsche had the genius to recognize, resentment of the centre is a moral reaction. The centre exists only because all participate equally in the designation of the scene. Resentment is thus a necessary feature of moral awareness, distinguishing it from mere contempt, which requires no similar awareness of moral reciprocity. As Coriolanus's behaviour in the first half of the play illustrates, contempt fixes the centre-periphery relationship into an unchanging and necessary ethical hierarchy. In converting his contempt of the plebeians into indignant resentment towards the entire social order, Coriolanus undergoes the moral revolution that Nietzsche associated with Christianity. The aristocratic warrior turns into the impotent slave. He becomes aware of the scandal of his insignificance before the immortal centre.

Why does Coriolanus abort his mission to burn Rome? Can we understand this reversal as a victory of love over resentment? I think we can, and I agree with Bradley when he says that "*Coriolanus* is as much a drama of reconciliation as a tragedy." As Bradley notes, Shakespeare simplified the story he found in Plutarch. He ignored the main intention of Plutarch's Coriolanus, which was to inflict a humiliating treaty upon his countrymen. Instead Shakespeare emphasized a single image that is not in Plutarch: the image of Rome in a "tower of flame." This idea captivates Coriolanus's imagination to the exclusion of all else. "What controls him," Bradley says, "is the vision that never leaves him and never changes, and his eye is red with its glare when he sits in his state before the doomed city." Coriolanus is a "hero enslaved by passion and driven blindly forward." The passion is resentment, and the magnitude of it is unmatched in all Shakespeare. As Bradley points out, we have a sense of the sheer size of it when we imagine its consequence. Coriolanus has abandoned everything he has loved: mother, wife, son, and Rome itself. He has allied himself with Rome's enemy, and he will burn the entire city, including every man, woman, and child. It matters not that his own family will perish in the flames.[36]

The point of the reconciliation scene is to test the hero's resolve. Is his resentment truly implacable? Will the love of his former attachments pull him from the brink? The scene is strongly allegorical in its construction. As the women approach, we get the only indication in the play of a moral struggle within the protagonist. Coriolanus has his first inner conflict and, as is typical in Shakespeare, it is represented by a soliloquy:

> My wife comes foremost; then the honored mold
> Wherein this trunk was framed, and in her hand
> The grandchild to her blood. But, out, affection!
> All bond and privilege of nature, break!
> Let it be virtuous to be obstinate.

What is that curtsy worth? Or those doves' eyes,
Which can make gods forsworn? I melt, and am not
Of stronger earth than others. My mother bows,
As if Olympus to a molehill should
In supplication nod, and my young boy
Hath an aspect of intercession which
Great Nature cries "Deny not." Let the Volsces
Plow Rome and harrow Italy, I'll never
Be such a gosling to obey instinct, but stand
As if a man were author of himself
And knew no other kin. (5.3.22–37)

The last sentence is frequently cited as an example of Coriolanus's overweening pride. But the context shows that Coriolanus's determination to stand as if a man were author of himself lacks conviction. The fact that he self-consciously presents the image of his self-sufficiency as a fiction already indicates that he is at odds with the thought. When his wife kneels before him, he finds he can no longer play the role: "Like a dull actor, / I have forgot my part, and I am out, / Even to a full disgrace" (5.3.40–2). Then, when she kisses him, his resentment melts: "Oh, a kiss / Long as my exile, sweet as my revenge!" (5.3.44–5).

Harold Goddard says that it is the silent wife rather than the voluble mother who has the greatest impact on Coriolanus.[37] If the scene is understood allegorically as an enactment on the stage of the internal struggle that has just occurred in Coriolanus's mind, then Goddard's remark makes a great deal of sense.[38] What we see depicted on the stage is a contest between love and resentment. This is why Shakespeare keeps Aufidius and his soldiers onstage. They say nothing but their presence is necessary for the allegory. They represent the forces of resentment, and they are arrayed against the women, who represent the forces of love. The latter, as Wilson Knight observes, represent the three stages of womanhood: maidenhood (Valeria), wifehood (Virgilia), and motherhood (Volumnia).[39] Meanwhile, the boy symbolizes innocence and, more specifically, the innocence of Coriolanus's lost childhood, which is now being given a second chance. Will he choose love, or will he commit his mother, wife, and child to the flames?[40] The struggle is protracted because Coriolanus's resentment is strong. The boy has only one line, but it is significant: "'A shall not tread on me; / I'll run away till I am bigger, but then I'll fight" (5.3.127–8). Allegorically, this is the old Coriolanus talking, the one ruthlessly bred in the wars. It almost succeeds in defeating the forces of love, for Coriolanus turns his back on the women: "Not of a woman's tenderness to be / Requires nor child nor woman's face to see" (5.3.129–30). But there is a new Coriolanus emerging from underneath the old, and in the end it triumphs. Volumnia shows a different side of herself to her son. She counsels mercy and reconciliation rather than war and destruction.[41] She kneels with the two other women; and then she points to the kneeling boy. It is a powerful image of Coriolanus's redeemed childhood. This boy will not run away and fight; instead he "kneels and holds up hands for fellowship" (5.3.175). The image of the kneeling boy symbolizes the change that occurs in Coriolanus. He cannot deny the women, which is to say, allegorically, he cannot deny love. He turns to Aufidius to tell him that though he cannot make true wars, he'll frame a convenient peace.

The allegorical interpretation emphasizes the hero's inner struggle, and this fits with the overall trajectory of the tragedy, which moves its hero away from the public and classically heroic conception of the centre and towards the romantic-Christian interpretation of it in terms of the individual's inner conscience. Without the participation of the latter in the scene, the public centre would not exist. Up to this point in the play, Coriolanus has never experienced a genuine moral conflict.[42] Thought had flowed spontaneously into ethical action. But this unproblematic conception of public honour as joyful life-affirming action runs up against the obstacle of the Roman citizens. The first hint of difficulty is the election, which forces Coriolanus into the unnatural role of dissembler and flatterer. Not insignificantly, when he goes before the people in the marketplace, he utters his first soliloquy, which gives us an introverted version of the contempt that would normally be vented directly on his inferiors:[43]

> Better it is to die, better to starve,
> Than crave the hire which first we do deserve.
> Why in this woolvish toge should I stand here
> To beg of Hob and Dick that does appear
> Their needless vouches? (2.3.113–17)

Instead of openly and, to quote Nietzsche again, "joyfully," expressing his contempt ("What's the matter, you dissentious rogues, / That, rubbing the poor itch of your opinion, / Make yourselves scabs?" [1.1.163–5]), Coriolanus represses it. It is an awkward role for Coriolanus to play, and he stumbles ungracefully through it. But it is Coriolanus's first step towards recognizing his dependency on others, including the lowborn plebeians.

His second soliloquy occurs, as we have seen, when he enters Antium. Aufidius personifies resentment, and Coriolanus's treacherous alliance with his enemy is Shakespeare's way of showing us that the hero is now consumed by this destructive passion. This is why Shakespeare emphasizes the closeness of the bond between the two: "so fellest foes ... shall grow dear friends / And interjoin their issues" (4.4.18–22). When Coriolanus declares that he will fight against his cankered country with the spleen of all the under fiends, Aufidius embraces him like a lover. We are reminded of Othello's oath to revenge:

> OTHELLO: Now art thou my lieutenant.
> IAGO: I am your own forever. (3.3.494–5)

Like Iago in the earlier play, Aufidius represents the perversion of the soul's dedication to love. When he enters Antium, Coriolanus embraces the false love of his sworn enemy.[44]

For Othello there was no hope; once committed to the path of vengeance, he remained steadfast until he had murdered Desdemona, his true love. In his last tragedy Shakespeare chose to reverse the hero's downward path. The reversal is the occasion for Coriolanus's third and final soliloquy, and it completes the protagonist's inward journey. Allied with the forces of resentment, Coriolanus stands on the threshold of his revenge. A battle unfolds between the forces of love and the forces of resentment; contrary to the tragic pattern, the hero wins a rare and precious victory for love. But the battle is not over; resentment has suffered a setback but it is realigning its forces. Aufidius turns darkly to the audience and utters an aside: "I am glad thou hast set thy mercy and thy honor / At difference in thee. Out of that I'll work / Myself a former fortune" (5.3.200–2). In the play's final scene, when Coriolanus returns in triumph to Corioles, the old rivalries flare up. Aufidius calls Coriolanus a boy of tears and a traitor. Coriolanus is incensed. He insults the Volscian people with the memory of how he fluttered them like an eagle in a dovecote. The people's admiration instantly turns to hatred. They cry for his death and Aufidius's conspirators hack him to pieces.

After the triumph of love in the reconciliation scene, the irony of the final scene, in which we abruptly return to the bleak pattern of resentment, might seem to overwhelm the tragic effect. Bradley is undaunted: "The effect of the previous scene, where he conquered something stronger than all the Volscians and escaped something worse than death, is not reversed."[45] Wilson Knight is yet more effusive: "Therefore Coriolanus now, as never before, enlists our sympathy, and can fling out his boast for the first time with a reckless joy and a new strength of pride which holds a magnificent finality."[46] Goddard, more subtly, emphasizes Coriolanus's conspicuous inaction, which shows that his redemption remains intact: "The old Coriolanus could have held off a dozen assassins, slaughtered them all perhaps, or at the very least sold his life dear. But he does not. And that he does not demonstrates that he is another man. His old self may echo in his last words. But his last act – or failure to act – is that of the new man created by Virgilia's kiss and the love of his child."[47] Each of these critics might be described as romantic, in that they emphasize the prominence of our identification with the hero's redeemed self. Bradley says that *Coriolanus* is peculiar in its emphasis on the inward transformation and redemption of its hero. A more strictly tragic ending would have "seen him amid the flaming ruins of Rome, awaking suddenly to the enormity of his deed and taking vengeance on himself." The fact that Shakespeare chose not to send his hero down that particular path suggests, Bradley says, that *Coriolanus* "marks the transition to his latest works, in which the powers of repentance and forgiveness charm to rest the tempest raised by error and guilt."[48] Harold Bloom, emphasizing rather the irony of Coriolanus's self-sacrifice, nonetheless agrees with Bradley when he says that *Coriolanus* marks the "twilight of tragedy."[49]

It seems that Shakespeare had pushed the genre to its limits. Tragedy requires the asymmetry between centre and periphery in order to maintain its aesthetic power over the spectator. As soon as this asymmetry is questioned, as it is throughout *Coriolanus*, tragedy turns into irony. A.P. Rossiter acknowledges this fact when he calls *Coriolanus* "the last and greatest of the Histories."[50] For Rossiter, the irony is simply too strong to sustain our identification with the hero through to the end; hence, Rossiter prefers to call *Coriolanus* a history play. In undermining Coriolanus's greatness, in consistently showing how history is made by little deeds, Shakespeare focused not on the big man, but on the *representation* of the big man. And in doing so, he turned the ethical paradox of tragedy into a problem that could be solved. Coriolanus's nobility begins to look slightly ridiculous when you set it beside the petty machinations of his "handlers," a group that includes both the patricians and the plebeians, and even, in the end, Aufidius and the Volscians.[51]

Shakespeare's most perverse big man is also his last. Having traced centrality back to its origin within the individual's desiring imagination, Shakespeare shifted his focus, in his last plays, to this more intimate scene. The tragic experiments of his middle period evolved into the tragicomic experiments of the late romances. Prospero is a duke and Leontes a king, but the narrative of their centralization has now shifted from the public scene of tragedy to the private scene of romance. Prospero's island is a thinly veiled allegory of the hero's inner struggle, as he attempts to come to terms with his banishment from Milan. Likewise, Leontes's jealousy, rather than being the occasion for the protagonist's destruction, as in *Othello*, becomes the occasion for his redemption. This redemption is depicted by the shift from winter to spring in the beautiful allegory of the fourth act.[52] Hermione's younger self Perdita is restored to life via the love of Prince Florizel, thereby providing the occasion for the redemption of Leontes and the restoration of Hermione. No similar redemption is possible for Shakespeare's tragic heroes, who are condemned to suffer the ritual agon for the centre that has defined tragedy from its beginning in ancient Greece. In the end this is the simplest definition one can give of Shakespeare's big men. They are condemned to suffer the sacrificial agon inherited from the ritual scene. Coriolanus's last action is to present himself self-consciously as a victim: "Cut me to pieces, Volsces. Men and lads, / Stain all your edges on me" (5.6.117–18). The sight of Shakespeare's most warlike and violent hero self-consciously embracing his sacrifice like a Christian martyr is, perhaps, too ironic to sustain the integrity of the tragic scene. Shakespeare's last big man is, at least in the final moments of the play, also his most contrived.[53]

Rossiter explains the contrived nature of the ending as Shakespeare's way of pointing out the reciprocity between centre and periphery that exists in the actual scenes of human history. Tragedy assumes the permanent asymmetry between centre and periphery, but history shows us that this asymmetry is constantly being undermined. I would certainly not disagree with Rossiter on this point, but I would modify it slightly by making explicit what remains implicit in his remarks. The reciprocity between centre and periphery that is to be found in *Coriolanus* reflects a general historical transformation taking place in the early modern era. This historical transformation is connected to an ethical transformation. The universally observed movement from compact ritual societies, in which exchange is centralized in ritual, towards the free market, which eschews centralization of any kind, leaves in its wake a vacuum.

This vacuum is filled by what we call high culture. Literature is the culture of the market because the market is the locus of cultural desacralization. The use of literature to explore the structure of human history is thus a modern phenomenon.[54] As many commentators have noted, the romantics were the first to take this idea seriously. They understood literature as an ethical discovery procedure. The significance of Shakespeare in the development of this idea needs no comment. The romantics turned to Shakespeare because they understood him to be the bearer of a new aesthetic, one that was richly responsive to the modern human predicament. Caught between, on the one hand, a scientific understanding of the world that ignored what was uniquely and characteristically human and, on the other, a theological understanding that was obsolete precisely because of the scientific world view, the romantics sought inspiration from literature and, in particular, from Shakespeare.

Today there are few romantics left. Harold Bloom is considered an aberration by most professional Shakespeareans. So is René Girard. At a time when so few believe in the romantic critical project, it is all too easy to dismiss these strong anthropological readers as bardolaters and monomaniacs. What is much harder to do is to replace their Shakespearean anthropologies with a Shakespeare equal to the task of human self-understanding. Before we dismiss Bloom or Girard as hopeless romantic bardolaters, we should ask ourselves what anthropological categories are assumed by our approaches to Shakespeare. Nor should we dismiss this task as merely idiosyncratic. On the contrary, at a time when the humanities have been invaded by pseudosciences of every stripe and colour, it is never more necessary.

In the final chapter of this book, I will examine more closely Girard's anthropological reading of Shakespeare. My main concern will be less with the details of Girard's analyses of the plays than with the basic anthropology underlying those analyses. It is one of the virtues of Girard's criticism that his readers are informed beforehand, in a clear and systematic fashion, of the basic anthropology underlying the many startling and original insights he finds in Shakespeare.

8 Coda: René Girard's Shakespeare

In what sense was Shakespeare an anthropologist? Harold Bloom credits Shakespeare with having "invented" the human.[1] This may be an overstatement. Anthropologists are supposed to study humans, not invent them. Of course, when Bloom says such things he is being deliberately belligerent. He presents himself as the last romantic, the last believer in the transcendence of art. As far as Bloom is concerned, Shakespeare provided us not merely with entertainment but also with ethical models for how to live the good life – good life here meaning above all an aesthetic life. "Shakespeare," Bloom writes, "teaches us how and what to perceive, and he also instructs us how and what to sense and then to experience as sensation."[2] Shakespeare teaches you how to see the world aesthetically.

The flip side to Bloom's unabashed romantic aestheticism is what Bloom calls "French Shakespeare," or the Shakespeare of the "school of resentment."[3] French Shakespeare is really a corollary of the romantic Shakespeare in which Bloom so fervently believes. For if Shakespeare did indeed invent the human, as Bloom claims, then presumably we can un-invent or deconstruct this invention by showing the ideological assumptions behind the idea of Shakespeare himself. This "hermeneutic of suspicion" has been the dominant mode of criticism for almost half a century. Michel Foucault argued in his 1966 *Les mots et les choses* that "man" is an invention of nineteenth-century anthropology.[4] The sooner we realize this, the better. It's not clear to me exactly what we are supposed to do after we have established the fact that man is a recent invention. Bloom clearly is happy with the idea. He just disagrees about who should be credited with the invention. It is not nineteenth-century anthropology that invented man but Shakespeare. Moreover, Bloom believes that since Shakespeare's intelligence vastly outmatches ours, we are better off accepting his version of humanity, at least for the time being. For all Bloom's romantic bombast, there is a certain humility in his belief that Shakespeare is the definitive anthropologist. But this humility before the aesthetic master (Shakespeare) is won at the cost of anthropology itself. Bloom's anthropological universe is a purely aesthetic one. You pay homage to the bard in the hope that some of his genius will rub off on you.

Like Bloom, René Girard believes in Shakespeare's transcendent status among literary authors. But unlike Bloom, Girard interprets Shakespeare's greatness in explicitly anthropological rather than purely aesthetic terms. Shakespeare is great not because he taught us how to perceive the world aesthetically, but because he discovered an otherwise nonobvious anthropological or sociological truth. If the social order is to survive, it needs to constrain the contagion of mimetic desire. So for Girard, Shakespeare is quite literally an anthropologist or sociologist. Presumably the only reason he didn't get his PhD in anthropology or some other related theoretical discipline, such as sociology, philosophy, or critical theory, was that these fields of study didn't exist in his day. Instead he was forced to make do with the medium he knew and loved best, which was the theatre.

The idea that Shakespeare was a keen student of human behaviour, a philosopher or anthropologist of sorts, is not new. But the more one emphasizes the idea that Shakespeare was a social theorist, the more tricky it becomes to explain the fact that he was also, quite obviously, a dramatist, an entertainer of the people. Bloom gets around this problem by making the strong romantic claim that human beings are fundamentally aesthetic creatures. Shakespeare teaches us how to perceive and feel. Hence for Bloom there is no contradiction between the two conceptions of Shakespeare. Dramatist and anthropologist are one. The two are the same because poetry defines – indeed creates – humanity. We are *homo aestheticus*, not *homo politicus*. As Bloom well knows, this stance puts him at odds with his anti-romantic contemporaries, which is precisely why Bloom's heroes don't go beyond the mid-twentieth-century Shakespeare critic Harold Goddard. Believers in *homo aestheticus* are a dying breed in the universities.

Still, at least Bloom has a tradition he can refer to, even if he is perceived as quaint and outmoded by the more advanced – postmodern – members of this tradition. In contrast, when Girard writes on Shakespeare, he appears to be writing in a vacuum. Let me quote from the introduction of his major work on Shakespeare, *A Theater of Envy*:

> My goal in this study is to show that the more quintessentially "mimetic" a critic becomes, the more faithful to Shakespeare he remains. To most people, no doubt, this reconciliation of practical and theoretical criticism seems impossible. This book is intended to demonstrate that they are wrong. All theories are not equal in regard to Shakespeare: his creation obeys the same mimetic principles I bring to bear upon his work, and it obeys them *explicitly* ... The mimetic approach solves the "problems" of many a so-called problem play. It generates new interpretations of *A Midsummer Night's Dream, Much Ado about Nothing, Julius Caesar, The Merchant of Venice, Twelfth Night, Troilus and Cressida, Hamlet, King Lear, The Winter's Tale*, and *The Tempest*. It reveals the dramatic unity of Shakespeare's theater and its thematic continuity. It discloses great variations in his personal perspective, a history of his oeuvre that points to his own personal history. Above all, the mimetic approach reveals an original thinker centuries ahead of his time, more modern than any of our so-called master thinkers.[5]

To the question, "Why do we need another book on Shakespeare?" Girard has a bulletproof reply: Because you've never seen a Shakespeare like this before.

But the persuasiveness of the reply really depends upon whether you accept the premise. Is Girard as original as he claims to be? What is to distinguish Girard's reading of Shakespeare from, for example, Francis Fergusson's reading of the ritual origins of Greek and Shakespearean tragedy, or John Holloway's remarks on the sacrificial origins of Shakespearean tragedy?[6] More generally, can't we see a connection between Girard's ideas about sacrifice and the work of James George Frazer or Émile Durkheim in the early twentieth century, both of whom were highly influential among critics of the early and mid-twentieth century? What about the ironic, late-romantic readings of Shakespeare by Wilson Knight or Harold Goddard? Finally, don't Girard's ideas about tragedy sound very similar to Kenneth Burke's?

But Girard's *Theater of Envy* is almost totally devoid of references to previous scholarship, and this has understandably upset Shakespeare specialists. Girard explicitly rejects the idea that he is just another "Shakespearean" humbly providing another interpretation to the ever-growing mountain of Shakespeare scholarship. *"Interpretation,"*

Girard writes, "is not the appropriate word for what I am doing. My task is more elementary. I am reading for the first time the letter of the text that has never been read on many subjects essential to dramatic literature: desire, conflict, violence, sacrifice."[7] Interpretation is an inadequate word for Girard because interpretation is what everybody else is doing. His task is, as he says, "more elementary."

When Girard says his task is more elementary, one is reminded of Durkheim's use of the word in the title of his magnum opus, *The Elementary Forms of Religious Life*. Girard's other key phrase, "for the first time," is also noteworthy. Girard is saying he is the *first* interpreter of Shakespeare to read him in this *elementary* fashion. Where others have merely interpreted Shakespeare in terms of the content of his works, Girard proposes to go beyond this content to explore the elementary anthropological conditions of the theatre itself. Girard proposes to trace literary content back to its elementary form in ritual sacrifice.

Let me briefly rehearse Girard's argument about the elementary structure of sacrifice. Sacrifice is necessary because desire is contagious. Desire, because it is always imitated from others, tends to get out of hand. If we all imitate each other, sooner or later a crisis of "undifferentiation" occurs, when all hands reach for the same object. To constrain the contagiousness of mimetic desire, it is necessary every now and again to punish those who seem to be responsible for it. It is not necessary that these victims really are the cause of the disorder. What is absolutely necessary, however, is that they are believed to be the cause. This "mimetic" account of desire leads Girard to his famous scapegoat hypothesis of culture outlined in his 1972 book, *La violence et le sacré*.[8]

With this simple theory Girard explains numerous puzzling facts in Shakespeare's plays. Consider, for example, his discussion of *The Two Gentlemen of Verona*. Proteus and Valentine are best friends. Proteus is in love with Julia, but he is torn between staying in Verona with Julia and following his best friend to Milan. Valentine goes to Milan and falls in love with Silvia. When Proteus decides to follow him there, he also falls in love with Silvia. Girard points out that Proteus, the more mimetic of the two friends, doesn't really have a choice. Valentine so praises Silvia that Proteus imitates his friend's desire and falls in love with the same woman. At the end Proteus tries to rape Silvia. She is saved only by the sudden appearance of Valentine, whose main concern seems to be that he has been betrayed by his best friend: "Oh, time most accurst, / 'Mongst all foes that a friend should be the worst!" (5.4.71–2). Proteus, embarrassed by his poor behaviour, begs forgiveness of his friend: "My shame and guilt confounds me. / Forgive me Valentine" (5.4.73–4). In a gesture that upsets audiences and critics alike, Valentine responds by offering Proteus the woman he (Proteus) has just attempted to rape: "And, that my love may appear plain and free, / All that was mine in Silvia I give thee" (5.4.82–3). Girard explains this apparently despicable action as a logical consequence of mimetic desire. Valentine feels guilty for having encouraged Proteus to desire Silvia in the first place. He realizes that he is partly responsible for what his friend has done. "The only peaceful solution," Girard says, "is to let the rival have the disputed object."[9] Girard reads this moment as a classic mimetic double bind. To remain friends, Proteus and Valentine must give up their rivalry *for the same object*. Valentine learns this more quickly than Proteus, which is why he is the first to give up Silvia. The important point, Girard says, is not that Valentine abandons Silvia to a would-be rapist, but that he abandons the rivalry of mimetic desire. By giving up the object, he gives up the rivalry. Luckily this spirit of renunciation is catching. Proteus refuses to accept Silvia. Instead he returns to the girl he originally loved, Julia. The play ends happily with Valentine marrying Silvia, and Proteus marrying Julia.

Girard's book is full of examples like this. Often the readings are quite brilliant. Highlights for me include his reading of *The Winter's Tale*, especially the final act in which Girard describes Leontes as a man tempted by the sight of Florizel and Perdita holding hands just as Polixenes and Hermione had sixteen years earlier. Will Leontes be able to withstand this second test of mimetic desire? Happily, sixteen years of repentance allow him to triumph over the temptation. He agrees to be a friend to Florizel without also falling in love with Florizel's fiancée, the beautiful Perdita, who is the mirror image of her mother, Hermione, the woman whom Leontes believes he has killed in a fit of jealous rage. As Girard says, "The entire past seems resurrected."[10] But this time there is a difference. Leontes does not make the same mistake the second time. Instead of treating Florizel as a rival, he treats him as a friend. The key lines for Girard occur when Leontes says to Florizel, "Your honor not o'erthrown by your desires, / I am friend to them and you" (5.1.230–1). Leontes has mastered his desire, and this is why he can be a friend to Florizel. Unlike his earlier self, or the Proteus of *The Two Gentlemen of Verona*, Leontes has renounced the object of mimetic desire.

I could easily cite more examples of Girard's reading of Shakespeare. But rather than simply repeat what Girard has said, I want to return to the question I began with. How does Girard justify his "mimetic" approach to Shakespeare? We have already seen that Girard claims that he is not simply offering another interpretation of Shakespeare. But if that is the case, then he can't justify himself by citing the self-evident plausibility of his reading of Shakespeare, because that would be to concede precisely what he finds objectionable: that is, the assumption that there is no way to go beyond the aesthetic. For many critics, of course, criticism is criticism of aesthetic texts, and that's the end of the matter. Critics differ on how much latitude they're willing to give to this idea of textuality. Bloom is a traditionalist because he restricts the text to Shakespeare, but many critics are willing to spread the wealth around a bit more. For this reason, I think it is wrong to read the new historicism as antithetical to aesthetic formalism. On the contrary, the new historicism is an attempt to expand the categories of aesthetic criticism beyond the canonical work to the surrounding cultural context. I think this is quite obvious, for instance, in the case of Stephen Greenblatt.[11]

Like the new historicists, Girard also claims that he is new. Implicit in this claim of newness is the sense that the aesthetic tradition has worn itself out and therefore needs renewing. Bloom's representation of contemporary cultural criticism as an exercise in resentment may be a caricature, but it has the virtue of identifying our general disenchantment with the aesthetic. Bloom compensates for this disenchantment by raising his voice and plugging his ears. He imagines himself transcending his contemporaries to take his rightful place in a tradition of criticism that stretches from Johnson and Hazlitt to Bradley, Wilson Knight, and Harold Goddard. Girard's claim to newness, however, is to present himself neither as the last romantic nor as a certified member of the disenchanted postmodern vanguard. Rather, his claim is that he is transcending the aesthetic tradition altogether. Shakespeare is great because he sees exactly what Girard sees: the futility of using art to conquer mimetic desire.

This conception of the aesthetic leads to a curious paradox. On the one hand, Shakespeare is a great dramatist who uncovers the mimetic structure of desire. On the other, he is a poor theorist because as a dramatist he is not at liberty to explain his theory in the straightforward logical fashion of a philosopher or anthropologist. Philosophers are not known for their capacity to earn a living by their writing alone. People are understandably unwilling to part with their hard-earned cash just to hear a philosopher lecture about the truth of his theory. Shakespeare's solution to this dilemma, Girard says, was to be fiendishly clever. Knowing that merely stating the principles of mimetic desire in sober, logical fashion is unlikely to satisfy the crowds, who are expecting something with a bit more gore, sensation, and slapstick, Shakespeare disguised the theory by cloaking it in good old-fashioned tragedy and comedy. In other words, he wrote two plays in one. The first version of the play was for the regular audience, who were looking for pure entertainment. The second, ironic version was for the philosophers, hoping for something more profound.

In principle there is nothing wrong with this "two-audience" theory to describe Shakespeare's method. You can strive to entertain everyone all the time, but if you wish to keep the attention of the more refined you will have to go beyond mere slapstick and gore. What is problematic in Girard's use of the two-audience theory, however, is his apocalyptic application of it to modernity. Consider, for example, this remark from his discussion of *Hamlet*. After commenting that Hamlet is caught in the double bind between revenge and no revenge, Girard goes on to generalize Hamlet's condition to all modernity:

> In *Hamlet*, the very absence of a case against revenge becomes a powerful intimation of what the modern world is really about. Even at those later stages in our culture when physical revenge and blood feuds completely disappeared or were limited to such marginal milieux as the underworld, it would seem that no revenge play, not even a play of reluctant revenge, could strike a really deep chord in the modern psyche. In reality the question is never entirely settled and the strange void at the center of *Hamlet* becomes a symbolic expression of the Western and modern malaise, no less powerful than the most brilliant attempts to define the problem, such as Dostoyevsky's underground revenge. Our "symptoms" always resemble that unnameable paralysis of will, that ineffable corruption of the spirit that affect[s] not only Hamlet, but the other characters as well. The devious ways of these characters, the bizarre plots they hatch, their passion for watching without being watched, their propensity to voyeurism and spying, the general disease of human relations make a good deal of sense as a description of an undifferentiated no man's land between revenge and no revenge in which we are still living.[12]

In his reading of Shakespeare, Girard remains blind to a key aspect of modernity: the capacity of its secular institutions to absorb resentment more effectively than its ritual precursors, including its precursors in Christian ritual. Girard tends to read modernity in a rather bleak either-or fashion. Either we must absorb the Christian lesson of forgiveness, or we must perish in a malaise of bad faith as we become increasingly disenchanted with the sacrificial institutions we no longer believe in but continue to use. The upshot is that the specifically aesthetic incarnations of modernity, in their various neoclassical, romantic, modernist, and postmodern guises, all get collapsed into one narrative of Christian demythologization.

Another way of putting this is to say that Girard subordinates his reading of literature to his reading of religion; in particular, to his reading of Christianity. The reason he can ignore the difference between classical, neoclassical, romantic, modernist, and postmodernist aesthetics is that next to Christianity, the difference between these aesthetic periods appears negligible. For Girard, the really significant difference, the one that trumps all others, is the difference between primitive religion and Judeo-Christianity. The role of literature in understanding this fundamental difference is at best ambivalent. Consider Girard's explanation of Shakespeare's turn to romance towards the end of the playwright's career. These last plays, especially *The Winter's Tale* and *The Tempest*, are (Girard says) resolutely self-undermining. *The Tempest* is an allegory of Shakespeare's career, beginning with Caliban who represents the monstrosity of mimetic desire, which Shakespeare had exploited to satisfy the audience's relentless appetite for mimetic violence. When Prospero breaks his staff and promises to leave off magic for good, this is Shakespeare's way of saying, "Enough already!" Tired of the mimetic games of the dramatist, Shakespeare announces his retirement. Presumably Shakespeare had learned his lesson; in particular, the lesson of the Gospels, in which forgiveness and love triumph over the violence and rivalry of mimetic desire. For Shakespeare, to continue to write drama would be merely bad faith.

I said just now that Girard doesn't really care about the difference between the various periods of literature because these seem insignificant when compared to the more fundamental anthropological problem of the origin of literature in sacrificial ritual. I think that the two-audience theory can help us unpack this problem. The theatre affords excellent opportunities for words to be supported by their actual flesh-and-blood contexts. This fact should not be underestimated. Despite what many philosophers believe, or used to believe, language is not primarily a means for communicating facts about the world. It is above all a means for producing what psychologists call "joint attention."[13] The most elementary form of language, the ostensive, is a pointing gesture. But what is worth pointing at? Girard believes it is the scapegoat, the first cultural and historical object of joint attention. But paradoxically he also insists that this form of attention is nonsymbolic. In *Things Hidden Since the Foundation of the World*, Girard writes, "I think that even the most elementary form of the victimage mechanism, prior to the emergence of the sign, should be seen as an exceptionally powerful means of creating a new degree of attention, the first non-instinctual attention."[14]

Here are the essential ingredients of sacrifice, all packed into a single primal scene. Again Girard stresses that he is looking at the most "elementary form" of culture, the very *first* moment of "non-instinctual attention." But there is a problem. The scapegoaters are both conscious and unconscious of what they are doing. They are conscious in the sense that this is a new moment of attention in which instinct has been superseded by something else, by a new type of attention that is therefore by definition the very first of its kind, unique in all human history. But they are also unconscious in the sense that this new type of attention is only a very minimal form of awareness. Girard really wants to say that they are in a state of semi-consciousness, a sort of liminal state between waking and sleeping where one is not really sure what one is doing. Perhaps noticing this ambivalence, Girard's interlocutor, Jean-Michel Oughourlian, asks a very good question: "Would this already be a sacred victim?" Girard responds:

> To the extent that the new type of attention is awakened, the victim will be imbued with the emotions provoked by the crisis and its resolution. The powerful experience crystallizes around the victim. As weak as it might be, the "consciousness" the participants have of the victim is linked structurally to the prodigious effects produced by its passage from life to death, by the spectacular and liberating reversal that has occurred at that instant. The double transference will determine the only possible meaning to take shape under the circumstances, and this will constitute the sacred and confer total responsibility for the event on the victim. It is necessary to conceive of stages, however, which were perhaps the longest in all human history, in which the signifying effects have still not truly taken shape. One would have to answer your question by saying that once the victim has appeared, however dimly, the process leading toward the sacred has begun, although concepts and representations are not yet part of it.
>
> There is no need to assume that the mechanism of awakening attention works right away; one can imagine that for a considerable period it produced nothing at all, or *next to nothing*. Nonetheless, even the most rudimentary signifying effects result from the necessity of controlling

> excessive mimesis; as soon as we grant that these effects can be in the slightest degree cumulative, we will have recognized them as forerunners of human culture.[15]

I don't think Girard has adequately answered Oughourlian's question. The key point is not the amount of violence in the scene, nor the tremendous contrast between violence and peace that Girard says the scene produces. Girard assumes that the sheer violence of the mimetic crisis is sufficient to generate an experience of the sacred. By bombarding your perceptual field with enough violence, you will eventually be compelled to see the sacred. But violence in itself is nothing new. On the contrary, nature is full of it. What is key is rather the *representation* of the violence and, more precisely, the *collective form of attention* that Girard says the violence leads to. For if the victim truly is to be represented as sacred, then this is already to say that the victim is an object of a collective attention, which is irreducible to the kind of indexical associations of purely individual perceptual experience.[16] Collective attention – symbolic representation – cannot originate unconsciously. On the contrary, the function it performs is by definition a conscious one – that is, to order and constrain the chaotic and largely unconscious associations of individual sensory experience. The joint scene of attention requires the individual not merely to attend to the object qua individual, but to attend to it as part of an intersubjective, collectively shared experience. In the scene of joint attention I attend to *your* attention to the object. And this relationship is reciprocal. Just as I attend to your attention to the object, so you attend to my attention to the object. Our relationship to the object is an instance of shared, collective attention, and this – the origin of joint attention – is indeed quite revolutionary in the history of hominid evolution. In the oscillation between other-model and central-object the word is born. This intersubjective oscillation is also what distinguishes the act of pointing from the indexical signals of animal communication. Animal signals remain unmediated by the intersubjective, joint attentional scene.

Girard's ambivalence towards the uniqueness of this originary event is reproduced in his ambivalence towards modernity and Shakespeare's place in it. Girard's paradoxical claim that the originary scene is both conscious and unconscious, both a unique event in human history and an intermediate stage in a series of endless intermediate stages, applies equally to his understanding of Shakespeare. On the one hand, Shakespeare is a vast intelligence who exposes ruthlessly and definitively the myth of romantic desire. On the other, Shakespeare is a dramatist who must hide this mimetic awareness behind the mythologizing narratives of tragic and comic form. Shakespeare has the potential to be a unique event in human history, but unfortunately the medium he selected for sharing his discovery of mimetic desire inevitably meant that his anthropological insights would be buried behind a wall of conventional theatrical pieties. If we read for the theatrical pieties, we will miss forever the mimetic intelligence. This is the fate of all Shakespeare criticism before Girard. If we read for the mimetic intelligence, we are forced to dispense with the theatre altogether, which is why Girard argues that Shakespeare's farewell to the stage in *The Tempest* is so critically self-referential. It is a deconstruction of the aesthetic myth of Shakespeare by Shakespeare himself.

So what can we learn from Girard's reading of Shakespeare? I think we can learn a great deal from Girard, but I have to add a significant caveat. Girard's ambivalence towards Shakespeare is a direct consequence of his ambivalence towards language. This is most clear in his hypothesis of the origin of sacrifice, which he sees as the fundamental cultural institution pre-existing even language itself. By claiming that the first act of scapegoating was unconscious and unrepresentable, Girard can say that all subsequent historical evidence that seems to contradict his hypothesis is merely a misrepresentation, a ruse distracting us from the reality of scapegoating. The technique of using the unconscious as a clever ruse has been made familiar to us by Freud. Because the unconscious is by definition elusive, it is always up to the one who is uniquely qualified in *sniffing it out* to let you know whether or not you have correctly identified the problem. The same rule applies to Girard's theory of the scapegoat. If you don't see how Shakespeare's plays demonstrate the scapegoating hypothesis, then you just have to look harder. And you do that by training yourself in the technique of Girard's peculiar brand of mimetic anthropology.

In the end, all claims to originality are by definition problematic. If you are the first to see things this way, then by definition nobody else does. But Girard's claim goes one step further. Not only is he the first, he is also the last. By making scapegoating unconscious, he absolves himself of the inconvenience of ever being refuted. For how can you refute something of which you are unconscious? Any refutation can be immediately dismissed as yet another confirmation of the unconscious at work. One has been hoodwinked yet again by the ruse of scapegoating.

What is the solution to this conundrum? The solution is to admit that scapegoating depends upon representation, and that representation itself cannot originate unconsciously. Once we have conceded this, it remains up to the individual to decide what elements to include in any particular formulation of the originary hypothesis. The real point of formulating such a hypothesis is not to be the first or the last, the most original or the most definitive. It is to provide a minimal starting point for dialogue on our fundamental humanity. That is the simplest way to define an anthropology. It is my hope that this book will be read in this sense: that is, as an attempt to initiate a dialogue concerning Shakespeare's contribution to human self-understanding – in other words, as a step towards a Shakespearean anthropology.

Notes

Preface

1 A.C. Bradley, *Shakespearean Tragedy: Lectures on "Hamlet," "Othello," "King Lear," "Macbeth"* (1904; repr., London: Penguin, 1991), 168.
2 Cary DiPietro, in *Bradley, Greg, Folger*, vol. 9 of *Great Shakespeareans* (London: Continuum, 2011), says that *Shakespearean Tragedy* "is arguably the most significant volume of Shakespeare criticism ever written" (8). In his review of *Great Shakespeareans*, B.J. Sokol, in "God's Plenty," *Shakespeare* 8 (2012), notes that Bradley "is not now highly regarded by many English Literature professionals, including Cary DiPietro whose essay on Bradley simply assumes that its readers will be complicit in an attitude of denigration" (349). Sokol is right to suggest that the denigration of Bradley is pretty much de rigueur for academic critics today.
3 Marshall Sahlins, "Poor Man, Rich Man, Big-Man, Chief: Political Types in Melanesia and Polynesia," *Comparative Studies in Society and History* 5, no. 3 (1963): 289.
4 The term is Michael Bristol's. I discuss Bristol's idea of "vernacular criticism" in chapter 1.

1. Why Shakespeare and Generative Anthropology?

1 This fact is rather dramatically illustrated by Laura Bohannan's, "Shakespeare in the Bush," which appeared in the August–September issue of *Natural History Magazine* in 1966. While conducting fieldwork among the Tiv in Africa, Bohannan was prompted by the chief of the village to tell the assembled villagers a story. She elected to tell the story of *Hamlet*, which she knew intimately. To her surprise, she discovered that the Tiv seemed familiar

with many aspects of the story. For example, upon hearing that Hamlet's "village" had been visited by a "dead man," the Tiv immediately declared that this was an omen sent by a witch. Furthermore, they were unsurprised to hear that Hamlet went mad, because "only witchcraft can make one mad." Interestingly, Bohannan's account is often interpreted as evidence of the untranslatable cultural differences between the Tiv and the West. For example, the Tiv had no problem with Claudius marrying Gertrude, since among the Tiv this is precisely what younger brothers do when their older brothers die prematurely. Who else will look after the dead brother's children? What seems more remarkable to me, however, is that these differences, while certainly not irrelevant, are no barrier to understanding the story. The Tiv had no difficulty grasping that the ghost was a bad omen for Hamlet. Indeed, seeing the story from the point of view of the Tiv perhaps makes us appreciate a little better why Shakespeare set the story in the more obviously primitive world of ancient Denmark, where primogeniture was not a given, rather than Elizabethan England, where it was. I agree with Naomi Conn Liebler, who says that it is a mistake to interpret Bohannan's story as "'proof' that Shakespeare can be understood only by a Western audience." Liebler's reference to Bohannan can be found in her pathbreaking *Shakespeare's Festive Tragedy: The Ritual Foundations of Genre* (New York: Routledge, 1995), 5–6.

2 Kiernan Ryan in his discussion of *The Merchant of Venice*, in *Shakespeare*, 3rd ed. (Basingstoke, UK: Palgrave, 2002), makes much the same point about the poverty of reducing the aesthetic text to the status of a historical document: "Few things are less riveting than mountains of meticulous research documenting the parallels or incongruities between some sphere of Elizabethan reality and Shakespeare's depiction of it in his drama. Unearthing and wheeling forth stacks of scholarship on the situation of Jews or women, on the law, or on usury in late sixteenth-century England doubtless has countless merits, but equipping us to gauge the effect of their metamorphosis into *The Merchant of Venice* rarely proves to be one of them" (25). Ryan's reservations echo what Patrick Murray said about the more extreme versions of historicism many years previously, in *The Shakespearian Scene: Some Twentieth-Century Perspectives* (London: Longmans, 1969): "The major reason why people are still interested in [Shakespeare's] plays is surely not that he is a great spokesman for Elizabethan commonplaces but that on the contrary he transcends the limitations of his age and is different from his fellows" (152). Few scholars today would defend Shakespeare's canonical significance so baldly. On the contrary, once you evacuate the aesthetic text of transcendence, there is no reason to elevate Shakespeare over the historical texts of his context.

3 Paul Kottman, in "Why Think about Shakespearean Tragedy Today?" in *The Cambridge Companion to Shakespearean Tragedy* (Cambridge: Cambridge University Press, 2013), puts the point well when he says that "the anxiety provoked by the disappearance of traditional justifications for the humanities has led humanists to retreat into quasi-scientific approaches that would allow us to amass truths about or around artworks" (240). Eschewing quasi-scientific or historicist approaches, Kottman instead takes his cue from the romantics and argues that Shakespearean tragedy is central for us today precisely because it addresses ethical questions that "scientific knowledge or theological tenets cannot fully decide" (241). Kottman's broadly romantic-anthropological approach to Shakespeare is, I think, wholly compatible with the generative-anthropological approach adopted in this book. In a penetrating analysis, Raymond Tallis, in *Aping Mankind: Neuromania, Darwinitis and the Misrepresentation of Humanity* (Durham, UK: Acumen, 2011), explores the philosophical and anthropological fallacies committed by the scientistic view that the human can be explained by reducing it to the ontology of the natural sciences.

4 Ernest Gellner, *Thought and Change* (Chicago: University of Chicago Press, 1964), 203. Here is the full paragraph: "Humanist thought is cognitively feeble. This is a crucial feature of it: the views of nature and society formulated in its terms are neither clear nor powerful nor universally convincing. They symbolise an allegiance more often than they apprehend a fact, and they provide an accompaniment for an activity more often than they really capture its principles. They do not provide a basis for effective manipulation of things, nor do they command general assent outside the social context in which they arose or gained popularity. This feature is clearly connected – though not in any simple way – with the three preceding ones: with the moral saturation, the practical effectiveness, and the human warmth and relevance of its concepts" (203–4).

5 Ernest Gellner, *Conditions of Liberty: Civil Society and Its Rivals* (New York: Penguin Books, 1994), 95.

6 Harold Bloom, *Shakespeare: The Invention of the Human* (New York: Riverhead Books, 1998).

7 Edward Pechter, *Shakespeare Studies Today: Romanticism Lost* (New York: Palgrave MacMillan, 2011), 23.

8 See, for example, the final sentence of *Shakespeare Studies Today*: "I should make it unequivocally clear now at the end of things that when the Introduction dismissed as naive the idea that the truth about Romantic Shakespeare would set us free, I was not abandoning the hope, however quixotic, that readers of *Romanticism Lost* might want to start working more

like Hazlitt and less like Bourdieu, and that I was not relinquishing the conviction that if they did so, the world, or that small and sequestered part of the world we call Shakespeare studies, would be a better place" (206).

9 See Edward Pechter, *Othello and Interpretive Traditions* (Iowa City: University of Iowa Press, 1999), especially chapter 4.

10 "Passionate engagement" is Pechter's phrase, which he uses to describe Greenblatt's desire, asserted at the beginning of *Hamlet in Purgatory*, to capture the "magical intensity" and "literary power" of *Hamlet*. Pechter also references Said's 1999 Presidential Address to the MLA ("An Unresolved Paradox"), and Fish's 2008 opinion piece for the *New York Times*, "French Theory in America, Part Two." See Pechter, *Shakespeare Studies Today*, 4–5, 26. On the face of it, these critics-turned-theorists may strike one as unlikely allies for Pechter. Didn't theory usurp the literary object as the privileged focus of attention in departments of literature in the 1980s? As the main figure of the new historicism, Greenblatt's case is particularly instructive. New historicism arose as a practical implementation of Jacques Derrida's notion of culture-as-text. What, since then, has prompted Greenblatt to return to a narrower and more exclusively "literary" idea of textuality? Interestingly, Fish, a stalwart supporter of Derrida's ideas in the 1970s and 1980s, provides the following back-cover blurb praising Pechter's book: "Pechter's story of how the discipline of literary studies has undermined the rationale for its existence by allowing its object to disappear in the solvent of historicist and materialist criticism is at once learned and sadly funny." Evidently, Fish now feels ambivalent about what theory has done to literature in the long run. High theory was okay, but "low" theory, in the form of countless new historicist and materialist readings of literature, is not. Pechter himself does not explain why these theorists have backtracked from their former positions. No doubt he would simply put it down to the mystery of the "contrariety" of human desire. But the mystery disappears when one understands theory as an attempt to wring the last dregs of sacrality from an institution that no longer commands the centrality it once did. The modernists were the last to believe, albeit in deliberately scandalizing and obtuse terms, in the transcendence of literature.

11 Richard C. McCoy, *Faith in Shakespeare* (Oxford: Oxford University Press, 2013), xii.

12 Ibid.

13 Ibid., 15.

14 Bristol, "Macbeth the Philosopher: Rethinking Context," *New Literary History* 42 (2011): 643–4.

15 Ibid., 644.

16 Ibid.
17 Michael Bristol, "Vernacular Criticism and the Scenes Shakespeare Never Wrote," in *Shakespeare Survey 53*, ed. Peter Holland (Cambridge: Cambridge University Press, 2000), 89–102.
18 Bristol, "Macbeth the Philosopher," 657.
19 Margreta de Grazia, *"Hamlet" without Hamlet* (Cambridge: Cambridge University Press, 2007).
20 Ibid., 163.
21 Mike Martin, *Self-Deception and Morality* (Lawrence: University of Kansas Press, 1986), 20.
22 Bristol, "Vernacular Criticism," 94.
23 Ibid.
24 Ibid.
25 Harry Berger Jr, *Making Trifles of Terrors: Redistributing Complicity in Shakespeare* (Stanford, CA: Stanford University Press, 1997).
26 See, for example, William Kerrigan, *Hamlet's Perfection* (Baltimore: Johns Hopkins University Press, 1994); John J. Joughin, ed., *Philosophical Shakespeares* (London: Routledge, 2000); Christy Desmet and Robert Sawyer, eds., *Harold Bloom's Shakespeare* (New York: Palgrave, 2001); Leon Harold Craig, *Of Philosophers and Kings: Political Philosophy in Shakespeare's "Macbeth" and "King Lear"* (Toronto: University of Toronto Press, 2001); Colin McGinn, *Shakespeare's Philosophy* (New York: HarperCollins Publishers, 2006); Tzachi Zamir, *Double Vision: Moral Philosophy and Shakespearean Drama* (Princeton: Princeton University Press, 2007); A.D. Nuttall, *Shakespeare the Thinker* (New Haven, CT: Yale University Press, 2007); Paul A. Kottman, *Tragic Conditions in Shakespeare: Disinheriting the Globe* (Baltimore: Johns Hopkins University Press, 2009); and Michael Bristol, ed., *Shakespeare and Moral Agency* (London and New York: Continuum, 2010).
27 Pechter, *Shakespeare Studies Today*, 1.

2. The Originary Hypothesis: Hierarchy, Resentment, and Tragedy

1 See, in particular, Eric Gans, *The End of Culture: Toward a Generative Anthropology* (Berkeley, CA: University of California Press, 1985); *Originary Thinking: Elements of Generative Anthropology* (Stanford, CA: Stanford University Press, 1993); and *Signs of Paradox: Irony, Resentment, and Other Mimetic Structures* (Stanford, CA: Stanford University Press, 1997). For a useful brief introduction to Gans's work, see Wolfgang Iser, "Anthropological Theory: Gans," in *How to Do Theory* (Oxford: Blackwell, 2006). A number of literary scholars have found Gans's ideas useful for the analysis of literature

and aesthetic history. See, for example, Ian Dennis, *Lord Byron and the History of Desire* (Newark: University of Delaware Press, 2009); Andrew Bartlett, *Mad Scientist, Impossible Human: An Essay in Generative Anthropology* (Aurora, CO: Davies Group Publishers, 2014); and the essays collected in Adam Katz, ed., *The Originary Hypothesis: A Minimal Proposal for Humanistic Inquiry* (Aurora, CO: Davies Group Publishers, 2007).

2 Ernest Gellner, *Plough, Sword and Book: The Structure of Human History* (Chicago: University of Chicago Press, 1989), 57.

3 Terrence Deacon, *The Symbolic Species: The Co-evolution of Language and the Brain* (New York: W.W. Norton, 1997). I take up Deacon's distinction between index and symbol in "Cognitive Science and the Problem of Representation," *Poetics Today* 24 (2003): 237–95, reprinted in *The End of Literature: Essays in Anthropological Aesthetics* (Aurora, CO: Davies Group Publishers, 2009). See also my "Stories, Jokes, Desire, and Interdiction: The Cognitive and Anthropological Origins of Symbolic Representation," *Fictions: Studi sulla narrativitià* 11 (2012): 91–113.

4 See Gellner, *Plough, Sword and Book*; and *Anthropology and Politics: Revolutions in the Sacred Grove* (Oxford: Blackwell, 1995).

5 Gellner, *Anthropology and Politics*, 48.

6 See Eric Gans, "Differences," *Modern Language Notes* 96 (1981): 792–808; and, especially, chapter 2 of *Signs of Paradox*.

7 Gellner, in *Plough, Sword and Book*, explains why the implementation of the moral model in the economic sphere required a double liberation of first the individual (in the form of Protestantism or moral egalitarianism) and then nature (in the form of science and technology). Without the first, the second would not be possible. On the close relationship between personal authenticity and the mass market for consumer goods, see Charles Lindholm, *Culture and Authenticity* (Oxford: Blackwell, 2008), especially chapter 4.

8 See, for example, Elizabeth A. Cashdan, "Egalitarianism among Hunters and Gatherers," *American Anthropologist* 82 (1980): 116–20; James Woodburn, "Egalitarian Societies," *Man* 17 (1982): 431–51; Richard B. Lee, *The Dobe !Kung* (New York: Holt, Rinehart and Winston, 1979); and Frank W. Marlowe, *The Hadza: Hunter-Gatherers of Tanzania* (Berkeley: University of California Press, 2010).

9 Richard Lee, in *The Dobe !Kung*, documents the practice of "insulting the meat." Hunters aggressively denigrate the hunting abilities of their peers to make sure no man believes himself to be better than his fellows: "Insulting the meat is one of the central practices of the !Kung that serve to maintain egalitarianism. Even though some men are much better hunters than others, their behavior is molded by the group to minimize

the tendency toward self-praise and to channel their energies into socially beneficial activities. As a result, the existence of differences in hunting prowess does not lead to a system of Big Men, in which a few talented individuals tower over others in terms of prestige" (50–1).

10 Gans, *The End of Culture*, 154.

11 James Woodburn, in "Egalitarian Societies," usefully distinguishes between aggressively egalitarian "immediate-return" and incipiently hierarchical "delayed-return" systems of economic distribution. The delayed-return system is equivalent to the big man's usurpation of the ritual centre; in appropriating the centre for himself, he "delays" his desire for immediate personal consumption.

12 Gans, *The End of Culture*, 158.

13 In a provocative discussion of Nietzsche's analysis of resentment, Mark Migotti, in "Slave Morality, Socrates, and the Bushmen: A Reading of the First Essay of *On the Genealogy of Morals*," *Philosophy and Phenomenological Research* 58, no. 4 (1998): 745–79, argues that there is some empirical evidence for Nietzsche's claim that the abstract (Christian) idea of morality depends upon a "slave revolt" against the big-man hierarchies of a pre-existing warrior culture. Migotti also asserts that reference to egalitarian hunter-gatherer societies does not constitute a knockdown argument against Nietzsche because in these societies resentment is purged via the ritual practice of ridiculing any pretensions to social superiority, as in the famous "joking relations" among the Bushmen. I will consider Nietzsche's anthropology and his analysis of resentment in my discussion of *Coriolanus* in chapter 7.

14 René Girard, *Violence and the Sacred* (Baltimore: Johns Hopkins University Press, 1977).

15 Simon Simonse, *Kings of Disaster: Dualism, Centralism and the Scapegoat King in Southeastern Sudan* (Leiden: E.J. Brill: 1992).

16 Gans, *Originary Thinking*, 127.

17 Ibid., 132.

18 See Marshall Sahlins, *Stone Age Economics* (Chicago: Aldine-Atherton, 1972); and "Poor Man, Rich Man, Big-Man, Chief: Political Types in Melanesia and Polynesia," *Comparative Studies in Society and History* 5, no. 3 (1963): 285–303. See also Charles Lindholm's study of envy among the Puktun tribal people in the Swat valley of Northwest Pakistan, "Culture and Envy," in *Envy: Theory and Research*, ed. Richard H. Smith (Oxford: Oxford University Press, 2008), 227–44.

19 Girard, *Violence and the Sacred*.

20 René Girard, *A Theater of Envy: William Shakespeare* (Oxford: Oxford University Press, 1991), 185.

21 In their introduction to a collection of papers by social scientists on the theme of envy, Richard H. Smith and Sung Hee Kim contrast the "benign envy" generated by the continually expanding consumer economy with the impotent and therefore "malicious" envy of more rigidly stratified societies. See Richard H. Smith and Sung Hee Kim, introduction to *Envy: Theory and Research*, ed. Richard H. Smith (Oxford: Oxford University Press, 2008), 3.
22 Gans, *Originary Thinking*, 21.
23 For an illuminating analysis of traditional and modern succession patterns in human society, see Robbins Burling, *The Passage of Power: Studies in Political Succession* (New York: Academic Press, 1974).
24 Gans, *Originary Thinking*, 133.
25 Ibid., 25, 126, 144, 184.
26 Ibid., 151. Gans uses the term "neoclassical" to distinguish classical art from medieval and Renaissance art. For Gans, the salient historical distinction is not given by the content of the artwork, but by the ethical context in which the art is produced. In this sense, what distinguishes classical art from all post-classical art in the West is Christianity.

3. Brutus's Neoclassical Irony

1 As Benoît Dubreuil observes, "Envy is an emotion that is difficult to study empirically. Being envious is not something with which most of us are comfortable. When we experience envy, we often transmute it into indignation and self-righteousness." Dubreuil is discussing the results of experimental economists who dispute the assumptions of rational choice theory. In experiments such as "public goods games," players are given a sum of money, a portion of which may be donated to a public good. Donations will be doubled by the experimenter and then fed back into the general pool. What the experimenters found is that cooperation tends to break down after a few rounds. However, if the players are given the opportunity to punish defectors, then the fund of public good can be sustained. Dubreuil suggests that punishment is not simply motivated by a desire for equality or equity. Envy at having less than others is also a key emotion. Indeed, it is very difficult to separate the two because players will always claim that their motivations are much nobler than they really are: "Punishers might conceive their decision as motivated by equity at the same time that their standard of equity is biased and rooted in contextual envy and spite." See Benoît Dubreuil, *Human Evolution and the Origins of Hierarchies: The State of Nature* (Cambridge: Cambridge University Press, 2010), 16.

2 Leslie H. Farber, "Faces of Envy," in *Lying, Despair, Jealousy, Envy, Sex, Suicide, Drugs, and the Good Life* (New York: Basic Books, 1976), 36. Helmut Schoeck, in *Envy: A Theory of Social Behavior* (Indianapolis, IN: Liberty Press, 1966), makes much the same point.
3 Harry Frankfurt, *On Bullshit* (Princeton: Princeton University Press, 2005).
4 Ibid., 54.
5 For the conflict between correspondence to the facts and correspondence to the priest, see Gellner, *Plough, Sword and Book: The Structure of Human History* (Chicago: University of Chicago Press, 1989), 39–49. Gellner's criticism of philosophy is that it is too wedded to the idea that our concepts are "operationalized" by reference to nature. As Durkheim understood, our concepts are constrained in the first place by society. Only much later are our concepts operationalized by scientific method. Gellner's point is that this is a very late and historically peculiar development. Failure to put "reference to the facts" into this anthropological context leads to all kinds of dead ends in philosophy.
6 According to research conducted by Robin Dunbar, people spend fully two-thirds of their time talking about social topics: personal relationships, their personal likes and dislikes, the behaviour of others, and so on. No other topic dominated more than 10 per cent of conversations. All other topics – including sports, leisure, politics, and work – made up just one-third of conversations. See Robin Dunbar, *Grooming, Gossip, and the Evolution of Language* (Cambridge, MA: Harvard University Press, 1996), 123. Dunbar's larger argument is that language is the way humans keep tabs on one another. The origin of language frees human societies from the constraints of primate societies, which must spend many hours cementing social relationships by laborious one-on-one grooming. Obviously, gossip is a far more efficient strategy. What is interesting about Dunbar's work is that unlike most scientists, who generally share the philosopher's obsession with reference and truth conditions, he ties the problem of language origin to the problem of social organization.
7 See, in particular, John Vyvyan, *The Shakespearean Ethic* (London: Chatto & Windus, 1959). Other critics who have emphasized the allegorical dimension include Roy W. Battenhouse, *Shakespearean Tragedy: Its Art and Its Christian Premises* (Bloomington: University of Indiana Press, 1969); Cherrell Guilfoyle, *Shakespeare's Play within Play: Medieval Imagery and Scenic Form in "Hamlet," "Othello," and "King Lear"* (Kalamazoo, MI: Medieval Institute Publications, 1990); Irving Ribner, *Patterns in Shakespearean Tragedy* (New York: Barnes & Noble, 1960); and Bernard Spivak, *Shakespeare and the Allegory of Evil: The History of a Metaphor in*

Relation to His Major Villains (New York: Columbia University Press, 1958). However, I find Vyvyan's treatment of allegory much more sensitive to the aesthetic context of Shakespeare's plays, and this means that he cannot be accused of reducing Shakespeare to his medieval precursors. For the latter critique of allegorical criticism, see Howard Felperin, *Shakespearean Representation: Mimesis and Modernity in Elizabethan Tragedy* (Princeton: Princeton University Press, 1977).

8 René Girard, *A Theater of Envy: William Shakespeare* (Oxford: Oxford University Press, 1991).

9 Vyvyan, *The Shakespearean Ethic*, 22.

10 Girard, *A Theater of Envy*, 213–14.

11 Ibid., 223.

12 Ibid., 216.

13 Kenneth Burke, *Kenneth Burke on Shakespeare*, ed. Scott Newstok (West Lafayette, IN: Parlor Press, 2007), 41.

14 Battenhouse, *Shakespearean Tragedy*, 260.

15 Harold Bloom, introduction to *William Shakespeare: The Tragedies*, ed. Harold Bloom (New York: Chelsea House Publishers, 1985), 5.

16 I mean this as a metaphor of course. Brutus does not literally sleepwalk, as Lady Macbeth does. But the comparison is worth noting. Lady Macbeth's guilt is unconscious and only shows itself in her sleep; Brutus's guilt hardly shows itself at all, but we know that he does not sleep well and he does briefly see Caesar's ghost, though he does not know what to make of it.

17 Geoffrey Miles, in *Shakespeare and the Constant Romans* (Oxford: Oxford University Press, 1996), observes that this is a habit of the characters in Shakespeare's Roman plays: they seek to emulate a heroic public self-conception that is often at odds with their much less heroic inner selves. Shakespeare, Miles argues, makes much of this gap between the public and private self, showing how frequently the characters end up betraying themselves in their attempt to emulate the heroic ideal, an ideal that Miles traces back to Stoicism. Miles makes much the same point about Caesar that I am making about Brutus when he usurps the centre: "When Caesar announces what 'Caesar' thinks, he is not expressing his personal feelings but issuing a press statement about a public figure. His shifts in 2.2 between the third person ('Caesar shall forth') and first person ('I will stay at home') suggest his wavering between the vulnerable human being and the immutable public Caesar" (142).

18 Michael Long, *The Unnatural Scene: A Study of Shakespearean Tragedy* (London: Methuen, 1976), 30. Long's larger argument is that Shakespeare's "derisive" irony makes him "a more and not a less humane

mind" (103) and that it is "essential" to understanding Shakespeare's "tragic vision" (122); the latter depends as much on an uncompromising comic intelligence as it does on a "determined compassion" for the tragic hero (122).

19 A.P. Rossiter, *Angel with Horns and Other Shakespeare Lectures*, ed. Graham Storey (London: Longmans, 1961), 238–9.

20 Ibid., 267.

21 A.C. Bradley, *Shakespearean Tragedy: Lectures on "Hamlet," "Othello," "King Lear," "Macbeth"* (1904; repr., London: Penguin, 1991), 168.

4. Hamlet's Filthy Imagination

1 Kenneth Burke, *Kenneth Burke on Shakespeare*, ed. Scott Newstok (West Lafayette, IN: Parlor Press, 2007), 40

2 Eric Gans, *Originary Thinking: Elements of Generative Anthropology* (Stanford, CA: Stanford University Press, 1993), 132–49. I summarize Gans's idea of aesthetic history at the end of chapter 2.

3 For example, John Dover Wilson, in *What Happens in "Hamlet,"* 3rd ed. (Cambridge: Cambridge University Press, 1951), argues that Claudius speaks "glibly" and "in rather embarrassed fashion" and that this is a clue that "something is amiss here," notably, that Claudius has usurped Hamlet's rightful place on the throne (31); L.C. Knights, in *An Approach to "Hamlet"* (Stanford, CA: Stanford University Press, 1961), writes that Claudius's speech has "the tone and accent of Milton's Belial; we need know nothing of Claudius's previous activities to react to those unctuous verse rhythms with some such comment as 'Slimy beast!'" (41–2); Madeleine Doran, in "The Language of *Hamlet,*" *Huntington Library Quarterly* 27, no. 3 (1964): 259–78, claims that Claudius is here seeking to make "acceptable … an action about which there might be some serious questions" and that the "strain is evident in the grotesque image of 'with an auspicious and a dropping eye'" (265); James I. Wimsatt, in "The Player King on Friendship," *Modern Language Review* 65, no. 1 (1970): 1–6, remarks that Claudius is seeking to imitate "Dame Fortune, who arbitrarily gives and takes away" (4); and R. Clifton Spargo, in *The Ethics of Mourning: Grief and Responsibility in Elegiac Literature* (Baltimore: Johns Hopkins University Press, 2004), states that Claudius "belittles the remembrance of the dead" by speaking with "oxymoronic flair and self-consciously apologetic language" (57).

4 G. Wilson Knight, *The Wheel of Fire: Interpretations of Shakespearian Tragedy* (1930; repr., London: Routledge Classics, 2001), 17–49.

5 As Dover Wilson points out, Hamlet takes care to explain to Claudius that the murderer Lucianus is *nephew* to the king. See Wilson, *What Happens in "Hamlet,"* 192.

6 Hamlet's headcount includes Polonius (stabbed), Ophelia (driven mad by Hamlet's actions), Rosencrantz and Guildenstern (by direct order), Laertes (stabbed by the poisoned sword), and Claudius (stabbed and poisoned). Claudius's includes Gertrude (who drank from the cup poisoned by the king) and Hamlet (who died from the poisoned sword Claudius had conspired to put in Laertes's hands).

7 This situation is slightly implausible, so John Updike, in his novel *Gertrude and Claudius* (New York: Ballantine Books, 2000), quite reasonably supposes that the affair has been going on for some time. Updike nonetheless stresses Claudius's great patience. He falls in love with Gertrude at his brother's wedding, and out of sheer decency spends his time as a mercenary in the Mediterranean trying to put her out of his head. Only much later does he finally give in and initiate an affair with Gertrude, who by this time is perfectly willing to reciprocate. Evidently the axe-wielding older brother lacks the romantic charm Gertrude finds in the rather more subtle and therefore exotic younger brother.

8 John Vyvyan, *The Shakespearean Ethic* (London: Chatto & Windus, 1959), 45.

9 Ibid., 45.

10 René Girard, *A Theater of Envy: William Shakespeare* (Oxford: Oxford University Press, 1991), 274–6.

11 Ibid., 286–9.

12 T.S. Eliot, *Selected Essays*, 2nd ed. (London: Faber and Faber, 1934), 145.

13 Ibid., 143.

14 For example, Roy W. Battenhouse, in *Shakespearean Tragedy: Its Art and Its Christian Premises* (Bloomington: Indiana University Press, 1969), agrees with T.S. Eliot that Hamlet's response is disproportionate to his mother's supposed crime (overhasty remarriage with the brother), but he disagrees with Eliot that this makes the play a failure. Could not the disproportionate response be indicative of a problem with Hamlet rather than Shakespeare? "Hamlet's responses," Battenhouse writes, "ought to be explained, not by supposing the play a failure, or by claiming that external events force a melancholy on the hero, or by hypothesizing a psychosis which eliminates responsibility, but rather by discerning the vice of soul which underlies Hamlet's encounter with his world" (224). Likewise, Howard Felperin, in *Shakespearean Representation: Mimesis and Modernity in Elizabethan Tragedy* (Princeton: Princeton University Press, 1977), argues that Eliot is right to see "the simultaneous resemblance and discrepancy

between the play and its older models" (60), but wrong to argue that this constitutes a failure. On the contrary, this ironic discrepancy between Hamlet's motive for action and his archaic models is precisely what constitutes, for Felperin, Shakespeare's modernity, his ironic *difference* from his sources. I am sympathetic to both these authors' viewpoints, especially Felperin's, but neither of these authors makes the next step towards a minimal anthropology. Battenhouse grounds his reading in Augustinian theology, while Felperin opts for Paul de Man's deanthropologized account of language. Thus Felperin criticizes Battenhouse for his reliance on a *restricted* allegorical mode of reading explicit in Shakespeare's source texts. But Shakespearean representation, Felperin maintains, is characterized by an *open* economy between sign and referent. It therefore follows that we cannot reduce Shakespeare to the restricted mode of reading. All this makes good sense, but without an account of the anthropological origin of the open economy of the aesthetic, Felperin risks making *all* language aesthetic. He thus leaves himself open to the criticism that his reading of Shakespeare is radically ahistorical. If all tragedy paradoxically refers both to itself and its source texts, what did the *first* tragedy refer to? More precisely, what did the first aesthetic sign refer to? The paradox of representation that Felperin associates with literature finds its minimal origin not in Shakespeare, or indeed Homer (to whom Felperin devotes his first chapter), but in an anthropological hypothesis for the origin of language.

15 Eliot, *Selected Essays*, 145.

16 Robert C. Solomon, in *The Passions* (Garden City, NY: Anchor Press / Doubleday: 1976), points out that the emotions frequently *determine* their objects. I am angry after a lousy day at work, so I come home looking for something to be angry at. Of course, I find it. I yell at my son for leaving his muddy shoes in the hallway. Solomon calls this "Verdict first; evidence afterward" (405). One can fruitfully compare Solomon's idea of the emotions preceding and creating their objects with Eliot's criticism that Hamlet lacks an objective correlative. On the contrary, Solomon would say, Hamlet creates his objective correlative. He is resentful, so he attacks his mother. Verdict first; evidence afterwards. Solomon adds that reflection offers the possibility of "seeing through" our more destructive emotions. But he cautions that reflection can also contribute, indeed amplify, the destructiveness of the emotions: for example, via self-deception or rationalization. But overall, he does offer a "therapy of reflection": "resentment understood is already resentment undermined" (415).

17 See Ernest Gellner, *Plough, Sword and Book: The Structure of Human History* (Chicago: University of Chicago Press, 1989).

18 James Calderwood, *To Be and Not to Be: Negation and Metadrama in "Hamlet"* (New York: Columbia University Press, 1983), xi–xii.
19 William Empson, in *Essays on Shakespeare*, ed. David B. Pirie (Cambridge: Cambridge University Press, 1986), puts this problem at the centre of *Hamlet*. Shakespeare solved the problem of how a tired old revenge play could be successfully revived by making this problem the very theme of the play. Hence Hamlet's self-consciousness about revenge.
20 Knight, *The Wheel of Fire*, 35.
21 It is surely no accident that Shakespeare gives Hamlet a speech about "some vicious mole of nature" (1.4.24) "breaking down the pales and forts of reason" (1.4.28) just prior to the ghost's second appearance. Like Brutus's reflections on young ambition's ladder, Hamlet's speech on the evil of Claudius's drinking is really a reflection of the protagonist's resentment. The ghost reflects Hamlet's overthrow by resentment.
22 W.W. Greg, "Hamlet's Hallucination," *Modern Language Review* 12 (1917): 393–421.
23 Johann Wolfgang von Goethe, *Wilhelm Meister's Apprenticeship*, trans. Thomas Carlyle (London: Francis Nicolls & Co., 1901). Carlyle's translation was first published in 1824. The first German edition was published in 1795.
24 Ibid., 1:302–3.
25 Ibid., 1:304.
26 A.C. Bradley, *Shakespearean Tragedy: Lectures on "Hamlet," "Othello," "King Lear," "Macbeth"* (1904; repr., London: Penguin Books, 1991), 104.
27 Ibid., 103
28 Ibid., 118.
29 Lionel Trilling, in *Sincerity and Authenticity* (Cambridge, MA: Harvard University Press, 1971), cites *Hamlet* as a key moment in the origin of sincerity. Trilling defines sincerity as the "congruence between an avowal and actual feeling" (2) and begins his account of its history by acknowledging that it is hard for us to reconcile Polonius's words – "to thine own self be true" – with this otherwise dull and unremarkable character. The words strike us as a revelation of the sincere self, but Polonius is not given to original or transcendent thought. So we say that "Polonius has had a moment of self-transcendence, of grace and truth. He has conceived of sincerity as an essential condition of virtue and has discovered how it is to be attained" (3). In contrast we have no difficulty identifying with Hamlet's sincerity: "The extent to which *Hamlet* is suffused by the theme of sincerity is part of everyone's understanding of the play. It is definitive of Hamlet himself that in his first full speech he affirms his sincerity, saying that he

knows not 'seems': there is indeed a discrepancy between his avowal of feeling over his father's death and what he actually feels, but it is not the one which, as he chooses to think, his mother is attributing to him – he feels not less but more than he avows, he has that within which passes show" (3–4). As Trilling notes, Hamlet's sincerity is apparent precisely because he feels divorced from his true self. This is the paradox of sincerity; we all wish to appear sincere, but as the public apologies of disgraced celebrities show, the public performance of an apology is by definition insincere.

30 Bradley, *Shakespearean Tragedy*, 118 n. 3.

31 Ibid.

32 Gans, *Originary Thinking*, 118.

33 Ibid., 167.

34 Dover Wilson's insistence that Shakespeare's ghost is an exercise in contemporary Elizabethan spirituality, in which there is something for everyone, whether Catholic, Protestant, or sceptic, seems to miss this elementary point. See Dover Wilson, *What Happens in "Hamlet,"* 52–86.

35 See, for example, Bradley, *Shakespearean Tragedy*, 368.

36 A.P. Rossiter also points out the paradox in the various senses of "To be, or not to be." See *Angel with Horns and Other Shakespeare Lectures*, ed. Graham Storey (London: Longmans, 1961), 175.

37 Bradley, *Shakespearean Tragedy*, 133.

38 Harold Goddard, *The Meaning of Shakespeare* (Chicago: University of Chicago Press, 1960), 1:370.

39 Ernest Jones, *Hamlet and Oedipus* (London: Victor Gollancz, 1949).

40 The irony is compounded, of course, by the likelihood that when the play was first performed, the actors who played Brutus and Caesar also played Hamlet and Polonius.

41 Girard, *A Theater of Envy*, 277.

42 For example, A.C. Bradley, in *Shakespearean Tragedy*, says, "We can observe a certain change, though it is not great" (139); John Dover Wilson, in *What Happens in "Hamlet,"* argues that "Hamlet returns from his voyage a changed man, with an air of self-possession greater than at any other time of the play" (266–7); and Harold Goddard, in *The Meaning of Shakespeare*, argues that after the murder of Polonius "Hamlet gives the impression of a man whose will has abdicated in favor of fate" (1:373).

43 It was, we recall, Greg's contention of the former that stimulated Dover Wilson to write in favour of the latter in *What Happens in "Hamlet."* See W.W. Greg, "Hamlet's Hallucination," *Modern Language Review* 12 (1917): 393–421.

44 Vyvyan, *The Shakespearean Ethic*, 40–1.

45 Bradley, *Shakespearean Tragedy*, 151.

46 I do not think it is insignificant that Laertes's outburst is prompted by his feeling that Ophelia's funeral lacks sufficient pomp and ceremony. "What ceremony else?" (5.1.225), he asks the priest, dumbfounded that the rites have ended so hastily. The question takes us back to Hamlet's outburst to his mother when she questioned his excessive mourning. "What ceremony else?" must have been exactly Hamlet's response to his father's funeral. Surely this is why Hamlet now feels compelled to challenge Laertes.

47 Vyvyan, *The Shakespearean Ethic*, 52.

48 Ibid., 53.

49 Ibid., 55.

50 Ibid., 136.

51 Many critics place the blame squarely on Ophelia. For example, Dover Wilson, in *What Happens in "Hamlet,"* invents a stage direction that enables Hamlet to overhear Polonius, Claudius, and Gertrude preparing their "trap" to unloose Ophelia upon Hamlet. Consequently, Hamlet's anger in the nunnery scene is wholly justified. But Wilson's invented stage direction seems like special pleading. For a more balanced assessment, see Harold Jenkins's essay "Hamlet and Ophelia," in *Structural Problems in Shakespeare: Lectures and Essays by Harold Jenkins*, ed. Ernst Honigmann, 137–55 (London: Arden Shakespeare, 2001). As Jenkins persuasively demonstrates, "it is not Ophelia who has abandoned [Hamlet] but he who abandons her" (146).

52 This question was first raised by W.W. Greg, who argued that Claudius's failure to react to the dumbshow proves that Hamlet must have "hallucinated" the ghost. If Claudius did not recognize his own highly unusual murder method (pouring poison into the victim's ear), then he cannot have murdered the old king in the manner the ghost reported. It follows that Hamlet's interview with the ghost is highly suspect. Indeed, it was hallucinated by Hamlet, who superimposes onto his hallucination the text of a play he previously knew, *The Murder of Gonzago*, in which this unusual murder method can be found. Furthermore, when Claudius does react and call for lights, it is because he is upset at the death threat Hamlet appears to be making towards him. See W.W. Greg, "Hamlet's Hallucination," *Modern Language Review* 12 (1917): 393–421. I think Greg makes a very keen and subtle observation, but I think the moral of the story is rather different from the one he draws. Shakespeare is not really disputing the "honesty" of the ghost; instead, he is showing that Claudius has been moved by the tragic representation of the death of a king.

53 This paradoxical oscillation between word and referent is also the main point made by Felperin in his analysis of Shakespeare (though Felperin does not

distinguish between the dumbshow and the spoken play, as I do). In general, I am in substantial agreement with Felperin in most of his critical observations. I do disagree with him, however, when it comes to grounding these critical remarks in a theory of language. Felperin's deconstructive premises are ultimately subject to the same criticism as are all such "metaphysical" hypotheses of language origin: they lack an anthropological conception of language. See Howard Felperin, *Shakespearean Representation*, and n. 14 above.

54 The connection between Claudius's appeal for light and his internal moral struggle is also made by Goddard and Vyvyan. See Goddard, *The Meaning of Shakespeare*, 1:368, and Vyvyan, *The Shakespearean Ethic*, 23.

55 Vyvyan, *The Shakespearean Ethic*, 62–94.

5. Iago, Our Co-Conspirator

1 For the argument in favour of Iago's medieval heritage, see Bernard Spivak, *Shakespeare and the Allegory of Evil: The History of a Metaphor in Relation to His Major Villains* (New York: Columbia University Press, 1958).

2 Picking up on Kenneth Burke's idea of Iago as an "impresario," A.D. Nuttall, in *Shakespeare the Thinker* (New Haven, CT: Yale University Press, 2007), notes how "eerily analogous" Iago is to "the dramatist, the manipulator of human beings" (281). This thought leads Nuttall to recall "a certain poet and novelist saying, with a slight shiver, 'You do realize that all writers of fiction identify at once with Iago'" (282).

3 Samuel Taylor Coleridge, *Shakespearean Criticism*, ed. Thomas Middleton Raysor (London: J.M. Dent & Sons Ltd., 1960), 1: 44.

4 William Hazlitt, *Characters of Shakespeare's Plays* (London: Oxford University Press, 1955), 41–2.

5 Algernon Charles Swinburne, *A Study of Shakespeare*, 4th ed. (London: Chatto & Windus, 1902), 177.

6 A.C. Bradley, *Shakespearean Tragedy: Lectures on "Hamlet," "Othello," "King Lear," "Macbeth"* (1904; repr., London: Penguin Books, 1991), 204.

7 See Ernest Gellner, *Thought and Change* (Chicago: University of Chicago Press, 1964).

8 Bradley, *Shakespearean Tragedy*, 204–5.

9 Ibid., 213.

10 Ibid., 209.

11 Michael Long, in *The Unnatural Scene: A Study of Shakespearean Tragedy* (London: Methuen, 1976), sees clearly that Iago's sense of moral injustice provides a rich breeding ground for anti-Semitism and racism: "For anyone who has heard the voice of the 'poor white man,' or who knows

what Jew-baiting and nigger-baiting are, Iago must represent a masterly social portrait. He has everything that Sartre describes as the social psychology of the anti-Semite – a man so degraded in self-image by social rejection that it becomes imperative for his ego to find somebody who is beneath him, like the Jew (or the Moor), onto whom he can project the unbearable view which society has of himself" (56).

12 *Firstness* is the term used by Adam Katz to describe the fact that, within the originary scene, one individual must be the first to convert his appropriative gesture into a sign. Firstness is thus an innovation that leads to various forms of social hierarchy, as when the big man usurps the role of central sacred distributor. See Adam Katz, "Remembering Amalek: 9/11 and Generative Thinking," *Anthropoetics* 10.2 (Fall 2004 / Winter 2005), accessed 23 January 2013, www.anthropoetics.ucla.edu/ap1002/amalek.htm.

13 Bradley, *Shakespearean Tragedy*, 167.

14 Girard, *A Theater of Envy: William Shakespeare* (Oxford: Oxford University Press, 1991), 277.

15 Bradley says that Iago and Hamlet are the same in that they both invent reasons to explain a perceived resistance to their desire. The difference is that Iago invents reasons for ignoring this resistance whereas Hamlet invents reasons for observing it: "I would venture to describe Iago in these soliloquies as a man setting out on a project which strongly attracts his desire, but at the same time conscious of a resistance to the desire, and unconsciously trying to argue the resistance away by assigning reasons for the project. He is the counterpart of Hamlet, who tries to find reasons for his delay in pursuing his design which excites his aversion" (211). I think this is a perceptive comment, but I would put it slightly differently. Both men are conscious of the ambivalence of the centre, which both attracts and repels. Where they differ is in their social status. Iago's relative inferiority gives him more room to manoeuvre when it comes to manipulating the centre to his advantage. This is why Hamlet so admires Horatio. In Horatio, Hamlet dimly perceives an aesthetic solution to his troubles in Denmark.

16 Iago's "consuming passion of resentment" (118) has been well described by Michael Neill in "Changing Places in *Othello*," in *Shakespeare Survey 37*, ed. Stanley Wells (Cambridge: Cambridge University Press, 1984). Neill writes that "resentment typically tends to reduce everything to its own level" (122). Consequently, Iago, who personifies resentment, reduces Othello to a version of himself. The point of accusing Cassio of adultery with Desdemona is not simply to bring Cassio down, but to bring the Moor down to Iago's level. As Neill puts it, "By putting Cassio in Othello's place, it puts Othello in Iago's own" (122). In other words, after the

temptation scene, Othello begins to see the world in the same resentful fashion as Iago.

17 Edward Pechter, in *Othello and Interpretive Traditions* (Iowa City: University of Iowa Press, 1999), notes that after having to work so hard to figure out exactly whom Iago and Roderigo are referring to, it suddenly becomes transparently clear in Iago's graphic image of "interracial copulation," which absorbs "all the feelings of angry resistance and resentment we have sensed till now" (32).

18 On this point, I agree with W.H. Auden and Harry Berger. In his essay "The Joker in the Pack," Auden writes, "I am inclined to think that the story Iago tells Roderigo about his disappointment over the lieutenancy is a deliberate fabrication" (260). See W.H. Auden, *The Dyer's Hand and Other Essays* (New York: Random House, 1962). Harry Berger also doubts the truth of Iago's story. Speaking of Iago's remark that he hates Othello because he's rumoured to have usurped his sexual function, Berger says, "This casual remark doesn't square with the story of being passed over for Cassio, and Othello's subsequent displays of confidence in Iago hardly substantiate the truth of the story. Maybe, then, the story he tells in 1.1 has the same doubtful status as the story of cuckoldry" (8). See Harry Berger Jr, "Acts of Silence, Acts of Speech: How to Do Things with Othello and Desdemona," *Renaissance Drama* 33 (2004): 3–35.

19 See Maurice Pope, "Addressing Oedipus," *Greece and Rome* 38 (1991): 156–70.

20 Kenneth Burke, *Kenneth Burke on Shakespeare*, ed. Scott Newstok (West Lafayette, IN: Parlor Press, 2007), 13.

21 For example, Wilson Knight, in *The Wheel of Fire: Interpretations of Shakespearian Tragedy* (1930; repr., London: Routledge Classics, 2001), calls Iago "cynicism incarnate" (129).

22 Burke, *Kenneth Burke on Shakespeare*, 70.

23 *Everyman* may not be the best example since it is the most "literary" of the moralities. But the basic point still stands. It is perhaps worth noting that students who read *Everyman* tend to enjoy the one character who is most like Iago – Death.

24 Harold Goddard, *The Meaning of Shakespeare* (Chicago: University of Chicago Press, 1960), 2:76–7.

25 René Girard, *A Theater of Envy*, 38.

26 Edward Pechter, picking up on the "sexual interest of recent criticism" (86), suggests that "we are encouraged to locate the origins of Othello's transformation in his sexual consummation" (87), which therefore must have occurred during the couple's first night on Cyprus. Pechter believes that this "impression is powerfully confirmed" (87) by Othello's

reference to Desdemona's genitals in his first soliloquy. Whether or not we can find the proximate cause of Othello's loathing in the act of sexual consummation, it is certainly true that it is only after the temptation scene that Othello begins to speak of Desdemona in highly sexualized terms.

27 Girard, *A Theater of Envy*, 184.

28 Ibid., 292.

29 The nostalgia and sentimentality evoked by Othello's tremendous distance from us is very well put by Bradley: "Othello is, in one sense of the word, by far the most romantic figure among Shakespeare's heroes; and he is so partly from the strange life of war and adventure which he has lived from childhood. He does not belong to our world, and he seems to enter it we know not whence – almost as if from wonderland. There is something mysterious in his descent from men of royal siege; in his wanderings in vast deserts and among marvellous peoples; in his tales of magic handkerchiefs and prophetic Sibyls; in the sudden vague glimpses we get of numberless battles and sieges in which he has played the hero and has borne a charmed life; even in chance references to his baptism, his being sold to slavery, his sojourn in Aleppo" (*Shakespearean Tragedy* 177–8).

30 Michael Long notes that the Venetian upper classes repress the "devil-beast nature" that lurks beneath their civilized ways, permitting themselves occasional sideways glimpses of "raging motions, carnal stings and unbitted lusts" in the "mollified" form of Othello's sentimental romance stories (*Unnatural Scene* 46–7). Long's larger argument is that Othello's tragedy is a product of Venetian "courtesy culture" (41), which is ill-equipped to deal with the anthropological reality of desire and resentment.

31 A.D. Nuttall, in *Shakespeare the Thinker*, puts the point nicely when he says that *Othello* is "a play about a hero who went into a house" (279). Othello's tragedy begins with his passage from the open skies of the battlefield to the close quarters of private domesticity. Iago relentlessly exploits Othello's unfamiliarity with the latter. As Nuttall says, "This man who should have died on the field of battle is destroyed by small-scale household stuff" (279).

32 See Bradley, *Shakespearean Tragedy*, 402–3.

33 The line is an attempt to negate Brabantio's last words to Othello: "Look to her, Moor, if thou hast eyes to see. / She has deceived her father, and may thee" (1.3.295–6), which Iago has just reminded him of: "She did deceive her father, marrying you" (3.3.220).

34 In a letter to his brothers, George and Tom Keats, on 21 December 1817, Keats writes, "I mean *Negative Capability*, that is when man is capable of being in uncertainties, Mysteries, doubts, without any irritable reaching

after fact & reason." *The Letters of John Keats*, ed. Robert Gittings (Oxford: Oxford University Press, 1970), 43.

35 See Harry Frankfurt, *On Bullshit* (Princeton: Princeton University Press, 2005). I discuss Frankfurt in chapter 3.

36 Pechter, *Othello and Interpretive Traditions*, 109.

37 Pechter has a strong ally in Janet Adamson, who feels that Bradley's sense of the drama is "much truer to our actual dramatic experience than the coolly analytic distance most anti-Othello critics suggest we can and should maintain" (67). See Janet Adamson, *"Othello" as Tragedy: Some Problems of Judgment and Feeling* (Cambridge: Cambridge University Press, 1980).

38 Pechter, *Othello and Interpretive Traditions*, 110.

39 Bradley, *Shakespearean Tragedy*, 196.

40 Ibid., 215.

41 Ibid., 220.

42 Girard, *A Theater of Envy*, 290.

43 Ibid., 291.

44 Bradley, *Shakespearean Tragedy*, 168.

45 See Harry Berger Jr, *Making Trifles of Terrors: Redistributing Complicity in Shakespeare* (Stanford, CA: Stanford University Press, 1997). For Berger's reading of *Othello*, see "Impertinent Trifling: Desdemona's Handkerchief," *Shakespeare Quarterly* 47 (1996): 235–50; and "Acts of Silence, Acts of Speech: How to Do Things with Othello and Desdemona," *Renaissance Drama* 33 (2004): 3–35.

46 Bradley, *Shakespearean Tragedy*, 215.

47 Ibid., 321.

6. Macbeth Unseamed

1 Eric Gans, *Signs of Paradox: Irony, Resentment, and Other Mimetic Structures* (Stanford, CA: Stanford University Press, 1997), 134.

2 Ibid., 144–5.

3 Kenneth Burke, *Kenneth Burke on Shakespeare*, ed. Scott Newstok (West Lafayette, IN: Parlor Press, 2007), 188.

4 Gans, *Signs of Paradox*, 140.

5 See Howard Felperin, *Shakespearean Representation: Mimesis and Modernity in Elizabethan Tragedy* (Princeton: Princeton University Press, 1977). Felperin uses *Macbeth* as a test case of his thesis that Shakespeare's modernity is apparent in "the residue of an untransmuted humanity" (131) that persists in his protagonists despite their apparent conformity to the models of the Christian allegorical tradition. Thus Felperin argues that

the major religious source of *Macbeth* – the tyrant plays of the mystery cycles in which Herod's massacre of the children is depicted – cannot be used as the allegorical model for interpreting the play. Macbeth's character always exceeds the predetermined role of the mad tyrant of the cycle plays. Notwithstanding its sophisticated deconstructive framework, Felperin's analysis is fully compatible with A.C. Bradley's more traditional emphasis on character.

6 A.C. Bradley, *Shakespearean Tragedy: Lectures on "Hamlet," "Othello," "King Lear," "Macbeth"* (1904; repr., London: Penguin Books, 1991), 329.

7 Ibid., 330.

8 Gans, *The End of Culture: Toward a Generative Anthropology* (Berkeley: University of California Press, 1985), 202.

9 Genesis 4:3–5 (New International Version).

10 Genesis 4:7.

11 Bradley, *Shakespearean Tragedy*, 330.

12 Ibid., 323–4.

13 Eric Gans, *The Scenic Imagination: Originary Thinking from Hobbes to the Present Day* (Stanford, CA: Stanford University Press: 2008), 166.

14 Eric Gans, "Originary Guilt," *Chronicles of Love and Resentment*, no. 333, accessed 2 December 2010, http://www.anthropoetics.ucla.edu/views/vw333.htm.

15 See Bradley, *Shakespearean Tragedy*, 452–6. The source of the debate is Lady Macbeth's lines at 1.7.48–60, when she alludes to an earlier occasion during which she and Macbeth had discussed Duncan's murder. Logically the lines seem to refer to an occasion before the play begins, but Bradley believes this seriously diminishes the magnitude of Macbeth's experience of guilt and his internal struggle. If he had already contemplated the murder, it is difficult to explain his uncanny yielding to the idea in the lines: "why do I yield to that suggestion / Whose horrid image doth unfix my hair / And make my seated heart knock at my ribs, / Against the use of nature?" (1.3.135–8).

16 Bradley, *Shakespearean Tragedy*, 348.

17 Ibid., 353.

18 Ibid., 348.

19 For an analysis of how the tragedy increasingly focuses our attention on the isolation of the central figure, see John Holloway's chapter on *Macbeth* in his *Story of the Night: Studies in Shakespeare's Major Tragedies* (London: Routledge & Kegan Paul, 1961).

20 G. Wilson Knight, *The Imperial Theme: Further Interpretations of Shakespeare's Tragedies including the Roman Plays* (London: Methuen, 1965), 125–53.

21 Picking up on Nietzsche's discussion of *ressentiment* in *The Genealogy of Morals*, trans. Walter Kaufmann and R.J. Hollingdale (New York: Vintage Books, 1989), Michael Bristol, in "Vernacular Criticism and the Scenes Shakespeare

Never Wrote," in *Shakespeare Survey 53*, ed. Peter Holland (Cambridge: Cambridge University Press, 2000), remarks that Macbeth's murder of Duncan is driven by rancour and envy rather than by what Nietzsche held to be the "noble morality" of "self-affirmation" of Homer's warrior aristocracy (100). I agree with Bristol's claim that resentment drives Macbeth to murder his king. As Bristol points out, far from being a test of noble self-affirmation, Macbeth's murder of Duncan is a "dirty little secret" (100). In this sense Macbeth is closer to Dostoyevsky's underground man than to a Homeric hero such as Achilles. I think, however, that Nietzsche underestimated the degree to which Homer's heroes were also driven by resentment. Shakespeare, it would seem, was not guilty of making the same mistake as Nietzsche – at least not on the evidence of *Troilus and Cressida* or *Coriolanus*.

22 Noting Macbeth's ambivalent status as both "Lord of Misrule" and scapegoat, John Holloway, in *The Story of the Night*, describes the banquet as a "mockery of a feast" (66).

23 Macbeth's powerlessness to resist the scene of violence that repels him illustrates the paradoxical nature of originary desire, which in tragedy compels the protagonist towards the centre he both admires and, in his displacement from it, resents. The debate about how we are to explain Macbeth's surrender to evil, despite his lucid realization that such evil cannot be morally justified, cannot be answered by appealing to such commonplace notions as self-deception or hypocrisy. Macbeth is not like the man who knows he shouldn't drink but gives into the impulse anyway. As A.P. Rossiter argues in *Angel with Horns and Other Shakespeare Lectures*, ed. Graham Storey (London: Longmans, 1961), such explanations merely trivialize Macbeth as a compulsive neurotic and so prohibit the kind of identification that tragedy requires of the audience. Rossiter himself is rather vague about what compels Macbeth's desire. He calls it an "impulsion" and sees it as a phenomenon of the will (217). Notions like "impulsion" and "will" can, I think, be better explained when situated in terms of the categories of the originary hypothesis.

24 Holloway puts the point well when he says that the dominant image of the play, an image that is from beginning to end associated with Macbeth, is the man of blood, the image of death: "This image, kept so much before our imagination that it seems without exaggeration to stalk the stage, is the image with which Macbeth is identified in the very first account we have of him. From the start, he may be valour's minion, but he impresses our minds as the bloody man, the image of death" (*The Story of the Night* 59).

25 Harry Berger Jr, "The Early Scenes of Macbeth: Preface to a New Interpretation," in *Making Trifles of Terrors: Redistributing Complicity in Shakespeare* (Stanford, CA: Stanford University Press, 1997), 70–97.

26 Ibid., 87.

27 See A.R. Braunmuller, ed. *Macbeth* (New Cambridge Shakespeare. Cambridge: Cambridge University Press, 1997), 16.

28 The general anthropological problem of succession is easily stated. If the king does not name a successor, the country will be thrown into chaos when he dies. If he does name a successor, he runs the risk of inviting his premature demise should his enemies decide to throw their lot in with the second-in-command. In a fascinating comparative study, the anthropologist Robbins Burling, in *The Passage of Power: Studies in Political Succession* (New York: Academic Press, 1974), analyses how this basic problem is dealt with in various African, Indian, and Chinese kingdoms. As Burling shows, primogeniture is far from being the only available pattern of succession. The situation in *Macbeth* suggests a society in transition between the big-man stage and a full-fledged inherited and sacralized monarchy.

29 Harry Berger Jr, "Text Against Performance: The Example of *Macbeth*," in *Making Trifles of Terrors*, 98–125.

30 I am in substantial agreement with J.L. Simmons, who argues, in *Shakespeare's Pagan World: The Roman Tragedies* (Charlottesville: University of Virginia Press, 1973), that Brutus's belief in his own perfection constitutes a failure of self-knowledge; Brutus refuses to admit that he is driven by imperfect emotions, such as envy and resentment. But Shakespeare has shown us otherwise in the temptation scene, which reveals that Brutus is not immune to the corrupting thoughts of envy. Simmons argues that Shakespeare deliberately presented his Roman heroes in an ethical "pagan" context that did not allow them to recognize original sin. Brutus's fleeting encounter with Caesar's ghost is an opportunity for Brutus to recognize his "fallen nature" (107), but the moment passes with no moral recognition on Brutus's part. The incident is thus dramatically ironic – we see the moral failure, but Brutus does not. As Simmons puts it, "Shakespeare, with no authority in Plutarch, identifies the spirit of Caesar, the spirit that Brutus wanted to destroy, with Brutus himself. Those qualities in Caesar that had caused Brutus to kill him – the attempted isolation from humanity, the presumptuousness, the potentiality of evil – are in Brutus. His full recognition of this spirit, however, would remove us from Shakespeare's pagan world. Like Coriolanus, Brutus must continue to behold himself only in the eyes of Rome" (107).

31 In Holinshed, Macbeth reigns for seventeen years.

7. Coriolanus's Impotence

1 As John Kekes observes, in the classical world the personal conception of honour was constrained by the public context in which it was demonstrated. Only those who possessed the traits necessary for success in battle (bravery, strength, cunning, etc.) could aspire to the public conception of honour. Honour was open to all, but the nature of the competition inevitably favoured a certain type of competitor – namely, able-bodied, physically fit young men. In the modern world, the notion of honour is considerably expanded, so much so that we no longer regard the military context as a reliable indicator of what is honourable. Kekes's main point is that honour should be defined in terms of personal character rather than in terms of social standing or occupation. See Kekes, *The Art of Life* (Ithaca, NY: Cornell University Press, 2002), 107–13.

2 Goethe's reflections on Hamlet in *Wilhelm Meister's Apprenticeship* spring to mind: "To me it is clear that Shakespeare meant, in the present case, to represent the effects of a great action laid upon a soul unfit for the performance of it" (1: 304) This view is ultimately not all that different from Girard's view of Hamlet as unfit for revenge because he sees the futility of the revenge ethic.

3 A.C. Bradley, *Coriolanus*, British Academy: Second Annual Lecture (London: Oxford University Press, 1912), 15.

4 I agree with Kenneth Burke, who argues that to understand Coriolanus's character one must first recognize that the play is fitted to perform a "symbolic action in which some notable form of victimage is imitated, for the purgation, or edification of an audience" (129). In a dazzling analysis, Burke argues that Coriolanus's character exploits the "malaise" (139) of complex agrarian societies in which social divisions are both necessary and the object of considerable resentment. In giving us a hero who so flagrantly exploits the superiority of the centre, Shakespeare compels both our admiration and our disgust. On the one hand, Coriolanus is a transparent example of nobility and therefore of aesthetic centrality; on the other, he makes insultingly clear our own inferiority and hence our resentment. As Burke points out, the hierarchical relationship between centre and periphery is implicit in all societies, but it is exaggerated in the complex agrarian societies of ancient Rome and Elizabethan England. For Burke's writings on Shakespeare, including the essay on *Coriolanus*, see Kenneth Burke, *Kenneth Burke on Shakespeare*, ed. Scott Newstok (West Lafayette, IN: Parlor Press, 2007).

5 Wilbur Sanders, in *Shakespeare's Magnanimity: Four Tragic Heroes, Their Friends and Families* (London: Chatto & Windus, 1978), makes a powerful case for retaining Folio's original line assignments to the first and second citizens.

Editors usually follow Edward Capell's 1768 emendation and reassign the second citizen's lines from line 55 onward to the first citizen. The argument for doing so is that these lines are consistent with the first citizen's more outspoken and rebellious character. In a subtle argument, Sanders counters that, in fact, Shakespeare wanted to show us multiple levels of irony, including the cowardly nature of the first citizen, who shrinks back into the crowd when confronted by one of his betters (Menenius), and the irony of Menenius berating the one plebeian who might be most inclined to reconcile himself to Coriolanus's point of view. I am inclined to agree with Sanders. Not only would this sequence be wholly typical of Shakespeare, but it also avoids the awkwardness of having to explain why emendation is necessary. Michael Warren, in "The Perception of Error: The Editing and the Performance of the Opening of *Coriolanus*," in *Textual Performances: The Modern Reproduction of Shakespeare's Drama*, ed. Lukas Erne and Margaret Jane Kidnie (Cambridge: Cambridge University Press, 2004), builds on Sanders's remarks and provides a balanced discussion of what is at stake in the reassignment of the speech prefixes. In any event, the question of the legitimacy of the emendation, which David Bevington follows in the text I am using, does not affect my argument.

6 As Michael Long notes, in *The Unnatural Scene: A Study of Shakespearean Tragedy* (London: Methuen, 1976), Coriolanus's characterization is inseparable from Shakespeare's vision of Rome as "a warrior aristocracy whose natural apotheosis is Marcius and whose value-system is adhered to with unquestioning attachment by all the members of the class which principally generates it" (62). Long's larger point is that Rome's obsessive attachment to the warrior ethic is pointedly used by Shakespeare to illustrate a "dehumanized" culture that creates heroes only so it can sacrifice them.

7 See Ernest Gellner, *Plough, Sword and Book: The Structure of Human History* (Chicago: University of Chicago Press, 1989).

8 Nor indeed does it apply to Volumnia, whose most famous lines are "Anger's my meat, I sup upon myself, / And so shall starve with feeding" (4.2.52–3). As explained in chapter 2, the big man is not the one who eats most or best, but the one who is willing to forgo appetitive satisfaction to enjoy the far greater pleasure of central significance. In her illuminating psychoanalytic reading of the play, Janet Adelman argues that Coriolanus suffers from an excessive castration anxiety, for which he compensates through self-inflicted starvation, food being associated with weakness, dependency, and effeminacy. As Adelman points out, the real source of Coriolanus's resentment is not the people, who merely consume, but his mother, whose refusal to eat is a sign of her desire for centrality; hence

the significance of the scene in which mother and son compete for honour before the gates of Rome. See Adelman, "'Anger's my meat': Feeding, Dependency, and Aggression in *Coriolanus*," in *Shakespeare: An Anthology of Criticism and Theory 1945–2000*, ed. Russ McDonald (Malden, MA: Blackwell, 2004), 323–37. Paul Cantor points out, in *Shakespeare's Rome: Republic and Empire* (Ithaca, NY: Cornell University Press, 1976), that Coriolanus's austerity is a peculiarly Roman virtue, one Shakespeare associated with the republic rather than the empire: "By considering the needs of the city in wartime we begin to see the connection between austerity and heroic or martial virtue in Rome" (35).

9 See, for example, Henry Hudson, who refers to Coriolanus's "modesty" or "aversion to being flattered" (introduction to *Shakespeare's Tragedy of Coriolanus* [Boston: Ginn & Company, 1909]). Hudson admits, however, that there is "something rather equivocal" about Coriolanus's "modesty" (23). Unhae Langis, in "Coriolanus: Inordinate Passions and Powers in Personal and Political Governance," *Comparative Drama* 44.1 (2010), also refers to Coriolanus's "magnanimity and modesty," though he too notices that there are "cracks" in this view of the hero (6).

10 A.D. Nuttall, in *Shakespeare the Thinker* (New Haven, CT: Yale University Press, 2007), points out that Coriolanus is a "primary wealth-creator" (297). His supremacy as a killer means that Rome's external food supply is guaranteed for as long as he serves Rome. Nuttall says that this fact distorts Rome's agrarian economy, but I would argue, with Ernest Gellner, that the close relationship between violence and food storage is implicit in any agrarian economy. As soon as there is a storehouse of food to be protected, the warriors will gain the upper hand. It matters not whether violence is inflicted on one's own people or neighbouring peoples; the basic situation remains the same – which is to say, the warriors remain in charge.

11 Matthew Proser, in *The Heroic Image in Five Shakespearean Tragedies* (Princeton: Princeton University Press, 1965), argues that Coriolanus is true to a perverted image of himself as a supreme killer. This belief is a betrayal of his basic humanity, but the deception is participated in by the entire community, including the plebeians, the patricians, Volumnia, Menenius, Aufidius, and, in the last scene, the Volscian mob. Proser allows a single exception: Virgilia. Her "gracious silence" (170) indicates both her difference and her impotence in the face of the violent image so relentlessly deployed by others. I agree with this assessment, but Virgilia, though clearly presented as a contrast to her dominant and ferocious mother-in-law, does have one violent outburst, which suggests that she is not totally free of resentment. Silence is no indication of the absence of

resentment, as Caesar realizes when he surveys Cassius's lean and hungry look. Michael Long, in *The Unnatural Scene*, notes that Virgilia, though "cowed into silence" by her dominating mother-in-law at the beginning of the play, learns to speak the same resentful language of Rome by the end when she joins in with Volumnia's vituperations against the tribunes (72). See also D.J. Gordon, "Name and Fame: Shakespeare's *Coriolanus*," in *Papers Mainly Shakespearean*, ed. G.I. Duthie (Edinburgh: Oliver and Boyd, 1964). Gordon connects the linguistic designation of the hero with the sacrificial violence of the *sparagmos*. After his banishment Coriolanus is a monster, "'a deed without a name,'" a being "from a realm that is not subjugated" (54), and for this reason he must be destroyed by the "voices" of the people: "the words that identify and bind become words that debase and destroy" (55). In Rome, Gordon says, "to speak is to be guilty" (55), and all are guilty "except Virgilia who is silent" (49).

12 Rossiter, in *Angel with Horns and Other Shakespeare Lectures*, ed. Graham Storey (London: Longmans, 1961), cites Menenius's description of Coriolanus: "The tartness of his face sours ripe grapes. When he walks, he moves like an engine, and the ground shrinks before his treading. He is able to pierce a corslet with his eye, talks like knell, and his hum is a battery" (5.4.17–21). "It is," Rossiter says, "a queer preparation for the death of the tragic hero" (245). Indeed it is. By emphasizing Coriolanus's resentment, Shakespeare makes it harder for us to identify with his hero.

13 In his lecture on *Coriolanus* Bradley says, "We may say of it, as of its hero, that, if not one of Shakespeare's greatest creations, it is certainly one of his biggest" (3).

14 Friedrich Nietzsche, *On the Genealogy of Morals*, trans. Walter Kaufmann and R.J. Hollingdale (New York: Vintage Books, 1989), especially Book 1. See also Max Scheler, *Ressentiment*, trans. Lewis B. Coser and William W. Holdheim (Milwaukee, WI: Marquette University Press, 1994).

15 On the notion that language originates as a negation of the object, see Gans, *Signs of Paradox: Irony, Resentment, and Other Mimetic Structures* (Stanford, CA: Stanford University Press, 1997), especially chapter 2; Kenneth Burke, *On Symbols and Society*, ed. Joseph R. Gusfield (Chicago: University of Chicago Press, 1989), especially chapter 2; and Ernest Gellner, *Anthropology and Politics: Revolutions in the Sacred Grove* (Oxford: Blackwell, 1995), especially chapter 4.

16 W.H. Auden says, in his *Lectures on Shakespeare* (Princeton: Princeton University Press, 2000), "The main contrast in the play is not of the aristocrats and plebeians, but of the one and the many, of Coriolanus and the crowd" (245).

17 In his lecture on *Coriolanus*, Bradley expresses unbounded disgust of Aufidius: "The unspeakable baseness of his sneer at the hero's tears is an injury to the final effect. Such an emotion as mere disgust is out of place in a tragic close; but I confess I feel nothing but disgust as Aufidius speaks the last words, except some indignation with the poet who allowed him to speak them and an unregenerate desire to see head and body of the speaker lying on opposite sides of the stage" (16). As usual, Bradley's romantic focus on the incomparable nobility of the tragic hero distracts him from observing that this nobility is self-consciously represented by Shakespeare as an artifice of the scene itself. A useful counterweight to Bradley is A.P. Rossiter, who is far more aware of the play's multiple ironies.

18 *Kenneth Burke on Shakespeare*, 137. Burke, however, does not go as far as Oscar Campbell, who believes that Menenius takes on the satiric role of ironizer and buffoon. See Oscar Campbell, *Shakespeare's Satire* (Hamden, CT: Archon Books, 1963), especially pages 206–10.

19 A.P. Rossiter, in *Angel with Horns*, makes much the same point about Menenius, whom he describes as "a humorous, ironical, experienced, sensible, critical commentator; and, simultaneously, in the Roman political world, an 'anti-type' and counterpoise to everything that is Marcius" (247). Rossiter's larger point is that Menenius can think dialectically, whereas Coriolanus cannot. Add to this point the many ironies in the play and you get the suggestion that "Menenius is 'greater' in mind than Marcius," at least when it comes to tackling the dialectical conflicts of history and politics (249).

20 Bradley, *Coriolanus*, 9.

21 See, for example, G. Wilson Knight's slightly sentimental account of Coriolanus's relationship with his mother, in *The Imperial Theme: Further Interpretations of Shakespeare's Tragedies including the Roman Plays* (London: Methuen, 1965), 154–98. Nuttall also emphasizes the relationship, going so far as to say that "the tragedy is largely of her making" (*Shakespeare the Thinker* 297). Sanders, however, argues that to reduce the play to a contest of wills between Coriolanus and his mother is to turn the tragedy into a farce: "It is no more 'tragic' than a play centering upon the moral consciousness of Idi Amin could hope to be" (*Shakespeare's Magnanimity* 180). I have some sympathy for Sanders, who shows very well that far from being the puppet of his mother, Coriolanus is complicit in the scene of his own destruction; he is both drawn to and alienated from the centre. Of the scene in the senate, Sanders says, "The sense of [Coriolanus's] being complicit could hardly declare itself more artlessly or profoundly. It is an unquiet conscience he carries with him out of the Senate-house" (178). Coriolanus both does and does not want centrality.

22 When Coriolanus returns to Rome, his mother says that she now expects the last of her "wishes" to be fulfilled (the consulship). Coriolanus responds by saying, "Know, good mother, / I had rather be their servant in my way / Than sway with them in theirs" (2.1.201–3). The plural pronoun suggests that Coriolanus is referring to her wishes rather than to Rome. He had rather serve her wishes in *his* way than simply bend to her desires.

23 After providing a brief overview of the critical responses to this problem, A. Luis Pujante, in "'No Sense Nor Feeling': A Note on *Coriolanus* in 4.1," *Shakespeare Quarterly* 41 (1990): 489, suggests that Shakespeare is simply following Plutarch. Pujante cites the following line from North's Plutarch: "he was so carried away with the vehemency of anger and desire for revenge that he had no sense nor feeling of the hard state he was in." What I have described as Coriolanus's romantic buoyancy is for Pujante merely delayed anger brought on by the shock of his banishment. I think that Pujante has rather missed Shakespeare's point, which was not to merely reproduce Plutarch but to modify him. In this case, I think the modification is explicit. Shakespeare's incipiently romantic hero is striving for something Plutarch's Coriolanus could never dream of – namely, a "world elsewhere," free of the violent burden of the public scene of ritual sacrifice.

24 Adelman argues that Coriolanus's "rage is properly directed toward his mother" (329). She is the one who has created him and continues to control him in his adulthood. His anger towards the plebeians is thus displaced resentment of his mother. This reading is an interesting one because it suggests that Coriolanus's violence on the battlefield is, paradoxically, an expression of his impotent rage towards his mother; her status as a rival becomes explicit in the final act when she defeats her son and is fêted like a hero by Rome.

25 Sanders expresses the point well when he says that "Shakespeare takes a keen pleasure in rendering the battle of adulation and censure and speculation, amidst which Martius lives. A very shrewd comic intelligence is at work, that is to say, in the interest *he* takes in the interest *others* take in his problematical protagonist" (*Shakespeare's Magnanimity* 143–4). This is another way of articulating Shakespeare's dramatic practice of putting the scene itself on stage. Rather than a centre unmediated by the periphery, Shakespeare shows that the centre is *dependent* upon the periphery. Sanders is right to observe that this kind of intelligence is essentially comic, which of course creates difficulties for tragedy. I will return to this point at the end of the chapter.

26 Carol Sicherman, in "The Failure of Words," *ELH* 39 (1972), observes that Coriolanus is "inarticulate" (199), his speech heavily dependent upon rote

proverbs and invective. Sicherman blames Volumnia for this impoverished linguistic state of affairs: "Her precepts have served him ill, teaching him to speak in formulas which create a disjunction between heart and brain" (197).

27 Bradley, *Coriolanus*, 5. James Calderwood, in "Wordless Meanings and Meaningless Words," *SEL* 6 (1966), observes that Coriolanus fastens on the literal meaning of words, and this is one reason why he hates the plebeians: they represent the polysemy of language, which Coriolanus cannot tolerate.

28 A.D. Nuttall, *A New Mimesis* (London: Methuen, 1983), 119.

29 Ibid., 116.

30 Bradley says that Coriolanus does not have "a drop of Stoic blood in his veins" (*Coriolanus*, 12). For an illuminating study of Shakespeare's treatment of the Stoic tradition in *Julius Caesar*, *Coriolanus*, and *Antony and Cleopatra*, see Geoffrey Miles, *Shakespeare and the Constant Romans* (Oxford: Oxford University Press, 1996). Placing Shakespeare with Montaigne in a tradition of Renaissance critiques of Stoicism, Miles argues that "*Coriolanus* is Shakespeare's definitive critique of the contradictions of 'constancy,' and its potentially destructive consequences for an individual or a society which hold it as the supreme virtue" (168).

31 This is also the argument of J.L. Simmons in his excellent study of the Roman plays, *Shakespeare's Pagan World: The Roman Tragedies* (Charlottesville: University of Virginia Press, 1973). Simmons argues that for Shakespeare's Roman heroes there is no "world elsewhere." Instead, they are confined to the ritual – or, as Simmons puts it, "pagan" – world of Rome and its culture of sacrifice. Rome perversely and cannibalistically sacrifices its own heroes. The only way out of this sacrificial cycle is to choose love rather than the resentful desire for recognition; but this is not an option for the Roman hero, whose identity cannot be separated from the warlike state that created him. In suggesting that Rome's heroic cult of the warrior is unsustainable, Simmons anticipates Stanley Cavell's argument, in *Disowning Knowledge in Six Plays of Shakespeare* (Cambridge: Cambridge University Press, 1987), that Coriolanus is a failed Christ figure. Comparing Coriolanus to Shylock, Simmons says, "Coriolanus becomes as consumed by the passion of revenge as the ignoble Jew; and, in the case of both Jew and Roman, Shakespeare makes it thematically clear that such a passion has developed because there is no access to the Christian ethos of love" (58).

32 In a well-known essay, Stanley Fish, in "How to Do Things with Austin and Searle: Speech Act Theory and Literary Criticism," *MLN* 91 (1976), notices the irony of the scene: "In a gesture intended to be revelatory, [Coriolanus] unmuffles, expecting, Satan-like, to be announced simply by

the transcendent brightness of his visage" (999). This is a fine insight, but unfortunately Fish remains too wedded to speech act theory to capitalize on it. He argues that Coriolanus's tragedy is about speech acts, and this is why the play lends itself so well to an interpretation informed by speech act theory. As we all know, we cannot use language effectively without submitting to collectively established rules and conventions. Having been named "Richard van Oort," I can't turn around and say to the immigration official at the airport that my name isn't Richard van Oort (as it says on my passport) but Jane Doe. Of course, I can say it, but my attempt to rename myself will be, as the speech act theorists say, "infelicitous." Drawing on John Searle's taxonomy of speech acts, Fish shows that the election scene, in which Coriolanus goes before the plebeians in the marketplace, is a "textbook discussion of the force and necessity of constitutive rules" (985). Coriolanus refuses to play by the rules, which leads to his downfall. One might be forgiven for asking why Fish needs forty-four pages to reach this rather self-evident conclusion. Ultimately, Fish's application of Searle's taxonomy, while often illuminating in some of its local insights, is too ad hoc to sustain any kind of anthropology, Shakespearean or otherwise. Sensing this, Fish ignores the many instances when speech act theory fails as an explanation of the play's action. To take only the example Fish himself cites, despite Coriolanus's flagrant abuse of rules for requesting the people's voices, he is in fact successful, at least initially. Why this is so is not explained by speech act theory, as Fish himself admits. In the end Fish's essay tells us more about Fish's theoretical constructivism than Shakespeare's *Coriolanus*. In itself this is not necessarily a problem, but it becomes a problem when one notes the self-evident nature of Fish's conclusions. Paradoxically, Fish seems to be perfectly happy with this state of affairs. He spends most of the essay arguing why speech act theory can do so little when it comes to explaining literature! John Plotz, in "*Coriolanus* and the Failure of Performatives," *ELH* 63 (1996), is right to point out that Fish, in his commitment to radical conventionalism and constructivism, ignores the possibility that Coriolanus's refusal to play by the rules can be interpreted as a criticism of the social order in which he exists. In other words, the ethical or anthropological question cannot be set aside so easily. Fish would have done well to have read James Calderwood's beautifully succinct fourteen-page essay discussing Coriolanus's attempt to exclude the public scene from his private sense of self-worth. Commenting insightfully on the scene in Aufidius's house, Calderwood observes that Aufidius's inability to identify Coriolanus without the name "reveals the futility of so exclusive a commitment to private meaning" and that precisely in his exile "Coriolanus becomes, not the autonomous individual he has striven to be, but a blank" ("Wordless Meanings and Meaningless Words" 221).

33 Rossiter, *Angel with Horns*, 249.

34 Applying an illuminating analogy between the promiscuity of language and high levels of currency inflation during social and economic crises, Calderwood argues that Coriolanus withdraws into his own private language in a futile effort to avoid being devalued on the open market; hence his fear of any public forum that might endanger his sense of his own worth. This fear includes the evaluations of the nobles, for "to accept praise would be to relinquish his right to total self-definition by acknowledging that his nobility is at least partly dependent upon the interpretations of others" ("Wordless Meanings and Meaningless Words" 218–19).

35 Compare Coriolanus's description of the citizens: "I would they were barbarians, as they are, / Though in Rome littered; not Romans, as they are not, / Though calved i'th' porch o'th' Capitol" (3.1.243–5).

36 The passages quoted in this paragraph come from Bradley's lecture on *Coriolanus*, 12–14.

37 See Goddard, *The Meaning of Shakespeare* (Chicago: University of Chicago Press, 1960), 2: 219–24. Sanders, in *Shakespeare's Magnanimity* (178–84), agrees.

38 Here I am inspired by John Vyvyan's example in *The Shakespearean Ethic* (London: Chatto & Windus, 1959). Vyvyan does not discuss *Coriolanus*, but his highly original and persuasive argument can easily be extended to include it.

39 Knight, *The Imperial Theme*, 194.

40 Leontes, in *The Winter's Tale*, is also possessed by the image of his wife and child in flames. When Paulina attempts to stir his sympathy by showing him his baby girl, he responds, "This brat is none of mine; / It is the issue of Polixenes. / Hence with it, and together with the dam / Commit them to the fire!" (2.3.93–6).

41 As Hermann Heuer points out in his useful little study of Shakespeare's sources, the emphasis on mercy is absent in Thomas North's English translation of Jacques Amyot's French translation of Plutarch. Heuer notes the addition of a significant psychological and moral dimension by Amyot, which was further enlarged by North. But the presentation of the political scene in terms of the hero's inner conflict between love and resentment is wholly Shakespeare's own. See Heuer, "From Plutarch to Shakespeare: A Study of *Coriolanus*," *Shakespeare Survey 10*, ed. Allardyce Nicoll (Cambridge: Cambridge University Press, 1957), 50–9.

42 I am only partially in agreement with Proser who argues that Coriolanus's self-image prevents him from "investigating his own moral stance" (*The Heroic Image*, 140). Clearly, in this scene he *is* investigating his moral stance. Proser's larger argument is that each of Shakespeare's tragedies is shaped by a conflict between the protagonist's representation of himself and his actual circumstances. This is another way of expressing the central problematic of the neoclassical aesthetic. The private scene of representation is shown to be in conflict with the public scene.
43 Coppélia Kahn, in *Roman Shakespeare: Warriors, Wounds, and Women* (New York: Routledge, 1997), observes that "for the first time in his life" Coriolanus must "mask the contempt he ordinarily heaps on them" (154).
44 Irving Ribner, in *Patterns in Shakespearean Tragedy* (New York: Barnes & Noble, 1960), also notes the symbolic significance of Coriolanus's alliance with Aufidius: "In joining with Aufidius Coriolanus gives himself to the evil side of his own personality, negating the noble elements which had counterbalanced it" (198). My only comment would be to add that Shakespeare traces this "evil" back to resentment, which Aufidius personifies. Simmons, in *Shakespeare's Pagan World*, calls the alliance between Coriolanus and Aufidius a "spiritual perversion" (62). Michael Long, in *The Unnatural Scene*, calls it "a grotesque parody of a betrothal" (67).
45 Bradley, *Coriolanus*, 15.
46 Knight, *The Imperial Theme*, 198.
47 Goddard, *The Meaning of Shakespeare*, 2:240.
48 Bradley, *Shakespearean Tragedy*, 88–9.
49 Harold Bloom, *Shakespeare: The Invention of the Human* (New York: Riverhead Books, 1998), 587.
50 Rossiter, *Angel with Horns*, 251. See also Leonard Tennenhouse, "*Coriolanus*: History and the Crisis of Semantic Order," in *Drama in the Renaissance: Comparative and Critical Essays*, ed. Clifford Davidson et al. (New York: AMS Press, 1986). Tennenhouse argues that Coriolanus suffers for his "linguistic solipsism" which makes him "impotent as a political man" (228); the hero's use of the "public language of the state" for purely private purposes leads to his downfall: "Shakespeare has come, as it were, to re-examine one of the persistent themes of the history plays in the mode of the great tragedies" (229). Of the play's ending, Tennenhouse says, "I for one … feel neither release nor resolution … His death does not bring understanding or insight to the other characters, nor does it bring closure to the historical narrative" (233). Campbell, in *Shakespeare's Satire*, goes even further than Rossiter and Tennenhouse, arguing that *Coriolanus* is pure satire. According to Campbell, Coriolanus is little

more than a dancing bear who reacts in hilariously Pavlovian fashion to all those who bait him (prod the bear and he growls). Campbell has a point, but he overstates his case so utterly that he becomes blind to any of Coriolanus's redeeming qualities; most notably, his moral transformation from contemptuous *Übermensch* to resentful and impotent slave. The reconciliation scene is manifestly *not* satire, and Campbell totally misses the exquisite allegory illustrating Coriolanus's inner conflict and redemption. Geoffrey Miles offers a more balanced view when he says that "Coriolanus is granted at least a moment of insight into his own failure, and at the climax of the play submits to universal nature" (*Shakespeare and the Constant Romans* 167). See also R.B. Parker, "*Coriolanus* and 'th'interpretation of the time,'" in *Mirror up to Shakespeare: Essays in Honour of G.R. Hibbard*, ed. J.C. Gray (Toronto: University of Toronto Press, 1984), who argues that Coriolanus "does realize fully what has happened to him and the price he is paying for it and will have to pay" (274).

51 Eugene Waith, in *The Herculean Hero in Marlowe, Chapman, Shakespeare and Dryden* (London: Chatto & Windus, 1962), acknowledges this fact when he suggests that what Coriolanus says of his submission to his mother in the reconciliation scene might be said of the final scene: "Behold, the heavens do ope, / The gods look down, and this unnatural scene / They laugh at" (5.3.183–5). Despite this sense of ridiculousness, Waith argues that there is no irony in the play's final scene, but rather the affirmation of a loss: "What the last scene affirms with compelling force is the value of what the world is losing in the death of the hero" (141). Obviously, given what I have just argued, I find Waith's position difficult to sustain. In the light of Coriolanus's persistent denial of his dependency on the public scene of representation, the irony of his last boast, in which he dares the Volsces to write their public annals true, is impossible to ignore. The man who had denied all need for public representation is now correcting the Volscian version of it!

52 See Vyvyan, *The Shakespearean Ethic*, 104–32.

53 John Holloway, in *The Story of the Night: Studies in Shakespeare's Major Tragedies* (London: Routledge & Kegan Paul, 1961), says that "the death of Coriolanus is almost as much a *sparagmos* of the ritual victim by the whole social group as was possible on the stage" (130), and he concludes that this tragedy, more sharply than the others, shows the "overt transformation of a hero into outcast through a ceremonial act of expulsion by the group" (130). Victor Kiernan, in *Eight Tragedies of Shakespeare: A Marxist Study* (London: Verso, 1996), makes a similar comment when he says, "Tragic irony could scarcely go any further; the apostle of war is killed preaching peace; more than any other hero he dies a martyr, a sacrificial offering" (184).

54 In a demanding reading, Stanley Cavell, in *Disowning Knowledge*, calls *Coriolanus* a "failed tragedy" (162) and a "failed sacrifice" (165). By this he seems to mean that Coriolanus is an inverted Christ figure. He is sacrificed for his self-consuming or "cannibalistic" narcissism. The key moment for Cavell is Coriolanus's silence as he is bombarded by the words of his mother in the reconciliation scene. His silence is not so much a moral awakening as an illustration of Coriolanus's failure to compete with Christ: "His sacrifice will not be redemptive; hence one may say his tragedy is that he cannot achieve tragedy" (161). But through Shakespeare's aesthetic representation of this failed sacrifice, the audience may find redemption; specifically, by participating in the performance itself, which thus becomes a kind of "rebirth of religion from the spirit of tragedy" (168). I find Cavell's argument at once enormously suggestive and frustratingly vague. Cavell seems to be considering what I have called the origin of high aesthetic culture out of ritual representations of the sacrifice of the big man.

8. Coda: René Girard's Shakespeare

1 Harold Bloom, *Shakespeare: The Invention of the Human* (New York: Riverhead Books, 1998).
2 Ibid., 8.
3 Ibid., 9.
4 "Les mots et les choses" was translated into English as "the order of things." See Michel Foucault, *The Order of Things: An Archeology of the Human Sciences* (New York: Vintage Books, 1994).
5 René Girard, *A Theater of Envy: William Shakespeare* (Oxford: Oxford University Press, 1991), 5–6.
6 Francis Fergusson, *The Idea of a Theater: A Study of Ten Plays: The Art of Drama in Changing Perspective* (Princeton: Princeton University Press, 1949); John Holloway, *The Story of the Night: Studies in Shakespeare's Major Tragedies* (London: Routledge & Kegan Paul, 1961).
7 Girard, *A Theater of Envy*, 5.
8 *La violence et le sacré* was preceded by Girard's 1961 study of the novel, *Mensonge romantique et vérité romanesque*, in which Girard first proposed his theory of mimetic desire. In *La violence et le sacré* Girard applied the "mimetic" model of desire he discovered in the novels of Stendhal, Flaubert, Dostoyevsky, and Proust to the general anthropological problem of human origin, proposing a global theory of human society. *Mensonge* was translated into English in 1965 as *Deceit, Desire, and the Novel: Self and Other in Literary Structure*. *La violence* was translated into English in 1977 as *Violence and the Sacred*.

9 Girard, *A Theater of Envy*, 16.
10 Ibid., 328.
11 I discuss Greenblatt's work in "The Critic as Ethnographer," *New Literary History* 35 (2004): 621–61, and "The Culture of Criticism," *Criticism* 49 (2007): 459–79. Both essays are reprinted in *The End of Literature: Essays in Anthropological Aesthetics* (Aurora, CO: Davies Group Publishers, 2009).
12 Girard, *A Theater of Envy*, 284.
13 See, for example, Michael Tomasello, *The Cultural Origins of Human Cognition* (Harvard, MA: Harvard University Press, 1999), or his more recent book, *A Natural History of Human Thinking* (Harvard, MA: Harvard University Press, 2014).
14 René Girard, *Things Hidden Since the Foundation of the World*, trans. Stephen Bann and Michael Metteer (Stanford, CA: Stanford University Press, 1987), 99.
15 Ibid., 100.
16 See Terrence Deacon, *The Symbolic Species: The Co-evolution of Language and the Brain* (New York: W.W. Norton, 1997).

Bibliography

Adamson, Janet. *"Othello" as Tragedy: Some Problems of Judgment and Feeling*. Cambridge: Cambridge University Press, 1980.

Adelman, Janet. "'Anger's my meat': Feeding, Dependency, and Aggression in *Coriolanus*." In *Shakespeare: An Anthology of Criticism and Theory 1945–2000*, edited by Russ McDonald, 323–37. Malden, MA: Blackwell, 2004.

Auden, W.H. *The Dyer's Hand and Other Essays*. New York: Random House, 1962.

– *Lectures on Shakespeare*. Edited by Arthur Kirsch. Princeton: Princeton University Press, 2000.

Bartlett, Andrew. *Mad Scientist, Impossible Human: An Essay in Generative Anthropology*. Aurora, CO: Davies Group Publishers, 2014.

Battenhouse, Roy W. *Shakespearean Tragedy: Its Art and Its Christian Premises*. Bloomington: University of Indiana Press, 1969.

Berger, Harry, Jr. "Acts of Silence, Acts of Speech: How to Do Things with Othello and Desdemona." *Renaissance Drama* 33 (2004): 3–35.

– "Impertinent Trifling: Desdemona's Handkerchief." *Shakespeare Quarterly* 47 (1996): 235–50.

– *Making Trifles of Terrors: Redistributing Complicity in Shakespeare*. Stanford, CA: Stanford University Press, 1997.

The Bible. New International Version. Accessed 8 August 2011. http://www.biblica.com/en-us/the-niv-bible/.

Bloom, Harold. Introduction to *Modern Critical Views: William Shakespeare: The Tragedies*. Edited by Harold Bloom, 1–10. New York: Chelsea House Publishers, 1985.

– *Shakespeare: The Invention of the Human*. New York: Riverhead Books, 1998.

Bohannan, Laura. "Shakespeare in the Bush." *Natural History Magazine*, August–September 1966. Accessed 30 September 2015. http://www.naturalhistorymag.com/picks-from-the-past/12476/shakespeare-in-the-bush.

Bradley, A.C. *Coriolanus*. British Academy: Second Annual Lecture. London: Oxford University Press, 1912.

– *Shakespearean Tragedy: Lectures on "Hamlet," "Othello," "King Lear," "Macbeth."* 1904; repr., London: Penguin, 1991.

Braunmuller, A.R., ed. *Macbeth*. New Cambridge Shakespeare. Cambridge: Cambridge University Press, 1997.

Bristol, Michael. "Macbeth the Philosopher: Rethinking Context." *New Literary History* 42 (2011): 641–62.

– "Vernacular Criticism and the Scenes Shakespeare Never Wrote." In *Shakespeare Survey 53*, edited by Peter Holland, 89–102. Cambridge: Cambridge University Press, 2000.

– ed. *Shakespeare and Moral Agency*. London: Continuum, 2010.

Burke, Kenneth. *Kenneth Burke on Shakespeare*. Edited by Scott Newstok. West Lafayette, IN: Parlor Press, 2007.

– *On Symbols and Society*. Edited by Joseph R. Gusfield. Chicago: University of Chicago Press, 1989.

Burling, Robbins. *The Passage of Power: Studies in Political Succession*. New York: Academic Press, 1974.

Calderwood, James. "Wordless Meanings and Meaningless Words." *Studies in English Literature* 6 (1966): 211–24.

– *To Be and Not to Be: Negation and Metadrama in "Hamlet."* New York: Columbia University Press, 1983.

Campbell, Oscar James. *Shakespeare's Satire*. Hamden, CT: Archon Books, 1963.

Cantor, Paul A. *Shakespeare's Rome: Republic and Empire*. Ithaca, NY: Cornell University Press, 1976.

Cashdan, Elizabeth A. "Egalitarianism among Hunters and Gatherers." *American Anthropologist* 82 (1980): 116–20.

Cavell, Stanley. *Disowning Knowledge in Six Plays of Shakespeare*. Cambridge: Cambridge University Press, 1987.

Coleridge, Samuel Taylor. *Shakespearean Criticism*. Edited by Thomas Middleton Raysor. London: J.M. Dent & Sons Ltd., 1960.

Craig, Leon Harold. *Of Philosophers and Kings: Political Philosophy in Shakespeare's "Macbeth" and "King Lear."* Toronto: University of Toronto Press, 2001.

de Grazia, Margreta. *"Hamlet" without Hamlet*. Cambridge: Cambridge University Press, 2007.

Deacon, Terrence. *The Symbolic Species: The Co-evolution of Language and the Brain*. New York: W.W. Norton, 1997.

Dennis, Ian. *Lord Byron and the History of Desire*. Newark: University of Delaware Press, 2009.

Desmet, Christy, and Robert Sawyer, eds. *Harold Bloom's Shakespeare*. New York: Palgrave, 2001.

DiPietro, Cary. "A.C. Bradley." In *Bradley, Greg, Folger*, edited by Cary DiPietro. Vol. 9 of *Great Shakespeareans*, edited by Peter Holland and Adrian Poole, 8–67. London: Continuum, 2011.

Doran, Madeleine. "The Language of *Hamlet*." *Huntington Library Quarterly* 27, no. 3 (1964): 259–78.

Dubreuil, Benoît. *Human Evolution and the Origins of Hierarchies: The State of Nature*. Cambridge: Cambridge University Press, 2010.

Dunbar, Robin. *Grooming, Gossip, and the Evolution of Language*. Cambridge, MA: Harvard University Press, 1996.

Durkheim, Émile. *The Elementary Forms of Religious Life*. Translated by Karen E. Fields. New York: The Free Press, 1995.

Eliot, T.S. *Selected Essays*. 2nd ed. London: Faber and Faber, 1934.

Empson, William. *Essays on Shakespeare*. Edited by David B. Pirie. Cambridge: Cambridge University Press, 1986.

Farber, Leslie H. "Faces of Envy." In *Lying, Despair, Jealousy, Envy, Sex, Suicide, Drugs, and the Good Life*, 35–45. New York: Basic Books, 1976.

Felperin, Howard. *Shakespearean Representation: Mimesis and Modernity in Elizabethan Tragedy*. Princeton: Princeton University Press, 1977.

Fergusson, Francis. *The Idea of a Theater: A Study of Ten Plays: The Art of Drama in Changing Perspective*. Princeton: Princeton University Press, 1949.

Fish, Stanley. "How to Do Things with Austin and Searle: Speech Act Theory and Literary Criticism." *Modern Language Notes* 91 (1976): 983–1025.

Foucault, Michel. *The Order of Things: An Archeology of the Human Sciences*. New York: Vintage Books, 1994.

Frankfurt, Harry. *On Bullshit*. Princeton: Princeton University Press, 2005.

Gans, Eric. "Differences." *Modern Language Notes* 96 (1981): 792–808.

– *The End of Culture: Toward a Generative Anthropology*. Berkeley: University of California Press, 1985.

– "Originary Guilt." *Chronicles of Love and Resentment*, no. 333. Accessed 2 December 2010. http://www.anthropoetics.ucla.edu/views/vw333.htm.

– *Originary Thinking: Elements of Generative Anthropology*. Stanford, CA: Stanford University Press, 1993.

– *The Scenic Imagination: Originary Thinking from Hobbes to the Present Day*. Stanford, CA: Stanford University Press: 2008.

– *Signs of Paradox: Irony, Resentment, and Other Mimetic Structures*. Stanford, CA: Stanford University Press, 1997.

Gellner, Ernest. *Anthropology and Politics: Revolutions in the Sacred Grove*. Oxford: Blackwell, 1995.

– *Conditions of Liberty: Civil Society and Its Rivals*. New York: Penguin Books, 1994.

– *Plough, Sword and Book: The Structure of Human History*. Chicago: University of Chicago Press, 1989.

– *Thought and Change*. Chicago: University of Chicago Press, 1964.

Girard, René. *Deceit, Desire, and the Novel: Self and Other in Literary Structure*. Translated by Yvonne Freccero. Baltimore: Johns Hopkins University Press, 1965.

– *A Theater of Envy: William Shakespeare*. Oxford: Oxford University Press, 1991.

– *Things Hidden Since the Foundation of the World*. Translated by Stephen Bann and Michael Metteer. Stanford, CA: Stanford University Press, 1987.

– *Violence and the Sacred*. Translated by Patrick Gregory. Baltimore: Johns Hopkins University Press, 1977.

Goddard, Harold. *The Meaning of Shakespeare*. 2 vols. Chicago: University of Chicago Press, 1960.

Goethe, Johann Wolfgang. *Wilhelm Meister's Apprenticeship*. 1795. Translated by Thomas Carlyle. 2 vols. London: Francis Nicolls & Co., 1901.

Gordon, D.J. "Name and Fame: Shakespeare's *Coriolanus*." In *Papers Mainly Shakespearean*, edited by G.I. Duthie, 40–57. Edinburgh: Oliver and Boyd, 1964.

Greg, W.W. "Hamlet's Hallucination." *Modern Language Review* 12 (1917): 393–421.

Guilfoyle, Cherrell. *Shakespeare's Play within Play: Medieval Imagery and Scenic Form in "Hamlet," "Othello," and "King Lear."* Kalamazoo, MI: Medieval Institute Publications, 1990.

Hazlitt, William. *Characters of Shakespeare's Plays*. London: Oxford University Press, 1955.

Heuer, Hermann. "From Plutarch to Shakespeare: A Study of *Coriolanus*." In *Shakespeare Survey 10*, edited by Allardyce Nicoll, 50–9. Cambridge: Cambridge University Press, 1957.

Holloway, John. *The Story of the Night: Studies in Shakespeare's Major Tragedies*. London: Routledge & Kegan Paul, 1961.

Hudson, Henry. "Introduction." *Shakespeare's Tragedy of Coriolanus*. Boston: Ginn & Company, 1909.

Iser, Wolfgang. *How to Do Theory*. Oxford: Blackwell, 2006.

Jenkins, Harold. *Structural Problems in Shakespeare: Lectures and Essays by Harold Jenkins*. Edited by Ernst Honigmann. London: Arden Shakespeare, 2001.

Jones, Ernest. *Hamlet and Oedipus*. London: Victor Gollancz, 1949.

Joughin, John J. *Philosophical Shakespeares*. London: Routledge, 2000.

Kahn, Coppélia. *Roman Shakespeare: Warriors, Wounds, and Women*. New York: Routledge, 1997.

Katz, Adam. "Remembering Amalek: 9/11 and Generative Thinking." *Anthropoetics* 10, no. 2 (Fall 2004 / Winter 2005). Accessed 23 January 2014. www.anthropoetics.ucla.edu/ap1002/amalek.htm.

– ed., *The Originary Hypothesis: A Minimal Proposal for Humanistic Inquiry*. Aurora, CO: Davies Group Publishers, 2007.

Keats, John. *The Letters of John Keats*. Edited by Robert Gittings. Oxford: Oxford University Press, 1970.

Kekes, John. *The Art of Life*. Ithaca, NY: Cornell University Press, 2002.

Kerrigan, William. *Hamlet's Perfection*. Baltimore: Johns Hopkins University Press, 1994.

Kiernan, Victor. *Eight Tragedies of Shakespeare: A Marxist Study*. London: Verso, 1996.

Knight, G. Wilson. *The Imperial Theme: Further Interpretations of Shakespeare's Tragedies including the Roman Plays*. London: Methuen, 1965.

– *The Wheel of Fire: Interpretations of Shakespearian Tragedy*. 1930; repr., London: Routledge Classics, 2001.

Knights, L.C. *An Approach to "Hamlet."* Stanford, CA: Stanford University Press, 1961.

Kottman, Paul A. *Tragic Conditions in Shakespeare: Disinheriting the Globe*. Baltimore: Johns Hopkins University Press, 2009.

– "Why Think about Shakespearean Tragedy Today?" In *The Cambridge Companion to Shakespearean Tragedy*, 2nd ed., edited by Claire McEachern, 240–61. Cambridge: Cambridge University Press, 2013.

Langis, Unhae. "Coriolanus: Inordinate Passions and Powers in Personal and Political Governance." *Comparative Drama* 44, no. 1 (2010): 1–27.

Lee, Richard B. *The Dobe !Kung*. New York: Holt, Rinehart and Winston, 1979.

Liebler, Naomi Conn. *Shakespeare's Festive Tragedy: The Ritual Foundations of Genre*. New York: Routledge, 1995.

Lindholm, Charles. *Culture and Authenticity*. Oxford: Blackwell, 2008.

– "Culture and Envy." In *Envy: Theory and Research*, edited by Richard H. Smith, 227–44. Oxford: Oxford University Press, 2008.

Long, Michael. *The Unnatural Scene: A Study of Shakespearean Tragedy*. London: Methuen, 1976.

Marlowe, Frank W. *The Hadza: Hunter-Gatherers of Tanzania*. Berkeley: University of California Press, 2010.

Martin, Mike W. *Self-Deception and Morality*. Lawrence: University Press of Kansas, 1986.

McCoy, Richard C. *Faith in Shakespeare*. Oxford: Oxford University Press, 2013.

McGinn, Colin. *Shakespeare's Philosophy*. New York: HarperCollins Publishers, 2006.

Migotti, Mark. "Slave Morality, Socrates, and the Bushmen: A Reading of the First Essay of *On the Genealogy of Morals*." *Philosophy and Phenomenological Research* 58, no. 4 (1998): 745–79.

Miles, Geoffrey. *Shakespeare and the Constant Romans*. Oxford: Oxford University Press, 1996.

Murray, Patrick. *The Shakespearian Scene: Some Twentieth-Century Perspectives*. London: Longmans, 1969.

Neill, Michael. "Changing Places in *Othello*." In *Shakespeare Survey 37*, edited by Stanley Wells, 115–31. Cambridge: Cambridge University Press, 1984.

Nietzsche, Friedrich. *On the Genealogy of Morals*. Translated by Walter Kaufmann and R.J. Hollingdale. New York: Vintage Books, 1989.

Nuttall, A.D. *A New Mimesis: Shakespeare and the Representation of Reality*. London: Methuen, 1983.

– *Shakespeare the Thinker*. New Haven, CT: Yale University Press, 2007.

Parker, R.B. "*Coriolanus* and 'th'interpretation of the time.'" In *Mirror up to Shakespeare: Essays in Honour of G.R. Hibbard*, edited by J.C. Gray, 261–76. Toronto: University of Toronto Press, 1984.

Pechter, Edward. *Othello and Interpretive Traditions*. Iowa City: University of Iowa Press, 1999.

– *Shakespeare Studies Today: Romanticism Lost*. New York: Palgrave MacMillan, 2011.

Plotz, John. "*Coriolanus* and the Failure of Performatives." *English Literary History* 63 (1996): 809–32.

Pope, Maurice. "Addressing Oedipus." *Greece and Rome* 38 (1991): 156–70.

Proser, Matthew N. *The Heroic Image in Five Shakespearean Tragedies*. Princeton: Princeton University Press, 1965.

Pujante, A. Luis. "'No Sense Nor Feeling': A Note on *Coriolanus* in 4.1." *Shakespeare Quarterly* 41 (1990): 489–90.

Ribner, Irving. *Patterns in Shakespearean Tragedy*. New York: Barnes & Noble, 1960.

Rossiter, A.P. *Angel with Horns and Other Shakespeare Lectures*. Edited by Graham Storey. London: Longmans, 1961.

Ryan, Kiernan. *Shakespeare*. 3rd ed. Basingstoke, UK: Palgrave, 2002.

Sahlins, Marshall. "Poor Man, Rich Man, Big-Man, Chief: Political Types in Melanesia and Polynesia." *Comparative Studies in Society and History* 5, no. 3 (1963): 285–303.

– *Stone Age Economics*. Chicago: Aldine-Atherton, 1972.

Sanders, Wilbur, and Howard Jacobson. *Shakespeare's Magnanimity: Four Tragic Heroes, Their Friends and Families*. London: Chatto & Windus, 1978.

Scheler, Max. *Ressentiment*. Translated by Lewis B. Coser and William W. Holdheim, with an Introduction by Manfred Fings. Milwaukee, WI: Marquette University Press, 1994.

Schoeck, Helmut. *Envy: A Theory of Social Behavior*. Indianapolis, IN: Liberty Press, 1966.

Shakespeare, William. *The Complete Works of Shakespeare*. 6th ed. Edited by David Bevington. New York: Pearson Longman, 2009.

Sicherman, Carol M. "The Failure of Words." *English Literary History* 39 (1972): 189–207.

Simmons, J.L. *Shakespeare's Pagan World: The Roman Tragedies*. Charlottesville: University of Virginia Press, 1973.

Simonse, Simon. *Kings of Disaster: Dualism, Centralism and the Scapegoat King in Southeastern Sudan*. Leiden: E.J. Brill: 1992.

Smith, Richard H., and Sung Hee Kim. Introduction to *Envy: Theory and Research*, edited by Richard H. Smith, 3–14. Oxford: Oxford University Press, 2008.

Sokol, B.J. "God's Plenty." Rev. of *Great Shakespeareans*, ed. Peter Holland and Adrian Poole, 18 vols. *Shakespeare* 8 (2012): 338–51.

Solomon, Robert C. *The Passions*. Garden City, NY: Anchor Press / Doubleday, 1976.

Spargo, R. Clifton. *The Ethics of Mourning: Grief and Responsibility in Elegiac Literature*. Baltimore: Johns Hopkins University Press, 2004.

Spivak, Bernard. *Shakespeare and the Allegory of Evil: The History of a Metaphor in Relation to His Major Villains*. New York: Columbia University Press, 1958.

Swinburne, Alergnon Charles. *A Study of Shakespeare*. 4th ed. London: Chatto & Windus, 1902.

Tallis, Raymond. *Aping Mankind: Neuromania, Darwinitis and the Misrepresentation of Humanity*. Durham, UK: Acumen, 2011.

Tennenhouse, Leonard. "*Coriolanus*: History and the Crisis of Semantic Order." In *Drama in the Renaissance: Comparative and Critical Essays*, edited by Clifford Davidson, C.J. Gianakaris, and John H. Stroupe, 217–35. New York: AMS Press, 1986.

Tomasello, Michael. *The Cultural Origins of Human Cognition*. Cambridge, MA: Harvard University Press, 1999.

– *A Natural History of Human Thinking*. Harvard, MA: Harvard University Press, 2014.

Trilling, Lionel. *Sincerity and Authenticity*. Cambridge, MA: Harvard University Press, 1971.

Updike, John. *Gertrude and Claudius*. New York: Ballantine Books, 2000.

van Oort, Richard. "Cognitive Science and the Problem of Representation." *Poetics Today* 24 (2003): 237–95.

– "The Critic as Ethnographer." *New Literary History* 35 (2004): 621–61.

– "The Culture of Criticism." *Criticism* 49 (2007): 459–79.

– *The End of Literature: Essays in Anthropological Aesthetics*. Aurora, CO: Davies Group Publishers, 2009.

– "Stories, Jokes, Desire, and Interdiction: The Cognitive and Anthropological Origins of Symbolic Representation." *Fictions: Studi sulla narrativitià* 11 (2012): 91–113.

Vyvyan, John. *The Shakespearean Ethic*. London: Chatto & Windus, 1959.

Waith, Eugene M. *The Herculean Hero in Marlowe, Chapman, Shakespeare and Dryden*. London: Chatto & Windus, 1962.

Warren, Michael. "The Perception of Error: The Editing and the Performance of the Opening of *Coriolanus*." In *Textual Performances: The Modern Reproduction of Shakespeare's Drama*, edited by Lukas Erne and Margaret Jane Kidnie, 127–42. Cambridge: Cambridge University Press, 2004.

Wilson, John Dover. *What Happens in "Hamlet."* 3rd ed. Cambridge: Cambridge University Press, 1951.

Wimsatt, James I. "The Player King on Friendship." *Modern Language Review* 65, no. 1 (1970): 1–6.

Woodburn, James. "Egalitarian Societies." *Man* 17 (1982): 431–51.

Zamir, Tzachi. *Double Vision: Moral Philosophy and Shakespearean Drama*. Princeton: Princeton University Press, 2007.

Index

www.ingramcontent.com/pod-product-compliance
Lightning Source LLC
LaVergne TN
LVHW090155080826
844660LV00013B/818/J

* 9 7 8 1 4 4 2 6 5 0 0 7 7 *